T0024406

TOP **10**
LONDON

Top 10 London Highlights

The Top 10 of Everything

CONTENTS

London Area by Area

Streetsmart

Within each Top 10 list in this book, no hierarchy of quality or popularity is implied. All 10 are, in the editor's opinion, of roughly equal merit.

Title page, front cover and spine *The Houses of Parliament and Elizabeth Tower at dusk*
Back cover, clockwise from top left *Autumn in Hyde Park; Gerrard Street in Chinatown; The Ship & Shovell pub; Tower Bridge and Shard; London Eye*

The rapid rate at which the world is changing is constantly keeping the DK Eyewitness team on our toes. While we've worked hard to ensure that this edition of London is accurate and up-to-date, we know that opening hours alter, standards shift, prices fluctuate, places close and new ones pop up in their stead. So, if you notice we've got something wrong or left something out, we want to hear about it. Please get in touch at **travelguides@dk.com**

Welcome to
London

River city. Royal city. City of palaces and pubs, museums and monuments. The world's first National Park City. Hotbed of art. Shopping mecca. Financial powerhouse. London is all these things and more... so who could argue when we say that it's the world's most exciting metropolis? With DK Eyewitness Top 10 London, it's yours to explore.

We love London: the culture, the history, the diversity. What could be better than strolling along the cobbled streets of **Covent Garden**, sailing along the Thames between the **Houses of Parliament** and **Tate Modern**, browsing the cutting-edge boutiques of **Spitalfields** and scouting the stalls for a bargain, walking in one of the city's 3,000 parks and open spaces, or time-travelling back to Shakes–peare's England at the **Globe Theatre**? It's all here, packed into a few square miles of the world's most energetic streetscape.

This city is a cultural colossus, with a buoyant theatre district, a bar or restaurant on every corner, and a packed calendar of eye-catching ceremonies and festivals, including the **Notting Hill Carnival**. It does history and pageantry like nowhere else, but for all its pomp and ceremony, London has always been a cosmopolitan capital. The city is a paradise for foodies, where you can sample street food from around the world, as well as dine in an enticing array of Michelin-starred restaurants.

Whether you're coming for a weekend or a week, our Top 10 guide brings together the best of everything that London can offer, from hip **Hoxton** to sophisticated **St James's**. The guide has useful tips throughout, from seeking out what's free to places off the beaten track, plus 13 easy-to-follow itineraries, designed to tie together a clutch of sights in a short space of time. Add inspiring photography and detailed maps, and you've got the essential pocket-sized travel companion. **Enjoy the book, and enjoy London**.

Clockwise from top: **British Museum**, **Big Ben**, **Red telephone boxes**, **St Paul's and the Millennium Bridge**, **Westminster Abbey**, **Tate Britain**, **Kew Gardens**

Exploring London

For things to see and do, visitors to London are spoiled for choice. Whether you're here for a short stay or you just want a flavour of this great city, you want to make the most of your time. Here are some ideas for two and four days of sightseeing in London.

Shakespeare's Globe is a replica of the original Globe Theatre.

Key
— Two-day itinerary
— Four-day itinerary

PADDINGTON

Portobello Road Market

NOTTING HILL

Kensington Gardens

Hyde Park

SO

ST JAMES

Green Park

Buckingham Palace

KNIGHTSBRIDGE

Science Museum

Natural History Museum

0 kilometres 1
0 miles 1

Trafalgar Square, a focal point for Londoners, is beautifully lit up at night.

Two Days in London

Day ❶

MORNING
Take a Beefeater tour of the **Tower of London** (see pp38–41), then visit St Paul's Cathedral (see pp42–5).

AFTERNOON
Cross **Millennium Bridge** (see p64), for a panorama of the River Thames. Explore the **Tate Modern** (see pp28–9) before walking along Bankside past **Shakespeare's Globe** (see p89).

Day ❷

MORNING
Begin at **Buckingham Palace** (see pp24–5), and then take a stroll through **St James's Park** (see p119). Afterwards, head to **Westminster Abbey** (see pp34–5) to see the monuments of English monarchs.

AFTERNOON
After lunch, spend two hours at the **National Gallery** (see pp16–17) in Trafalgar Square. Then take a "flight" on the **London Eye** (see pp26–7).

Four Days in London

Day ❶

MORNING
Start with a full morning exploring the **Tower of London** (see pp38–41), then cross the imposing **Tower Bridge** (see p141) and stroll along the river past **HMS Belfast** (see pp64–5).

AFTERNOON
Take lunch at **Borough Market** (see p91), just around the corner from the towering **Shard** (see p27). Roam the **Tate Modern** (see pp28–9) before enjoying an alfresco evening meal on the South Bank.

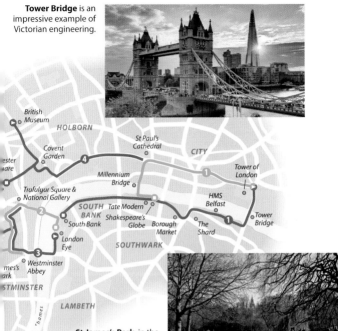

Tower Bridge is an impressive example of Victorian engineering.

St James's Park, in the heart of London, is popular for its immaculate flower beds and great views.

Day ❷
MORNING
Begin in Notting Hill, with a morning turn around **Portobello Road** market *(see pp126–7)*. Walk south from there through the stately expanse of **Kensington Gardens** *(see p54)*.
AFTERNOON
Exit the park into South Kensington's museum quarter, for an afternoon exploring the **Science Museum** *(see pp22–3)* and the **Natural History Museum** *(see pp20–21)*.

Day ❸
MORNING
Choose between the **London Eye** *(see pp26–7)* or **Westminster Abbey** *(see pp34–5)*. Not far away is **Trafalgar Square** *(see p95)*, where you can admire Nelson's Column before taking in the magnificent artworks at the **National Gallery** *(see pp16–17)*.

AFTERNOON
Meander through **St James's Park** *(see p119)* before enjoying tea and cake at St James' Café. Peek through the gates at **Buckingham Palace** *(see pp24–5)*, then hit swish **St James's** *(see pp118–23)* for dinner and cocktails.

Day ❹
MORNING
Start at the **British Museum** *(see pp12–15)*, a two-million-year trove of human endeavour, then head down to **Covent Garden** *(see pp104–11)* for a leisurely stroll around the Apple Market and stop for lunch at one of the area's many eateries.
AFTERNOON
St Paul's Cathedral *(see pp42–5)* is a short way by Tube. In the evening, return west to **Leicester Square** *(see p97)*, where the bright lights of London's Theatreland await.

Top 10 London Highlights

The blue whale skeleton in the Hintze Hall, Natural History Museum

TOP **10** London Highlights

A city of infinite colour and variety, London is both richly historic, tracing its roots back over 2,000 years, and unceasingly modern, at the forefront of fashion, music and the arts. A selection of the best London has to offer is explored in the following chapter.

British Museum ①
The oldest national public museum in the world contains a rich collection of treasures and artifacts *(see pp12–15)*.

② National Gallery and National Portrait Gallery
The nation's most important art collections are held here, including this c 1592 portrait of Queen Elizabeth I *(see pp16–19)*.

③ Natural History Museum
The enormous and varied collection here explores the history of life on Earth *(see pp20–21)*.

Science Museum ④
A huge museum with fascinating interactive exhibits that explain and demonstrate the wonders of science *(see pp22–3)*.

⑤ Buckingham Palace
The official London home of the monarch, where the Changing the Guard takes place *(see pp24–5)*.

6 London Eye

One of the world's tallest observation wheels, the Eye offers stunning views of the city *(see pp26–7)*.

7 Tate Modern and Tate Britain

London's two Tate galleries house collections of British and modern international art *(see pp28–31)*.

8 Westminster Abbey and Parliament Square

This royal abbey has, since 1066, hosted the coronations of nearly all Britain's monarchs *(see pp34–7)*.

9 Tower of London

The Tower has been a royal palace, fortress and prison, and is the home of the Crown Jewels *(see pp38–41)*.

10 St Paul's Cathedral

Sir Christopher Wren's Baroque masterpiece still stands out and takes pride of place on the City skyline *(see pp42–5)*.

0 kilometres 1
0 miles 1

🔟 ⭐ British Museum

The world's oldest national public museum has over 8 million items spanning the history of the world's cultures, from the stone tools of early humans to 21st-century artworks. The collection was started with the bequest of a physician and antiquarian, Sir Hans Sloane, in 1753. In the 18th and 19th centuries, travellers and emissaries added treasures from around the world, though in recent decades calls for some items of contested provenance to be returned have grown louder. The central courtyard is used as a public space.

Parthenon Sculptures **1**
This spectacular 5th-century BC frieze from the Parthenon **(right)** was made under Pericles and shows a procession in honour of the goddess Athena. It was taken in 1801 by Lord Elgin, Ambassador to Constantinople.

2 Mummified Cat
Cats and sacred cows were mummified in Ancient Egypt. This cat **(left)** comes from Abydos and dates from the 1st century AD. Many Egyptian deities took on animal shapes, as seen on wall paintings and other artifacts.

3 Ram in a Thicket
Decorated with shells, gold leaf, copper and lapis lazuli, this priceless ornament comes from Ur in Sumer, one of the world's earliest civilizations. Games and musical instruments are also displayed.

4 Double-Headed Serpent Mosaic
Carved in wood and covered with turquoise mosaic, this Aztec ornament was probably worn on the chest on ceremonial occasions.

5 Rosetta Stone
In 196 BC Egyptian priests wrote a decree about Ptolemy V on this granite tablet in Greek, in demotic and in Egyptian hieroglyphics. Found in 1799, it proved crucial in deciphering Egyptian pictorial writing.

6 Portland Vase
Probably discovered in a funerary monument at Monte del Grano, near Rome, this exquisite 1st-century blue-and-opaque-glass vase is so called because it came into the possession of the Duchess of Portland. It had to be reassembled after a visitor smashed it into 200 pieces in 1845.

7 David Vases
These blue and white porcelain altar vases dating from c 1351, were made in Jingdezhen, China. They feature elephant-head handles in addition to various motifs.

8 Mildenhall Treasure

Some of the greatest early English treasures are these silver plates **(left)** from the 4th century, found at Mildenhall in Suffolk. Their decorations include sea nymphs, satyrs and Hercules.

Ramesses II 9

This is all that remains of the colossal granite statue **(right)** of Ramesses II (c 1250 BC) from his memorial temple at Thebes. Its arrival in England in the 19th century is said to have inspired the poet Shelley to write the poem *Ozymandias*.

British Museum

Ram in a Thicket ❸

Mummified ❷
Cat

Portland ❻
Vase

Mildenhall
Treasure
❽

David ❼
Vases

Ramesses II ❾

Parthenon ❶
Sculptures

❺ Rosetta
Stone

❿ Lewis Chessmen

❹ Double-Headed
Serpent Mosaic

Key to Floor Plan
- Lower floor
- Ground floor
- Upper floor

10 Lewis Chessmen

These 12th-century carved chess pieces originate from Norway and were discovered in Scotland's Western Isles. The Lewis Chessmen set includes seated kings, queens, bishops, knights and standing warders, which are fashioned from walrus ivory.

NEED TO KNOW

MAP L1 ■ Great Russell St WC1 ■ 020 7323 8000
■ www.britishmuseum.org

Open 10am–5pm Sat–Thu, 10am–8:30pm Fri

Adm for major temporary exhibitions

■ The Great Court's Reading Room is closed to public.

■ There are two cafés, a pizzeria and the fine-dining Great Court Restaurant.

■ Free "eye-opener" tours (40 mins) focus on specific rooms. Highlights tours (£14) introduce the collection. Other tours also available; check website for details.

■ The British Museum shop sells reproduction artifacts, books and gifts.

Museum Guide

Free maps are available and guides are on sale at the information desks. Start to the left of the main entrance with the Assyrian, Egyptian, Greek and Roman galleries. The upper floor has Egyptian mummies. The Asian collections provide a change from Classical material, as do the British and European galleries on the east side.

British Museum Collections

 Middle East
Highlights include the spectacular 2,600-year-old carved reliefs depicting a variety of scenes from the Assyrian palace of Nineveh.

 Ancient Egypt and Sudan
An array of mummies and sarcophagi are found in one of the world's biggest collections.

 Africa
The gallery holds a remarkable collection of sculpture, textiles and graphic art, including the famous Benin bronzes, looted in 1897 and under calls to be returned to Nigeria.

 Asia
Buddhist limestone reliefs, Chinese porcelain, objects from the Mughal court and a jaw-dropping array of Japanese artifacts are displayed across several galleries.

5 **Greece and Rome**
Several rooms cover the marvels of the Classical world. Highlights include the sculptures that once decorated the outside of the Parthenon and colossal statues from the Mausoleum at Helicarnassus.

British Museum Collections

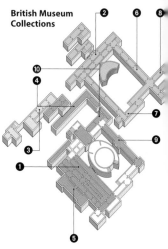

Ancient Greek vase

 Prehistory and Europe
This collection includes Lindow Man – the body of a 1st-century man found preserved in a peat bog – and the burial hoard of a 7th-century Anglo-Saxon king found at Sutton Hoo in Suffolk. There are also fine decorative arts, including medieval jewellery and Renaissance clocks.

 Money
The exhibit traces the history of money over 4,000 years - from shell currency to digital payment methods.

8 **Islamic World**
This stunning display of objects ranges from West Africa to Southeast Asia covering the period from the 7th century to the present.

9 **Enlightenment**
The museum's oldest room features the original 18th-century collection from around the world.

10 **Americas**
Highlights of the Mexico collection include reliefs from Yaxchilán, depicting ritual bloodletting.

THE GREAT COURT

Designed by architect Sir Norman Foster and unveiled in 2000, the architectural highlight of the museum is the Great Court, a stunning conversion of the original 19th-century inner courtyard. The court is covered by a glass roof, making it Europe's largest indoor square, and contains shops, cafés, and the museum's main ticket and information desk. In the centre is the domed Reading Room, built in 1857. It was formerly home to the British Library – one of the world's most important collections of books and manuscripts and the workplace of some of London's greatest writers. The collection is now housed in a purpose-built building in St Pancras and in Yorkshire.

TOP 10
LIBRARY READERS

1 Karl Marx
(1818–83), German revolutionary

2 Mahatma Gandhi
(1869–1948), Indian leader

3 Oscar Wilde
(1854–1900), playwright and wit

4 Virginia Woolf
(1882–1941), Bloomsbury novelist

5 W B Yeats
(1865–1939), Irish poet and playwright

6 Thomas Hardy
(1840–1928), English novelist

7 George Bernard Shaw
(1856–1950), Irish playwright

8 E M Forster
(1879–1970), English novelist

9 Marcus Garvey
(1887–1940), Jamaican political activist

10 Leon Trotsky
(1879–1940), Russian revolutionary

The Reading Room, at the centre of the Great Court, was based on the domed Pantheon in Rome.

The Great Court, at the centre of the museum, has a tesselated roof constructed out of 3,312 unique panes of glass. It surrounds the Reading Room.

🔟 ⭐ National Gallery

The National Gallery houses one of the world's greatest collections of European paintings. The collection was established in 1824, when a small group of paintings was gifted to the nation, and after rapid expansion it was moved to the present building in Trafalgar Square in 1838. The gallery is now home to over 2,300 paintings dating from the 13th to the 20th centuries. In 2024–5, it will celebrate its bicentenary with an exciting programme of events, culminating in a dramatic rehang of all its works.

1 The Arnolfini Portrait

One of the most famous paintings from the extensive Flemish collection is this unusual portrait of an Italian banker and his wife in Bruges. Jan van Eyck (c 1390–1441) brought oil painting to a new and colourful height.

2 The Wilton Diptych

A highlight of Gothic art, this exquisite royal painting (below), by an unknown artist, shows Richard II being recommended to the Virgin by saints John the Baptist, Edward and Edmund.

3 The Rokeby Venus

Painted in Rome to replace a lost Venetian painting, *The Rokeby Venus* (above) is the only nude by Diego Velázquez (1599–1660), court painter to Spain's Philip IV. Venus, the goddess of love, is sensually depicted here with her son, Cupid, who holds a mirror up for her to see her reflection and that of the viewer.

4 The Virgin of the Rocks

This Renaissance masterpiece by Leonardo da Vinci (1452–1519) was originally painted, along with two other panels, for a partly sculpted altarpiece in a church in Milan. The Virgin and Child, with St John the Baptist and an angel, are depicted within a strange cavernous landscape.

⑤ Self Portrait as St Catherine of Alexandria

The Italian painter Artemisia Gentileschi (1593–1653) portrays herself as a martyred saint in this work. Her expression is one of determination and resilience, having broken free from the spiked wheel on which she was bound and tortured.

⑥ A Young Woman Standing at a Virginal

Dutch painter Johannes Vermeer's (1632–75) works carry a sense of calm. Many of his interiors were painted in his home.

⑦ Self Portrait at the Age of 63

Rembrandt's (1606–69) self-portrait, created in the last year of his life, is among his most poignant works. He painted many self-portraits during his lifetime, and two of these are on display at the National Gallery.

⑧ The Ambassadors

Symbols, such as the distorted skull fore-telling death, abound in this 1533 double portrait by Hans Holbein the Younger (c 1497–1543).

⑨ Sunflowers

Displaying his inimitable expressive style, van Gogh (1853–90) painted this work **(below)** in Arles, France during a period of rare optimism while he was awaiting the arrival of his hero, the avant-garde painter Paul Gauguin.

⑩ Bathers at La Grenouillière

Claude Monet (1840–1926), the original Impressionist, explored the effect of light on water at La Grenouillière, a popular bathing spot on the Seine close to Bougival to the west of Paris, where he worked alongside fellow painter Pierre-Auguste Renoir.

NEED TO KNOW

MAP L4 ■ Trafalgar Sq WC2 ■ 020 7747 2885 ■ www.nationalgallery.org.uk

Open 10am–6pm daily (until 9pm Fri)

Adm for major temporary exhibitions

Free guided tours at 3pm Tue–Thu (1 hr; meet at the Portico entrance)

■ To avoid long queues, it is advisable to book a timed ticket online.

■ There is an espresso bar, a self-serve canteen and a good fine-dining restaurant, Ochre.

■ There is an excellent art bookshop on level 0 and a gift shop on level 2.

■ Special events are often run during Friday Lates.

Gallery Guide
Most of the collection is housed on Level 2, with temporary exhibitions also on Level 0. Some major works will be on tour around the UK in summer 2024. Expect room closures in the lead-up to the rehang in 2025; check the website or ask a gallery assistant if looking for a specific work.

![TOP 10] ⭐ National Portrait Gallery

Reopened in 2023 following a three-year renovation, the National Portrait Gallery showcases Britain's most famous and historically important figures through a series of portraits. Royalty is depicted, from Richard II (1367–1400) to the House of Windsor, and the collection also holds a 1554 miniature, England's oldest self-portrait in oils. As part of the refurbishment, the entire collection has been redisplayed, bringing to the fore lesser-known figures and stories from British history and encompassing more works from the gallery's vast photographic archive.

Queen Elizabeth I
This anonymous portrait **(right)** is one of several of Elizabeth I (1533–1603), who presided over England's Renaissance.

2 Horatio Nelson
The portrait by Sir William Beechey is considered to be a great likeness of the admiral, who died at the Battle of Trafalgar in 1805. After Queen Victoria and the Duke of Wellington, Nelson was the most painted British figure of the era.

3 William Shakespeare
Known as the "Chandos portrait" **(below)**, this is the only depiction of England's famous playwright with a strong claim to have been painted during his lifetime (1564–1616). It was the first portrait to be acquired by the gallery on its foundation in 1856.

4 The Whitehall Mural
The cartoon of Henry VIII and his father Henry VII by Hans Holbein (1537) was drawn for a large mural in the Palace of Whitehall. The mural was lost when the palace burnt down in 1698.

5 Brontë Sisters
Painted c 1834 by their teenage brother Branwell (1817–48), this is the only surviving portrait (see p58) of all three of the famous literary sisters: Anne, Emily and Charlotte. It lay forgotten and neglected for many years in a wardrobe in Ireland until its rediscovery in 1914.

Queen Victoria ⑥
This regal-looking portrait by Sir George Hayter (1792–1871) is an 1863 replica of an earlier work by the artist and depicts the 19-year-old queen **(right)** as she was at her Coronation in 1838. Shown wearing the Imperial State Crown and carrying the Sceptre with the Cross, the young queen looks strong and determined on what she later described as the proudest day of her life.

⑧ Mary Seacole
Painted by Albert Charles Challen, this portrait is the only known oil painting of

Mary Seacole **(left)**, a Jamaican nurse who went to extraordinary lengths to care for the sick and wounded during the Crimean War.

⑨ Prince Charles Edward Stuart
This portrait of "Bonnie Prince Charlie" (1720–1788), grandson of the Catholic King James II, was painted by French artist Louis Gabriel Blanchet (1705–72). It was a splendid piece of propaganda during the Jacobite rising, a doomed attempt to restore Catholic rule to the British throne.

⑦ Oliver Cromwell

Robert Walker's oil painting shows Oliver Cromwell (1599–1658) posing in armour. The portrait is believed to date from 1649 – the year Charles I, whose death warrant Cromwell signed, was executed. It is ironic therefore that the pose and dress strongly echoes the earlier royalist portraits of Van Dyck, probably in order to emphasize Cromwell's fitness to rule.

⑩ Charles Darwin
John's Collier's 1883 portrait of the scientist **(right)**, regarded by Darwin as the best made of him, was based on a work he had completed a year before the scientist's death. Collier was the son-in-law of naturalist T H Huxley, an advocate of Darwin's theory of evolution.

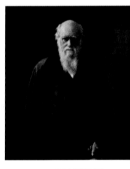

NEED TO KNOW

MAP L3 ◼ St Martin's Place WC2 ◼ 020 7306 0055 ◼ www.npg.org.uk

Open 10:30am–6pm daily (until 9pm Fri & Sat)

Adm for major temporary exhibitions

◼ **The Portrait Restaurant on the top floor** has great views across Trafalgar Square to Parliament.

◼ There is a café with its own dedicated entrance in the Weston Wing.

◼ The bookshop stocks a range of fashion, history and biography titles.

◼ The ground-floor gift shop has good postcards.

Gallery Guide
The permanent collection is arranged chronologically, starting at the top. The second floor houses the Tudor and Stuart galleries, as well as some 19th-century works. The first floor Blavatnik Wing features key British figures from the period 1840–1945. The ground-floor and basement galleries display later 20th- and 21st-century portraiture and temporary exhibitions. Part of the contemporary portraiture collection is displayed in the newly opened Weston Wing.

🔟 ⭐ Natural History Museum

There are some 80 million specimens in the Natural History Museum's fascinating collections. Originally the repository for items brought back by Charles Darwin and botanist Joseph Banks, among others, the museum combines traditional displays with innovative, hands-on exhibits. It remains one of London's most popular museums and has a number of attractions for kids, such as the impressive dinosaur collection and the life-sized model of a blue whale. A hot-house of research, it employs more than 300 scientists and librarians.

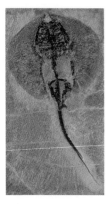

3 Treasures (Cadogan Gallery)

Treasures is an apt title for this extraordinary collection, which has a rare first edition of Darwin's *On the Origin of Species* and an Archeopteryx fossil, the first specimen of a dinosaur skeleton found. The exhibits on display **(right)** were chosen for their scientific and historical importance and are true movers and shakers of natural history.

1 Fossils

Marine reptiles that existed at the time of the dinosaurs have survived as some remarkable fossils **(above)**, such as the pregnant female Ichthyosaur, found in a Dorset garden, which lived 187–178 million years ago.

4 Earthquake Simulator

Board the escalator from the Earth Hall through a giant partially formed Earth to the top of the Red Zone, where you can experience the rumblings of the 1995 Kobe earthquake inside a mock-up of a Japanese supermarket.

5 Images of Nature Gallery

This gallery showcases the museum's collection of historic and modern artworks, including prints from micro-CT scanners, watercolours and photographs. More than 100 exhibits span 350 years to the present day.

Hintze Hall 2

After a major renovation in 2017, the museum's cathedral-like hall **(right)** replaced "Dippy", the Diplodocus skeleton cast, with a giant blue whale skeleton. In alcoves along the sides of the hall are other stars of the museum, including an American mastodon.

6 Spirit Collection
Get a fascinating glimpse of the museum's vast collection of zoological specimens preserved in spirit, including creatures collected by Charles Darwin.

7 Darwin Centre
One of the centre's many attractions is the eight-storey Cocoon, shaped like a giant egg, where visitors can see hundreds of butterfly, insect and plant specimens.

8 Blue Whale
The Mammals gallery houses this fascinating exhibit, where both modern mammals and their fossil relatives are dwarfed in comparison to the astounding life-sized model of a blue whale, the largest animal that's ever lived.

Key to Floorplan
- Ground floor
- First floor
- Second floor

9 Dinosaurs
T. Rex, one of the museum's life-like animatronic models, lurches and roars in this popular gallery. More traditional exhibits of fossilized skeletons are also on display. Taking pride of place in the Earth Hall is 6-m (19.5-ft) *Sophie* (above), the most intact Stegosaurus fossilized skeleton ever found.

10 Giant Sequoia
Over 5 m (16 ft) wide, this segment from a 101-m- (330-ft-) tall tree was over 1,300 years old when it was felled in California in 1891. It had to be split into 12 sections to be shipped to the UK. It is found on the upper balcony of the Hintze Hall.

Natural History Museum

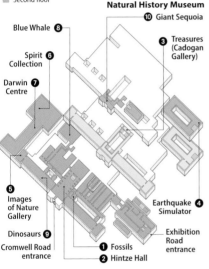

Blue Whale **8**
Spirit Collection **6**
Darwin Centre **7**
10 Giant Sequoia
3 Treasures (Cadogan Gallery)
5 Images of Nature Gallery
Dinosaurs **9**
Cromwell Road entrance
1 Fossils
2 Hintze Hall
4 Earthquake Simulator
Exhibition Road entrance

NEED TO KNOW

MAP B5 ■ Cromwell Rd SW7 ■ 020 7942 5000 ■ www.nhm.ac.uk

Open 10am–5:50pm daily. Last admission 5:30pm

Closed 24–26 Dec

Adm for some special exhibitions

■ There is a restaurant in the Green Zone, and several cafés and snack bars.

■ A number of different self-guided trails are available. Details at the Central Hall information desk. The outdoor Wildlife Garden is closed until 2024.

Museum Guide
The Natural History Museum is divided into four zones: the Blue Zone, which includes the Dinosaurs and Mammals galleries and Images of Nature; the Green Zone, featuring the Treasures gallery; the Orange Zone, with the Darwin Centre; and the Red Zone, incorporating the geological displays.

The Cromwell Road entrance leads to the Hintze Hall with its grand staircase.

An additional entrance on Exhibition Road leads to the Red Zone.

🔟 ⭐ Science Museum

Packed with hands-on exhibits, this museum explores the world of science through centuries of scientific and technological development. The collection showcases how Britain led the Industrial Revolution, with looms and steam engines, navigation and early flight. It also has displays on contemporary science, medicine, mathematics, space and cutting-edge technologies. Opening in 2023, the Energy Revolution gallery examines how the world can tackle climate change.

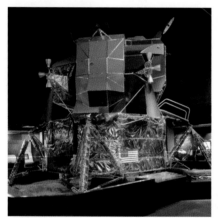

5 Apollo 10 Command Module

The Apollo 10 Command Module, which went around the moon in May 1969, is on display, as is a replica of the Apollo 11 Lunar Lander **(left)**. Buzz Aldrin and Neil Armstrong stepped onto the moon from the original in July 1969 and became the first humans to set foot on the lunar surface.

6 Wonderlab: The Equinor Gallery

With its 50 hands-on exhibits, this interactive gallery captivates 7- to 14-year-olds, to whom it primarily caters. From the friction slides to the lightning strike, learning about science has never been so much fun.

1 Exploring Space

Rockets, satellites, space probes and landers can all be explored, and you can learn about Sputnik, the world's first satellite, how we sent spacecrafts to other planets and walked on the moon.

2 Information Age

The late Queen Elizabeth II opened this gallery with her first tweet in 2014. The gallery is divided into six themes and covers 200 years of communication and modern information technology from the earliest telegraph messages to the internet and mobile phones.

3 Medicine

Exhibits include a real Victorian pharmacy, a walk-in padded cell, and artifacts from the extraordinary medical collection of pharmaceutical entrepreneur Henry Wellcome.

4 Puffing Billy

Puffing Billy **(below)** is the world's oldest remaining steam locomotive. It was built in England in 1813 and used to transport coal. Countless other engineering marvels, from a Model T Ford to the V-2 rocket, are also on display.

7 Who Am I?

The continually updated Who Am I? gallery presents the latest in brain science and genetics through interactive exhibits and object-rich displays.

8 Fly Zone

This zone offers three kinds of flight simulators. With the adrenaline-pumping Fly 360°, take the controls of a jet plane, performing barrel rolls and loop-the-loops.

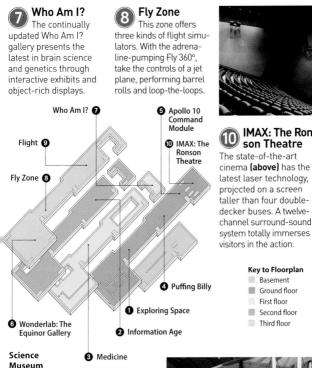

Who Am I? 7

Flight 9

Fly Zone 8

5 Apollo 10 Command Module

10 IMAX: The Ronson Theatre

4 Puffing Billy

1 Exploring Space

6 Wonderlab: The Equinor Gallery

2 Information Age

Science Museum

3 Medicine

10 IMAX: The Ronson Theatre

The state-of-the-art cinema **(above)** has the latest laser technology, projected on a screen taller than four double-decker buses. A twelve-channel surround-sound system totally immerses visitors in the action.

Key to Floorplan
- Basement
- Ground floor
- First floor
- Second floor
- Third floor

9 Flight

This gallery is filled with extraordinary aircraft reflecting both UK and international achievements in aviation. Highlights include Amy Johnson's *Gipsy Moth* and the *Vickers Vimy* biplane **(right)**, which in 1919 became the first aircraft to cross the Atlantic non-stop.

NEED TO KNOW

MAP B5 ■ Exhibition Rd SW7 ■ 0330 058 0058 ■ www.sciencemuseum.org.uk

Open 10am–6pm daily (last entry 5:15pm)

Closed 24–26 Dec

Adm for special exhibitions, Wonderlab, simulator rides and IMAX cinema

■ There is a diner, several cafés and a picnic area.

■ Printed maps with a guide provide details of exhibits.

■ The museum shop is good for innovative gifts.

Museum Guide
The museum's exhibits are spread across five floors. Space exploration, steam engines and the IMAX cinema are on the ground floor. Who Am I?, the Medicine galleries and special exhibitions are on the first floor. Information Age, Mathematics and Science City (covering London's connection to science) are on the second floor. Flight and the Fly Zone's interactive games and simulators can be found on the third floor, along with Wonderlab.

🔟⭐ Buckingham Palace

London's most famous residence, and one of its best recognized landmarks, Buckingham Palace was built as a townhouse for the first Duke of Buckingham around 1705. In 1825, George IV commissioned John Nash to extend the house into a substantial palace, and its first resident was Queen Victoria who moved in upon her accession to the throne in 1837. The extensive front of the building was refaced by Sir Aston Webb in 1913. The palace is now the official residence of the monarch, and its State Rooms and the Royal Mews are open to the public during summer, while the Queen's Gallery is open year-round.

1 **The Balcony**
On special occasions, the King and other members of the Royal Family step on to the palace balcony to wave to the crowds below.

2 **Queen's Gallery**
The gallery hosts a changing programme of exhibitions of the Royal Collection's master-pieces, including works by artists such as Johannes Vermeer and Leonardo da Vinci.

3 **Changing the Guard**
The palace guards, in their red tunics and tall bearskin hats **(below)**, change over at 11am on Monday, Wednesday, Friday and Sunday (and most days in summer), weather permitting. They march to the palace from the Wellington Barracks.

Façade of Buckingham Palace

4 **State Rooms**
The Ambassadors' Entrance leads into the Grand Hall. From here the Grand Staircase, with gilded balustrades, rises to the first floor where the regal State Rooms are found.

5 **Throne Room**
This houses the throne chairs used by Prince Philip and Queen Elizabeth for her coro-nation. Designed by John Nash, the room has an ornamented ceiling and magnificent chandeliers.

6 **Picture Gallery**
One of the largest rooms in the palace it has a barrel-vaulted glass ceiling and feat-ures some of the finest paintings from the Royal Collection, including works by Rembrandt, Rubens and Van Dyck.

8 State Ballroom
Banquets for the visiting heads of state are held here **(left)**. The largest annual event is the Diplomatic Reception in November, attended by around 1,000 dignitaries from about 130 countries.

7 Brougham
Every day a horse-drawn Brougham carriage sets out to collect and deliver royal packages between Buckingham Palace and St James's Palace.

PALACE LIFE
The official business of the monarchy takes place in Buckingham Palace, which employs over 800 staff. Several members of the royal family have offices in the palace but due to ongoing restoration work, these have had to move to St James's Palace. The work is due to finish in 2027. The most senior member of the Royal Household is the Lord Chamberlain. The Master of the Household and the Palace's domestic staff organize many functions every year, including Investitures for recipients of awards which are given by the King.

10 Royal Mews
The finest working stables in Britain care for horses that pull the royal coach on state occasions. The collection of coaches, motorcars and carriages includes the Gold State Coach, used at every coronation since 1821.

9 Palace Garden
The 16-ha (39-acre) palace garden **(below)** is an oasis for wildlife and includes a 1-ha (3-acre) lake. It can be visited on tours. There are at least three royal garden parties each year, attended by over 30,000 people.

NEED TO KNOW

MAP J6 ■ Buckingham Palace SW1 ■ 0303 123 7300 ■ www.rct.org.uk

Adm under 5 free; combined tickets available; for family tickets see website

State Rooms: open Wed & Fri–Mon: mid-Jul–Aug 9:30am– 7:30pm (last adm 5:15pm), Sep to 6:30pm (last adm 4:15pm); adm: adults £30, ages 18–24 £19.50, under 18 and visitors with specific requirements £16.50

Royal Mews: open Mar–Oct: 10am–5:30pm daily (last adm 4pm); adm: adults £14, ages 18–24 £9, under 18 and visitors with specific requirements £8

Queen's Gallery: open 10am–5:30pm Thu–Mon (last adm 4:15pm); adm: adults £17, ages 18–24 £11, under 18 and visitors with specific requirements £9

TOP 10 ⭐ London Eye

An amazing feat of engineering, this 135-m- (443-ft-) high cantilevered observation wheel offers fascinating views over the whole of London. Towering over the Thames opposite the Houses of Parliament, it was built to celebrate the millennium year, and has proved enormously popular. Its 32 enclosed capsules each hold up to 25 people and offer total visibility in all directions. A rotation on the London Eye takes 30 minutes and, on a clear day, you can see up to 40 km (25 miles) across the capital and the south of England.

2 Houses of Parliament

The London Eye rises high above the Houses of Parliament (see p36) on the far side of the Thames. From here you can look down on Big Ben **(left)** and see the Commons Terrace – historically a place for Members of Parliament to drink, dine and discuss policy by the river.

1 BT Tower

This 190-m (620-ft) tower, built for the Post Office in 1961–4 to carry telecommunications traffic, is still in use, primarily for TV broadcasting. Its existence was officially a secret until it was "outed" in Parliament in the 1990s.

3 One Canada Square

With its distinctive pyramid roof, One Canada Square is the tallest of an ever-growing array of skyscrapers in Canary Wharf, the financial centre at the heart of the Docklands area to the east of the City.

The London Eye, South Ba

4 Wren Churches

The enormous dome of St Paul's Cathedral **(left)** stands out as the star of the City churches (see pp42–5). You'll also spot the spires of some of Wren's other churches, including St Bride's, which has a tiered design said to have inspired the traditional wedding cake, and Wren's favourite, St James's on Piccadilly.

5 Alexandra Palace

The BBC transmitted the world's first high-definition public television broadcasting service from Alexandra Palace in 1936. There are exhibition halls, a large theatre and an ice rink here.

6 Crystal Palace

This TV and radio transmission mast, to the south of the city, is near the site of the original "Crystal Palace", built for the 1851 Great Exhibition. It was moved here from Hyde Park and burned down in 1936.

7 The Shard
Designed by Renzo Piano, this towering 306-m (1,004-ft) glass spire (left) rises from London Bridge station and gives the city skyline a new defining point. The 95-storey building houses offices, restaurants and a hotel. There is an observation deck on the 72nd floor.

MILLENNIUM LEGACY
The London Eye was one of a number of nationwide projects designed for the year 2000. The focus in London was on the enormous Millennium Dome, a spectacular structure – controversial at the time – built in Greenwich to house a national exhibition. It is now the O2 arena. Other projects included Tate Modern (see pp28–9) and Millennium Bridge, the Great Court at the British Museum (see pp12–15) and the opening up of Somerset House (see p105).

8 Heathrow
To the west of the city, London's main airport is one of the busiest international airports in the world. The Thames acts as a kind of runway, as planes line up overhead to begin their descent.

NEED TO KNOW

MAP N5 ■ South Bank SE1
■ www.londoneye.com

Open 11am–6pm daily; closed 25 Dec and 2 weeks in Jan

Adm: adults £36, children £32.50, under 3s free; book online in advance for discounts

Timed tickets every 15 minutes

■ There are cafés in County Hall and on the South Bank.

■ Tickets are available on the day but advance booking is advisable to avoid standing in long queues. Combined tickets with other London sights or a river cruise are also available; check the website for details.

9 Queen Elizabeth II Bridge
On a clear day you can just make out the easternmost crossing on the Thames, a huge cable-stayed bridge at Dartford, some 32 km (20 miles) away. Traffic flows north in a tunnel under the river, south over the bridge.

10 Windsor Castle
Windsor Castle (below) sits by the Thames to the west of London. The largest occupied castle in the world, it is still a favourite residence of the royal family.

TOP 10 ⭐ Tate Modern

Looming over the southern bank of the Thames, Tate Modern is one of London's most exciting galleries and is housed in the former Bankside power station. In 2016, the Blavatnik Building was added to this site. The galleries provide an airy space for the collection of international modern art and installations, and includes works by Dalí, Picasso, Matisse, and Pollock, as well as work by many acclaimed contemporary artists. With an increased focus on the global art scene, the displays are changed frequently.

① Three Dancers
Pablo Picasso (1881–1973) was noted for the different painting styles he mastered as he pushed the boundaries of modern art. The energetic, unsettling painting **(above)** *Three Dancers* (1925) followed the most serene stage of his work, and marked the beginning of a radical phase of distortion and emotional violence in his art.

② Fish
Romanian artist Constantin Brâncuși (1876–1957) created *Fish* in 1926. The sculpture presents a bronze "fish" on a polished metal disk balanced on a smooth, carved wooden base. The play of light on both the metal disk and the bronze adds a sense of movement.

③ Turbine Hall Installations
The power station's original and vast turbine hall is an iconic space used for large-scale as well as specially commissioned monumental art installations, which are very often interactive. With a new installation each year or so, the Turbine Hall has hosted some of the world's most acclaimed works and revolutionized public perceptions of 21st-century contemporary art.

④ Whaam!
Inspired by an image from *All American Men of War*, published by DC Comics in 1962, Roy Lichtenstein (1923–97) created *Whaam!* **(below)** in 1963. He was inspired by comics and advertisements, presenting powerful or emotive scenes in an impersonal and detached style.

The Tate Modern

⑤ Lobster Telephone
This iconic Surrealist work by Salvador Dalí (1904–1989) is made from steel, plaster, rubber, resin and paper. Created in 1938, this combination of objects with sexual overtones is one that Dalí returned to many times. For Dalí, such objects could reveal desires of the unconscious.

6 Fountain

One of the most iconic works of 20th-century art on display, Marcel Duchamp's much discussed *Fountain* is a urinal simply signed 'R. Mutt 1917'. This is a 1964 replica – the original, which consisted of a standard urinal, is lost. Made from glazed earthenware, it was painted to resemble the original porcelain. The ordinary object, presented largely unchanged but out of its usual context, is often used as an example to debate what constitutes a "work of art".

7 The Snail

This 1953 collage is one of the final works of Henri Matisse (1869–1954), completed while he was bedridden. The paper shapes represent a snail's shell.

10 Babel

The modern Tower of Babel (2001) is a creation of Brazilian artist, Cildo Meireles (b 1948). The immense pillar **(above)** of hundreds of radios produce a constant hum of noise as they all broadcast different frequencies. This installation is a part of Tate's themed exhibit Media Networks.

8 untitled: up-turnedhouse2, 2012

This unsettling, large-scale sculpture of a deconstructed shed by British artist Phyllida Barlow (b 1944) leans precariously, with a slab of concrete looming threateningly inches away from the viewer's head.

9 Composition B (No. II) with Red

The Dutch painter Piet Mondrian (1872–1914) gradually refined his art to a rigorous and pure abstract language of straight lines and squares of primary colours, an example of which is this painting, completed in 1935.

NEED TO KNOW

MAP R4 ■ Bankside SE1 ■ 020 7887 8888 ■ www.tate.org.uk

Open 10am–6pm daily (till 9:30pm last Fri of the month); closed 24–26 Dec

Adm for temporary exhibits

■ Tours run most days at noon, 1pm and 2pm.

■ Stores in both buildings have a wide selection of art and culture books.

■ A river boat service from Bankside connects the Tate Modern with the Tate Britain *(see p30)*

Gallery Guide
The main entrance, from the river, leads to the Turbine Hall on Level 0, where the information and ticket offices are located. There is also an entrance to the Blavatnik Building on Sumner Street. There are seven levels in the main Natalie Bell Building and eleven levels in the Blavatnik Building, though only five are currently in use.

The Start Display on Level 2 of the Natalie Bell Building is an introduction to the collection. Special exhibitions are displayed on Level 3 of the Nathalie Bell Building and Level 4 of the Blavatnik Building.

Level 6 of the Natalie Bell Building has a restaurant.

TOP 10 ⭐ Tate Britain

Opened in 1897 as the National Gallery of British Art, the magnificent collection at London's first Tate gallery ranges from 1545 to the present day. It was founded by the sugar merchant, Henry Tate (1819–99). The collection has works by major British painters and was greatly added to by J M W Turner, one of Britain's most revered artists. Paintings are often moved to Tate's other galleries, loaned out or removed for restoration. The works on these pages, therefore, may not always be on display.

1 Norham Castle, Sunrise

J M W Turner (1775–1851) was the great genius of English landscape painting. This c 1845 work **(above)** typifies his use of abstraction and luminosity of colour.

2 A Bigger Splash

British artist David Hockney (b 1937) celebrates his love affair with California with this 1960 work depicting the state's climate through the use of colour and light.

3 Standing Figure with African Masks

This monumental work in pastel and gouache by Black British artist Claudette Johnson (b 1959) depicts the artist in a defiant pose in front of abstract masked figures – a repudiation of western appropriation of African art forms.

4 Works by William Blake

Poet, mystic, illustrator and engraver William Blake (1757–1827) claimed to be guided by visions. Tate has a large collection of his works, including *Elohim Creating Adam*, which illustrates the Book of Genesis and shows Adam growing out of the earth.

5 Ophelia

Detailed and accurate observation of nature was a key element of the Victorian Pre-Raphaelite painters, as in this tragic scene from Shakespeare's *Hamlet* **(above)** by John Everett Millais (1829–96), painted in 1851–2.

6 Flatford Mill

Painted near his home in Dedham Vale, and depicting a mill on the Stour, this **(left)** is one of the first landscapes that John Constable (1776–1837) painted outdoors rather than in his studio.

The Cholmondely Ladies

One of the earliest works on display that dates from the early 1600s, this is a painting by an unknown artist of two almost identical noble women and their babies. Despite the strong likeness, there are subtle differences.

9 Carnation, Lily, Lily, Rose

John Singer Sargent (1856–1925) moved to London from Paris in 1885 and adopted Impressionist techniques. The title of this 1886 work **(right)** was taken from a popular song of the time.

10 Three Studies for Figures at the Base of a Crucifixion

Leading light of the Soho arts scene, Francis Bacon (1910–1992) was uncompromising in his view of life. When first shown, this triptych caused an immediate sensation, shocking audiences with its savage imagery **(below)**. It is now among his best-known works.

8 Recumbent Figure

Henry Moore (1898–1986) was a sculptor whose work is on public display around London. Figures such as this became a recurrent theme of Moore's prolific output.

NEED TO KNOW

MAP E5 ■ Millbank SW1 ■ 020 7887 8888 ■ www.tate.org.uk

Open 10am–6pm daily; Closed 24–26 Dec

Adm for temporary exhibitions

River boat service between Tate Britain and Tate Modern every 30 minutes from Millbank Pier

■ The excellent Djanogly café is located on the lower floor.

■ Free guided tours most days at noon, 1pm and 2pm, and regular talks.

■ The Tate's art bookshop is very comprehensive.

Gallery Guide
The permanent collection occupies most of the Main Floor. Starting in the north-west corner, it follows a broad chronological sweep from the 16th century to the present. Alongside the permanent collection are a smaller number of regularly changing displays focusing on individual artists, movements or topics. The Turner Collection – made up of 300 oil paintings and about 20,000 watercolours and sketches by J M W Turner – is displayed in the adjoining Clore Gallery.

Following pages Changing the Guard in front of Buckingham Palace

TOP 10 ★ Westminster Abbey

A glorious example of medieval architecture on a truly grand scale, this former Benedictine abbey church stands on the south side of Parliament Square *(see pp36–7)*. Founded in the 11th century by Edward the Confessor, it survived the Reformation and continued as a place of royal ceremonials. Queen Elizabeth II's coronation was held here in 1953 and her state funeral in 2022. It was also the venue for the wedding of Prince William and Catherine Middleton in 2011.

1 St Edward's Chapel
The shrine of Edward the Confessor (c 1003–66), last of the Anglo-Saxon kings, lies at the heart of Westminster Abbey. He built London's first royal palace at Westminster.

2 Coronation Chair
This chair was made in 1301 for Edward I. It is placed in front of the high-altar screen on the 13th-century mosaic pavement when used for coronations. Four gilt lions **(above)**, dating from 1727, form the chair's legs.

3 Nave
At 31 m (102 ft), this is the tallest vaulted nave **(right)** in England and took 150 years to build. Designed by the great 14th-century architect Henry Yevele, it is supported externally by flying buttresses.

4 Poets' Corner
This corner of the south transept contains memorials to literary giants, including Shakespeare and Dickens.

5 Lady Chapel
The spectacular fan vaulting **(below)** above the nave of this eastern addition to the church is late Perpendicular in style. Built for Henry VII (1457–1509), it includes two side aisles and five smaller chapels and is the burial place of 15 kings and queens.

6 Tomb of Elizabeth I
England's Tudor Protestant queen (1533–1603) is buried in a huge marble tomb complete with recumbent effigy on one side of the Lady Chapel. The tomb of her Catholic rival and first cousin once removed, Mary, Queen of Scots (beheaded in 1587), is on the other side of the chapel. Mary's remains were brought to the abbey by James I in 1612.

7 The Queen's Diamond Jubilee Galleries

These grand galleries in the abbey's medieval triforium display treasures from the abbey's collection. The triforium offers arresting views to the Houses of Parliament and into the church. Access to the galleries is via the Weston Tower by a staircase or lift.

8 Tomb of the Unknown Warrior

The body of an unknown soldier from the battlefields of World War I was buried here in 1920. His grave **(above)** represents all those of have lost their lives in war.

9 Chapter House

This octagonal building with a 13th-century tiled floor is where the abbey's monks once gathered. The House of Commons met here for a time in the 14th century. The door in the covered entrance is said to be the oldest in Britain.

10 Cloisters

The cloisters were located at the heart of the former Benedictine monastery and would have been the monastery's busiest area. On the east side are the only remaining parts of the Norman church, the Undercroft and the Pyx Chamber, where coinage was tested in medieval times.

ABBEY HISTORY

A Benedictine monastery was established by St Dunstan (AD 909–988) on what was the marshy Isle of Thorney. King Edward the Confessor re-endowed the monastery, and founded the present church in 1065. William the Conquerer was crowned here in 1066. Henry III's architect Henry of Reyns began rebuilding the church in 1245. The nave was completed in 1376. The eastern end of the church was extended by Henry VII, who had the Lady Chapel built. Finally, in 1734–45, the twin towers on the west front were completed by Nicholas Hawksmoor.

Westminster Abbey

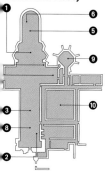

NEED TO KNOW

MAP L6 ■ 20 Dean's Yard SW1 ■ 020 7222 5152 ■ www.westminster-abbey.org ■ Guided tours (£10)

Open 9:30am–3:30pm Mon–Fri (from 9am Sat), Sun for worship only; times vary (check website)

Adm: adults £27; students and over 65s £24; children 6–17 £12 (under 6 free); family (1 adult, 1 child) £27

Cellarium Café and Terrace: open 8am–4pm Mon–Fri, 9am–4pm Sat

Queen's Diamond Jubilee Galleries: open 10am–3pm Mon–Fri, 9:30am–2:30pm Sat

■ Hear the choir sing at the 5pm Evensong service weekdays except Wednesday, 3pm some Saturdays and at Sunday services.

■ Listen to free organ recitals at 5pm every Sunday.

TOP 10 ⭐ Parliament Square

The Palace of Westminster, dominating Parliament Square and better known as the House of Commons, is the political heart of the nation, with a history stretching back a thousand years. The original palace, built by Edward the Confessor, served as a royal household until the reign of Henry VIII, after which the House of Commons moved into its St Stephen's Chapel. Parliament Square was planned as part of the rebuilding programme after fire destroyed the old palace in 1834.

1 Westminster Abbey

See pp34–5.

2 St Margaret's Church

Winston Churchill was among many eminent figures to marry in this 16th-century church (below). William Caxton (c 1422–92), who set up the first printing press in England, and the writer and explorer Sir Walter Raleigh are both buried here. Charles I is also remembered.

3 Big Ben

Reopened after restoration in 2023, the huge Elizabeth Tower of the Palace of Westminster is known as Big Ben (left). The name refers to the clock's 13.7-tonne bell, cast in 1858 and thought to be named after Sir Benjamin Hall, Chief Commissioner of Works.

4 Houses of Parliament

A Gothic Revival building by Sir Charles Barry and Augustus Welby Pugin, built between 1840 and 1870, the Houses of Parliament (right) cover 3 hectares (8 acres) and have 1,100 rooms around 11 courtyards. The Commons Chamber is where Members of Parliament sit and debate policy.

5 Westminster Hall

This lofty hall is one of the few remnants of the original palace that survived the 1834 fire. For centuries the courts of law sat beneath its grand 14th-century hammerbeam roof.

6 Central Hall

This large assembly hall, built in 1905–11 in Beaux-Arts style, was funded by a collection among the Methodist Church to commemorate its founder John Wesley (1703–91).

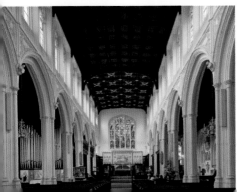

7 Jewel Tower

Built in 1365 to safeguard the treasure of Edward III, this is an isolated survivor of the 1834 fire. A museum about the history of the tower **(left)** is housed inside.

8 Millicent Fawcett Statue

A women's suffrage activist, Fawcett (1847–1929) is the only woman represented in the square. Other figures include Winston Churchill and Nelson Mandela.

PARLIAMENT

The 650 elected Members of Parliament sit in the House of Commons, where the Prime Minister and his or her government occupy the benches on the right-hand side of the Speaker, who ensures the House's rules are obeyed. The opposition parties sit on the Speaker's left. The 780 or so members of the House of Lords, most appointed by the government, have limited powers. The Prime Minister attends a weekly audience with the monarch, who today has largely a symbolic role.

10 Dean's Yard

Buildings around this square were used by monks until the Dissolution of the Monasteries. The square is now used by students at Westminster School, founded by Elizabeth I and one of the country's top public schools.

Parliament Square

NEED TO KNOW

MAP M6 ■ Parliament Sq SW1
■ www.parliament.uk

Tickets for tours on Saturdays and at other times during recess are available online or call 020 7219 4114.

Adm: adults £29, ages 16–18 and concessions £24.50, ages 5–15 £13; multimedia tours: £22.50/£19.50/£9.50

UK residents can arrange free guided tours through their MPs

■ The Public Galleries at the Houses of Parliament have limited seating for visitors during debates. Check times online or call 020 7219 4272.

■ Wesley's Café in Central Hall is a good place for a snack.

9 Statue of Oliver Cromwell

Oliver Cromwell (1599–1658) presided over England's only republic, which began after the Civil War. He was buried in Westminster Abbey, but after the monarchy was restored in 1660, his corpse was taken to the gallows at Tyburn and hanged as a criminal.

TOP 10 ⭐ Tower of London

London's great riverside fortress is usually remembered as a place of imprisonment, but it has a much more varied past. Originally a moated fort, the White Tower was built for William I (the Conqueror) and begun around 1078. It became home to the city arsenal, the Crown Jewels, a menagerie and the Royal Mint – and was enlarged by later monarchs, including Henry VIII, who sent two of his wives to their deaths on Tower Green.

③ The White Tower

The heart of the fortress is a sturdy keep, 30 m (90 ft) tall with walls 5 m (15 ft) thick. Constructed under William I, it was completed in 1097, and is the Tower's oldest surviving building. In 1240 it was whitewashed inside and out, hence its name.

① Yeoman Warders

The men and women who make up the Tower's 32 Yeoman Warders (above), known as Beefeaters, are drawn from the armed services. They organize guided tours of the Tower that are included in the ticket.

④ Imperial State Crown

This is the most dazzling of a dozen crowns in the Jewel House. It contains 2,868 diamonds, and the sapphire at its top is said to have belonged to Edward the Confessor (r 1042–66). The crown was made for the coronation of George VI in 1937.

The Tower of London

⑤ Chapel of St John the Evangelist

The finest Norman place of worship in London (left), which remains much as it was when it was built, is on the upper floor of the White Tower. In 1399, in preparation for Henry IV's coronation procession, 40 noble knights held vigil here. They then took a purifying bath in an adjoining room and Henry made them the first Knights of the Order of the Bath. It is still used as a royal chapel today.

② The Bloody Tower

The displays here explore the dark history of the Bloody Tower where murderous deeds, including the alleged killing of the little princes, took place (see p40).

6 Ravens

The saying goes that if the ravens leave the Tower the building and the monarchy will fall. Currently, there are nine ravens in residence, looked after by the Ravenmaster.

Tower of London

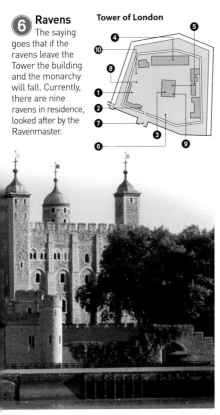

TOWER HISTORY

William I's White Tower was intended to defend London against attacks – and to be a visible sign to the native Anglo-Saxon population of the conquering Normans' power. Henry III (r 1216–72) built the inner wall with its 13 towers and brought the Crown Jewels here. The city arsenal was kept here, and under Henry VIII (r 1509–47) the Royal Armouries were improved. James I (r 1603–25) was the last monarch to stay in residence. All coinage in Great Britain was minted in the Tower's Outer Ward until 1810, when the Royal Mint was established on Tower Hill.

9 The Line of Kings

Drawn from the Royal Armouries' collection, this exhibition showcases the arms and armours of centuries of monarchs, displayed on and alongside carved horses.

NEED TO KNOW

MAP H4 ■ Tower Hill EC3 ■ www.hrp.org.uk

Open Mar–Oct: 9am–5:30pm Tue–Sat, 10am–5:30pm Sun & Mon; Nov–Feb: to 4:30pm; from 9am daily in school hols; last adm: 3:30pm year-round; closed 24–26 Dec

Adm: adults £29.90; children 5–15 £14.90 (under 5s free); family (1 adult, 3 children) £52.20, (2 adults; 3 children) £82.10

■ Beefeater tours set off from the main entrance every 30 min.

7 Traitors' Gate

The oak and iron water gate in the outer wall **(right)** was used to bring many prisoners to the Tower, and became known as Traitors' Gate.

8 Beauchamp Tower

The walls here are engraved with graffiti made by real prisoners of the Tower, including powerful nobles. The tower takes its name from Thomas Beauchamp, Earl of Warwick, who was imprisoned here between 1397 and 1399 by Richard II.

10 Tower Green

The place of execution for nobility, including Lady Jane Grey (1554) and two of Henry VIII's wives – Anne Boleyn (1536) and Catherine Howard (1542).

Tower Prisoners

1 Bishop of Durham
The first political prisoner to be held in the White Tower was Ranulf Flambard, Bishop of Durham. Locked up by Henry I in 1100, he was seen as responsible for the unpopular policies of Henry's predecessor, William II.

2 Henry VI
During the Wars of the Roses, between the rival families of York and Lancaster, Henry VI was kept in Wakefield Tower for five years, and died as a prisoner there in 1471.

3 The Little Princes
The alleged murder of Edward, 12, and Richard, 10, in 1483, gave the Bloody Tower its name. Some believe their uncle, Richard III, was responsible.

4 Sir Thomas More
Chancellor Thomas More's refusal to approve Henry VIII's marriage to Anne Boleyn led to his imprisonment in the lower Bell Tower. He was beheaded in 1535.

Anne Boleyn

Sir Thomas More

5 Henry VIII's Wives
Some of the Tower's most famous victims, such as the beheaded wives of Henry VIII, Anne Boleyn and Catherine Howard, are buried in the Chapel Royal of St Peter ad Vincula.

6 Lady Jane Grey
In 1553 Lady Jane Grey was queen for just nine days. Aged 16, she was held in the gaoler's house on Tower Green and later executed by order of Queen Mary I.

7 Catholic Martyrs
Under the reign of Elizabeth I (1558–1603), many Catholics were executed. Some, including Jesuits, were held in the Salt Tower.

8 John Gerard
Jesuit priest Gerard escaped from the Cradle Tower with a fellow prisoner in 1597, using a rope strung over the moat by an accomplice.

9 Guy Fawkes
The most famous of the Catholic conspirators, Guy Fawkes tried to blow up King James I and Parliament in 1605. He is burned in effigy each year on 5 November.

10 Rudolf Hess
The Tower's last prisoner was Hitler's deputy. He was held in the Queen's House in 1941, after flying to the UK to ask for peace.

Sites of Imprisonment

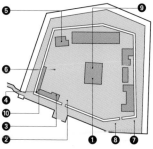

THE CROWN JEWELS

The lavish, bejewelled items that make up the sovereign's ceremonial regalia are all in the care of the Tower of London. The collection dates from 1661 when a new set was made to replace those destroyed by Cromwell following the execution of Charles I in 1649. St Edward's Crown was the first subsequent crown to be made of pure gold, and is the oldest of the 10 crowns here. Other coronation jewels on display include a gold, jewel-studded orb, made in 1661, and a

sceptre containing the 530-carat Cullinan 1, the biggest colourless cut diamond in the world. The Sovereign's Ring, made for William IV, is sometimes called "the wedding ring of England".

TOP 10 JEWELS

1 Imperial State Crown
2 St Edward's Crown
3 Imperial Crown of India
4 Queen Victoria's Crown
5 Royal Sceptre
6 Jewelled State Sword
7 George IV's Crown
8 The Sovereign's Ring
9 The Sovereign's Orb
10 The Sovereign's Sceptre

The Imperial State Crown is heavily encrusted with 2,868 diamonds, 17 sapphires, 11 emeralds, 4 rubies and 269 pearls. It is worn by the monarch during the State Opening of Parliament.

Queen Elizabeth II wore the Imperial State Crown at her coronation on 2 June 1953.

TOP 10 ⭐ St Paul's Cathedral

This is the great masterpiece of Christopher Wren, who rebuilt the City's churches after the Great Fire of 1666. Completed in 1711, it was England's first purpose-built Protestant cathedral, but the exterior design shares similarities with St Peter's in Rome, most notably its ornate dome. One of its bells, Great Paul, is the largest bell ever cast in Britain. Three clock bells strike the hour; the largest, Great Tom, marks the death of royalty and senior church officials. The cathedral is renowned for its music and draws its choristers from St Paul's Cathedral School.

3 Dome
One of the largest domes in the world **(left)**, it is 111 m (365 ft) high and weighs 65,000 tonnes. The Golden Gallery at the top, and the larger Stone Gallery, both have great views.

4 Whispering Gallery
Inside the dome is the famous Whispering Gallery **(right)**. Words whispered against the wall can be heard on the gallery's opposite side.

1 Quire
The beautiful choirstalls and organ case in the Quire are by Grinling Gibbons. Handel and Mendelssohn both played the organ, which dates from 1695.

2 The Light of the World
This painting by the Pre-Raphaelite artist William Holman Hunt shows Christ knocking on an overgrown door that opens from inside, meaning that God can enter our lives only if we invite him in.

5 Geometric Staircase
Located in the south-west bell tower, the remarkable Dean's Staircase, hewn from Portland stone, appears to float up to the ceiling. It is accessible on tours.

6 West Front and Towers
The imposing West Front **(right)** is dominated by two huge towers. The pineapples at their tops are symbols of peace and prosperity. The Great West Door is 9 m (29 ft) high and is used only for ceremonial occasions.

High Altar ⑦
The magnificent High Altar **(right)** is made from Italian marble, and the canopy, constructed in the 1950s after the cathedral was bombed during World War II, is based on one of Wren's sketches.

⑧ Tijou Gates
The French master metal worker Jean Tijou designed these ornate wrought-iron screens in the South and North Quire, along with the railings in the dome galleries and other cathedral metalwork.

⑨ Mosaics
Colourful mosaic ceilings were installed in the Ambulatory and Quire in the 19th century. They are made with glass tesserae, angled so that they sparkle.

⑩ Moore's Mother and Child
This piece is one of a growing number of works of art that have been introduced into St Paul's since the 1960s. The sculptor, Henry Moore, is commemorated in the crypt.

ST PAUL'S HISTORY

The first known church dedicated to St Paul was built on this site in AD 604. Made of wood, it burned down in 675 and a subsequent church was destroyed by Viking invaders in 962. The third church was built in stone. Following another fire in 1087, it was rebuilt under the Normans as a much larger cathedral, with stone walls and a wooden roof. This was completed in 1300. In 1666 Sir Christopher Wren's plans to restore the building had just been accepted when the Great Fire of London burned the old cathedral beyond repair.

St Paul's Cathedral

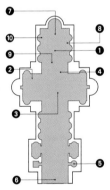

NEED TO KNOW

MAP R2 ■ Ludgate Hill EC4 ■ 020 7246 8350 ■ www.stpauls.co.uk

Adm: adults £21; children 6–17 £9 (under 6s free); students & over 60s £18.50; family £51; book online in advance for reduced rates. Services are free.

Cathedral: open 8:30am–4:30pm Mon–Sat (from 10am Wed); Sun for services only

Galleries: open 9:30am–4:15pm (from 10am Wed)

■ Guided tours run between 11am and 3pm and are included in the price of admission.

■ Food and drink are served in the café.

■ Choral evensong services are held at 5pm Mon–Sat, 3pm Sun; check the website for a full schedule of services.

■ Multimedia guides are included in the price of admission.

St Paul's Monuments

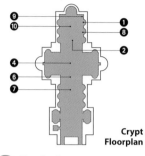

Crypt Floorplan

1 Tomb of Christopher Wren

St Paul's architect, Christopher Wren's (1632–1723), tomb inscription reads, "*Lector, si monumentum requiris, circumspice*" – "Reader, if you seek his monument, look around you".

2 Wellington's Tomb

The UK's great military leader and prime minister, Arthur Wellesley, 1st Duke of Wellington (1769–1852), lies in the crypt. He also has a monument in the nave.

3 John Donne's Memorial

The metaphysical poet John Donne (1572–1631) was made Dean of St Paul's in 1621. His effigy is in the South Quire Aisle on the cathedral floor.

4 Nelson's Tomb

Preserved in brandy and brought home from Trafalgar, naval commander Admiral Lord Nelson's (1758–1805) black sarcophagus is in the centre of the crypt.

5 American Memorial

Behind the High Altar on the cathedral floor, the American Memorial Chapel's roll of honour lists the US servicemen killed while stationed in the UK in World War II.

Detail, American roll of honour

6 Gallipoli Memorial

This memorial is dedicated to those who died in the 1915 Gallipoli campaign of World War I.

7 Churchill Memorial Gates

These gates commemorate Sir Winston Churchill (1874–1965), who during the 1940–41 Blitz said "at all costs, St Paul's must be saved".

8 The Worshipful Company of Masons Memorial

This City guild's plaque near Wren's tomb reads, "Remember the men who made shapely the stones of Saint Paul's Cathedral".

9 J M W Turner's Tomb

The great painter is buried in the Artists' Corner in the crypt.

10 OBE Chapel

At the eastern end of the crypt is a chapel devoted to those appointed to the Order of the British Empire, an honour established in 1917, and the first to include women.

Nelson's Tomb, St Paul's Cathedral

ST PAUL'S ROLE IN HISTORY

St Paul's, as the Cathedral for the Diocese of London, belongs to the parishes all across London, as well as to the nation. It is run by a Dean and Chapter of priests. One of the cathedral's main functions is as a place of national mourning and celebration. In the 19th century, 13,000 people filled the cathedral for the funeral of the Duke of Wellington. Queen Victoria's Jubilee was a spectacular occasion held on the steps of the cathedral. The then Prince of Wales and Lady Diana Spencer chose to be married at St Paul's rather than the royal Westminster Abbey. The decision helped to portray the couple as the people's prince and princess.

TOP 10 MOMENTS IN ST PAUL'S HISTORY

1 Elizabeth II's Platinum Jubilee (2022)

2 Prince Charles' and Lady Diana's wedding (1981)

3 Winston Churchill's funeral (1965)

4 Martin Luther King Jr preaches (1964)

5 Cathedral bombed (1940)

6 Queen Victoria's Diamond Jubilee (1897)

7 Duke of Wellington's funeral (1852)

8 Nelson's funeral (1806)

9 First service in the rebuilt cathedral (1697)

10 Gunpowder Plotters executed in the churchyard (1606)

The wedding of the future King Charles III and Lady Diana Spencer, 1981

The Duke of Wellington's funeral at St Paul's Cathedral

The Top 10 of Everything

**The Lady Chapel,
Westminster Cathedral**

TOP 10 Moments in History

Painting depicting Charles I being taken for his execution

1 AD 43: Roman Invasion
The Romans built a bridge across the Thames from Southwark and encircled Londinium with a wall, fragments of which are still visible in the City (see pp140–45). Their forum was near Cornhill and their amphitheatre lies beneath the Guildhall.

2 1066: Norman Conquest
The last successful invasion of England came from northern France. It was led by William, Duke of Normandy ("the Conqueror"), who was crowned King of England in the newly completed Westminster Abbey (see pp34–5) on Christmas Day 1066.

3 1381: Peasant's Revolt
Rebels marched on London, storming the Tower of London and beheading the Archbishop of Canterbury. The revolt ended in failure after its leader, Wat Tyler, was killed.

4 1534: The Reformation
A quarrel between Henry VIII and Pope Clement VII over the king's divorce led to Henry breaking with Rome and declaring himself head of the church in England. Today, the sovereign remains the head of the Church of England.

5 1649: Charles I Executed
Charles I's belief in the divine right of kings led to civil war. The royalist cause was lost and the king was beheaded in 1649. After 11 years of the Commonwealth, the monarchy was restored to power under his son, Charles II.

6 1666: Great Fire of London
Much of the city, including the medieval St Paul's Cathedral (see pp42–5) and 87 parish churches, were destroyed in the fire, which raged for nearly five days. Afterwards, Sir Christopher Wren replanned the cathedral, alongside 51 new churches.

7 1863: First Underground
The world's first underground railway was opened, operating between Paddington and Farringdon

Baker Street Underground station

Street. Carriages were pulled by steam locomotives until the early 20th century.

8 1940–41: The Blitz

Between September 1940 and May 1941, German air raids left 30,000 Londoners dead. The bombers destroyed much of the docks, the East End and the City. The House of Commons, Westminster Abbey and the Tower of London were all hit. Many Londoners sought shelter in Underground stations at night.

An air warden watching for bombers

9 2012: Olympic Games

The Olympic and Paralympic Games were held in London in 2012, with many of the city's iconic land-marks playing host to sporting events. Part of Stratford was transformed into a world-class Olympic Park, with a magnificent stadium and velodrome, and a spectacular aquatic centre with a wave-shaped roof.

10 2022: A New Royal Era

In 2022, numerous celebrations, including a joyful pageant and a concert outside Buckingham Palace, were held to mark Queen Elizabeth II's Platinum Jubilee. Her death in Sept-ember ended her reign, the longest in British history, and ushered in a new king. The state funeral for the Queen was held inside Westminster Abbey, which then also hosted the coronation of King Charles III in May 2023.

TOP 10 CULTURAL HIGHLIGHTS

The Great Exhibition of 1851

1 Shakespeare Arrives
William Shakespeare (1564–1616) was established as a London actor and dramatist by 1592.

2 Van Dyck Knighted
The Flemish artist Anthony Van Dyck moved to London and was knighted by Charles I in 1632 for his service as the court painter to the king.

3 Purcell's Appointment
The greatest English composer of his time, Henry Purcell was appointed organist at Westminster Abbey in 1679.

4 Handel's Water Music
George Frideric Handel composed *Water Music* for a performance on King George I's royal barge in 1717.

5 Great Exhibition
In 1851, the expanding Empire was celebrated in an exhibition held in a massive glass structure in Hyde Park.

6 J M W Turner Bequest
Turner's paintings *(see pp30–31)* were left to the nation in 1851 on condition that they be displayed together.

7 Royal Opera Highlight
In 1892 Gustav Mahler conducted the first UK performances of Wagner's *Ring* cycle at the Royal Opera House.

8 First Radio Broadcast
The BBC began broadcasting daily in November 1922.

9 Festival of Britain
In 1951, the Festival of Britain was held to mark the centenary of the Great Exhibition.

10 Royal National Theatre
The National Theatre company was founded in 1963 and temporarily housed at the Old Vic near Waterloo under Laurence (later Lord) Olivier.

🔟 Churches

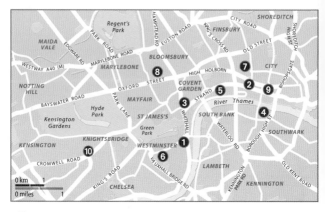

1 Westminster Abbey
See pp34–5.

2 St Paul's Cathedral
See pp42–5.

3 St Martin-in-the-Fields
MAP L4 ■ Trafalgar Sq WC2 ■ Open 9am–5pm daily (noon–7:30pm Wed) ■ www.stmartin-in-the-fields.org

This impressive parish church is famous for its music. There's been a church on the site since the 13th century, and the present building was designed by James Gibbs in 1726. The crypt café is award-winning.

St Martin-in-the-Fields

4 Southwark Cathedral
MAP S4 ■ London Bridge SE1 ■ Open 9am–6pm Mon–Sat, 8:30am–5pm Sun ■ www.cathedral.southwark.anglican.org

This priory church became a cathedral in 1905. It has many connections with local Elizabethan theatres, and with Shakespeare, who is commemorated in a memorial and a stained-glass window. US college founder John Harvard was baptised here and is remembered in the Harvard Chapel.

5 Temple Church
MAP P2 ■ 1 Inner Temple Lane EC4 ■ Open Mon–Fri; check website for times ■ Adm ■ www.templechurch.com

The original circular church was built in the 12th century for the Knights Templar. Effigies of the knights are embedded in the floor. A chancel was added in the 13th century. The church has been maintained by the Inns of Court since 1608, and was rebuilt after wartime bomb damage.

6 Westminster Cathedral
MAP D5 ■ Victoria St SW1 ■ Cathedral: open 7:30am–6:30pm Mon–Fri, 7:30am–7pm Sat, 7:30am–8pm Sun ■ Tower: check website for opening times; adm ■ www.westminstercathedral.org.uk

The main Roman Catholic church in England, Westminster Cathedral was designed in Byzantine Revival style by John Francis Bentley and completed in 1903. Intricate mosaics and over 100 varieties of marble decorate the interior, while the exterior features horizontal bands of white stone across red brickwork. Take the lift up the tower for spectacular views.

Inside St Bartholomew-the-Great

⑦ St Bartholomew-the-Great

A survivor of the Great Fire, this is London's only Norman church apart from St John's Chapel in the Tower of London. It was founded in 1123 by the monk Rahere, a courtier of Henry I, and its solid pillars and Norman quire have remained unaltered since. The 14th-century Lady Chapel, restored by Sir Aston Webb in 1890, once housed a printing press where US statesman Benjamin Franklin worked. The church *(see p144)* has also featured in films, including *Four Weddings and a Funeral* and *Shakespeare in Love*.

⑧ All Saints Margaret Street

MAP J1 ■ 7 Margaret St W1 ■ Open 11am–7pm Mon–Fri; Sat & Sun during services only
■ www.asms.uk

Designed by William Butterfield and completed in 1859, this is a fine example of High Victorian Gothic architecture, with a patterned brick exterior and an interior decorated with inlaid marble, mosaics and stained glass.

Reredos detail, All Saints Margaret Street

⑨ St Stephen Walbrook

MAP S3 ■ 39 Walbrook EC4
■ Open 10am–3:30pm Mon–Fri
■ www.ststephenwalbrook.net

Unspectacular on the outside, the interior of St Stephen Walbrook is the best-preserved and most beautiful of all Wren's churches – it was his own parish church. Designed as a prototype for St Paul's Cathedral, the space is dominated by its deep, coffered dome with ornate plasterwork, which is raised above a set of twelve Corinthian columns. A simple, white modern altar by Henry Moore sits in the centre of the church. There are free lunchtime musical recitals on Tuesdays and Fridays.

⑩ Brompton Oratory

MAP C5 ■ Brompton Rd SW7 ■ Open 6:30am–7pm daily
■ www.bromptonoratory.co.uk

Renowned for its rich musical tradition, this Italianate church was established by a Catholic convert, John Henry Newman (1801–90). He introduced to England the Oratory of St Philip Neri, a community of priests and lay brothers founded in Rome. The building opened in 1884, and houses many Italian treasures.

Rich interior of Brompton Oratory

Royal London

Main entrance to Hampton Court

1 Hampton Court
The finest example of Tudor architecture in Britain, Hampton Court *(see p153)* was given to Henry VIII by the king's ally Cardinal Wolsey. It was enlarged by Henry and then later rebuilt by William and Mary, who employed Christopher Wren as architect. Highlights include the huge Tudor kitchens, the Cumberland Art Gallery, the Chapel Royal and the royal apartments. The stunning gardens, with their famous maze, are as much an attraction as the palace.

2 Buckingham Palace
(see pp24–5).

3 Kensington Palace
Famous as the home of Princess Diana, this intimate royal palace's first sovereign residents were William and Mary in 1689, and Queen Victoria was born here in 1819. The interior preserves William and Mary's State Apartments, as well as the childhood rooms of Victoria, restored to their appearance in the early 19th century *(see p125)*. The Kensington Palace Pavilion is delightful for tea.

4 St James's Palace
Although closed to the public, St James's Palace *(see p119)* has a key role in royal London. Its classic Tudor style sets it in the reign of Henry VIII, and while it has had many royal residents, every monarch since Victoria has lived at Buckingham Palace.

5 Kew Palace and Queen Charlotte's Cottage
Kew, Surrey TW9 ■ Palace: open Apr–Sep: 11am–4pm daily; Cottage: open Apr–Sep: 11:30am–3:20pm Sat, Sun & public hols ■ Adm ■ www.hrp.org.uk
The smallest royal palace, Kew was built in 1631 and was a residence of George III and Queen Charlotte. Queen Charlotte's Cottage was used as a tea-time stop during walks. The palace is in Kew Gardens *(see p153)*.

6 Banqueting House
MAP M5 ■ Whitehall SW1 ■ Open for guided tours on specific days ■ Adm ■ www.hrp.org.uk
Built by Inigo Jones, this magnificent building is particularly noted for its

Sunken Garden, Kensington Palace

Rubens ceiling. It was commissioned by Charles I, who stepped from the Banqueting House onto the scaffold for his execution in 1649.

7 Queen's House
Romney Rd SE10 ■ Train to Greenwich or Maze Hill; DLR Cutty Sark ■ Open 10am–5pm daily ■ www.rmg.co.uk

This delightful home in the middle of Greenwich Park was the first Palladian building by Inigo Jones, and once home to the wife of Charles I. Restored to its 17th-century glory, it houses the art collection of the National Maritime Museum (see p56).

Queen's House, Greenwich

8 Royal Mews

(see p25).

9 Queen's Chapel
MAP K5 ■ Marlborough Rd SW1

This royal chapel is open only to its congregation (visitors welcome as worshippers). Built by Inigo Jones and operational from 1626, its furnishings include a beautiful altarpiece by Annibale Carracci.

10 Clarence House
MAP K5 ■ St James's Palace SW1

John Nash designed this house for the Duke of Clarence, who lived here after becoming King William IV in 1830. It was home to the Queen Mother until her death in 2002, and remains the preferred residence of King Charles III and the Queen Consort. It is closed to the public.

TOP 10 ROYAL MONUMENTS AND MEMORIALS

Albert Memorial, Kensington

1 Albert Memorial
Prince Albert, beloved consort of Queen Victoria, has a splendid memorial (see p125) in Kensington Gardens.

2 Queen Anne's Gate
A delightful small Westminster street with a statue of the queen who gave her name to a style of furniture.

3 Queen Elizabeth I's Statue at St Dunstan-in-the-West
Sculpted in 1586, this is one of the only statues to have been created during Elizabeth's reign.

4 Duke of York Steps
A statue of the "Grand Old Duke of York", subject of the nursery rhyme, is elevated above these steps off The Mall.

5 Queen Victoria Statue at Blackfriars
This regal statue at the northern end of Blackfriars Bridge shows Victoria in her pomp holding a sceptre and orb.

6 Queen Elizabeth II's Birthplace Plaque
At 17 Bruton Street in Mayfair, a simple plaque marks Elizabeth II's birthplace.

7 George VI and Queen Elizabeth Memorial
A statue of the late Queen's mother was positioned next to that of her husband, George VI, on The Mall in 2009.

8 Charles I Statue, Whitehall
Over the road from Trafalgar Square is a mounted Charles I.

9 The Henry VIII Gate at St Barts
The only outdoor statue of Henry VIII in London is at St Bartholomew's Hospital.

10 Princess Diana Memorial Fountain
This popular cascade in Hyde Park was opened in 2004.

TOP 10 Parks and Gardens

Tazza Fountain in the Italian Gardens, Kensington Gardens

1 Kensington Gardens
MAP A4–B4 ▪ W2 ▪ Open 6am–dusk daily ▪ www.royalparks.org.uk

A succession of queens living in Kensington Palace between 1689 and 1837 appropriated parts of Hyde Park for their palace gardens. Since opening in 2000, the Diana, Princess of Wales, Memorial Playground has proved a great hit with children. The park is also home to the Serpentine Galleries (see p59).

2 St James's Park
 London's oldest and most elegant park (see p119) was re-designed by John Nash in 1828. Its lake is home to many species of water-fowl, including pelicans which are fed daily at 2:30pm. It has an attractive café (see p123).

3 Hyde Park
MAP B3–D4 ▪ W2 ▪ Open 5am–midnight daily ▪ www.royal parks.org.uk

One of the most popular features of this huge London park is its lake, the Serpentine, with boats for hire in summer and a swimming area. Horses can be rented and ridden in the park. On Sundays at Speakers' Corner, near Marble Arch, you can get up on a soapbox and address the crowds who gather there.

4 Green Park
MAP D4 ▪ SW1 ▪ Open 24 hours daily ▪ www.royalparks.org.uk

This park was enclosed by Charles II in 1668 to create a link between Hyde Park and St James's Park, and opened to the public in 1826. There are deckchairs for hire in summer.

5 Regent's Park
 Home to London Zoo, an open-air theatre and a boating lake, Regent's Park (see p135) is surrounded by John Nash's Classical terraces. The fragrant Queen Mary's Garden is a delight.

The bandstand at Regent's Park

6 Richmond Park
Kingston Vale
TW10 ■ Open 24 hours
daily (Nov & Feb
7:30am–8pm) ■ www.
royalparks.org.uk

Covering an area
of 10 sq km
(4 sq miles), this is
by far the largest
Royal Park. Herds
of red and fallow

Fallow deer, Richmond Park

deer roam freely across the heath. In
late spring, the Isabella Plantation is
a blaze of colourful azaleas, camel-
lias and rhododendrons, plus many
rare shrubs. Pembroke Lodge is an
elegant spot for refreshment.

7 Victoria Tower Gardens
MAP E5 ■ SW1 ■ Open 24
hours daily ■ www.royalparks.org.uk

Although little heralded, this small
pocket of green just south of Parliament's Victoria Tower is utterly
charming. Beyond the entrance,
which features a memorial to suffra-
gette Emmeline Pankhurst, is a cast
of Rodin's *The Burghers of Calais*.

8 Primrose Hill
MAP C1 ■ NW1
■ Open 5am–dusk daily
■ www.royalparks.org.uk

North of Regent's Park, Primrose
Hill offers spectacular views of the
city skyline from its 63-m
(207-ft) summit. Once a
popular venue for duels,
this small park was pur-
chased by the Crown in
1841 to provide outdoor
space for the poor of
north London.

9 Bushy Park
Hampton Court Rd,
Hampton TW11 ■ Open
24 hours daily (Sep & Nov
8am–dusk Mon–Fri) ■
www.royalparks.org.uk

Chestnut Sunday in May,
when the blossoms are
out, is one of the best
times to come to Bushy
Park, near Hampton Court.

This is also the perfect time to visit
the magical Waterhouse Woodland
Gardens. Deer roam this
park, too.

10 Greenwich Park
SE10 ■ Open
6am–6pm or dusk
daily ■ www.
royalparks.org.uk

The 0° longitude
meridian passes through the Royal
Observatory Greenwich, located on a
hill in this sprawling 73-ha (183-acre)
park. It offers great views of the Old
Royal Naval College *(see p153)*, the
River Thames and over London.

The expansive Greenwich Park

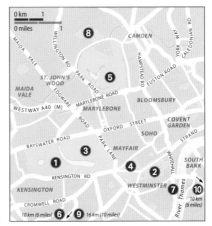

☰ Museums

Main entrance of the British Museum

① British Museum

The oldest national public museum in the world, and one of the most fascinating in London, the British Museum *(see pp12–15)* contains treasures from far and wide.

② Natural History Museum

Life on Earth and the Earth itself are vividly explained here *(see pp20–21)* using hundreds of traditional and interactive exhibits.

③ Science Museum

This exciting museum traces centuries of scientific and technological development *(see pp22–3)*, with impressive and educational displays throughout.

④ Victoria and Albert Museum

One of London's great pleasures, this museum of art and design *(see p125)* contains astonishingly eclectic collections covering many periods and styles. Highlights include the Medieval and Renaissance Galleries, with their remarkable collections, and

Chalice, V&A

the rooms full of Indian and Far Eastern treasures. There are also displays of ornate jewellery, fashion, textiles, metalwork, glass, paintings, prints and sculpture.

⑤ Horniman Museum

This award-winning museum *(see p154)* features a gallery of music instruments, a butterfly house and world culture displays, but the highlight is a natural history gallery that contains a remarkable collection of taxidermy and skeletons, including the famous Horniman Walrus. It also puts on fun workshops and events for kids.

⑥ National Maritime Museum

Greenwich SE10 ■ Train to Greenwich or Maze Hill; DLR Cutty Sark ■ Open 10am–5pm daily ■ www.rmg.co.uk

The world's largest maritime museum, part of the Maritime Greenwich World Heritage Site *(see p152)*, depicts Britain's seafaring past. One of the most famous exhibits is the coat that was worn by Nelson at the Battle of Trafalgar, complete with a bullet hole on the left shoulder. Four stunning galleries, opened in 2018, examine British and European sea exploration from the 15th century to the present day.

Spitfire, Imperial War Museum

7 Imperial War Museum

Some of the larger highlights in the four-level atrium of this museum *(see p89)*, housed in part of the Bethlehem ("Bedlam") Royal Hospital, include aircraft suspended from the ceiling, armoured vehicles and missiles, along with hundreds of smaller items in exhibitions covering World War I to the present day. The objects on display range from weapons, uniforms and equipment to diaries and letters, photographs and art. A highlight is the walk through a "trench" with a Sopwith Camel fighter plane swooping low overhead.

8 Design Museum

Located in a 1960s architectural landmark with beautifully converted interiors, this museum *(see p128)* is the only one in Britain devoted solely to 20th- and 21st-century British and inter-national design. There's a small but engaging free permanent exhibition, called Designer Maker User. The regularly changing exhibitions feature the very best of modern design, including both product and graphic design, fashion, furniture and engineering.

9 London Transport Museum

In this former flower-market building *(see p106)*, the history of London's transport system is illustrated with posters, photographs, films and examples of early buses, Tube carriages and horse-drawn vehicles. There are plenty of hands-on exhibits and activities available for children of all ages.

Exhibit, London Transport Museum

10 Sir John Soane's Museum

The former home *(see p113)* of Neo-Classical architect John Soane is filled with his collection of paintings, sculptures and ancient artifacts. An Act of Parliament negotiated by Soane preserves the house and collection as he left it, for the benefit of the nation.

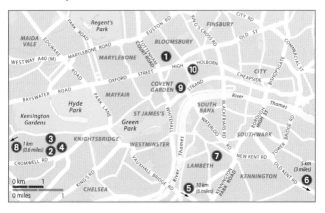

Art Galleries

Tiger in a Tropical Storm (Surprised!) by Rousseau, National Gallery

1 National Gallery

Located adjacent to the National Portrait Gallery, this Neo-Classical building with a "pepper pot" dome, houses one of the world's finest collections of European art *(see pp16–17)*.

2 Tate Modern

Housed in a huge converted power station *(see pp28–9)*, this exciting gallery with a modern extension covers modern international art of the 20th and 21st centuries. The exhibits are curated thematically, with an increasing focus on artists from across the globe.

3 Tate Britain

The oldest Tate gallery *(see pp30–31)* focuses on British art from 1500 to the present, has, among its many treasures, the largest collection of J M W Turner's works.

4 Courtauld Gallery

MAP N3 ▪ Somerset House, Strand WC2 ▪ Open 10am–6pm daily ▪ Adm ▪ www.courtauld.ac.uk

The Courtauld *(see p105)* is most famous for its exquisite collection of Impressionist and Post-Impressionist paintings, with world-famous works by Manet, Van Gogh, Modigliani, Cézanne, Monet and Renoir on display, among many others.

5 Wallace Collection

This wonderful Victorian mansion *(see p135)* belonged to Sir Richard Wallace (1818–90). In 1897, his widow bequeathed the house and the amazing art collection inside it to the nation. Covering three floors, the beautifully furnished rooms encompass an astonishing array of European paintings from the 15th to the 19th centuries, as well as porcelain, sculpture and armour – notable works include Nicolas Poussin's *A Dance to the Music of Time* and Frans Hals' *The Laughing Cavalier*. There are English portraits by Gainsborough and Reynolds.

6 National Portrait Gallery

Reopened in 2023 following a major refurbishment, this is the world's most extensive collection of portraits *(see pp18–19)*, home to over 220,000 paintings, drawings, sculptures, photos and mixed-media works. It is a virtual "Who's Who" of important British people.

The Brontë Sisters by Patrick Branwell, National Portrait Gallery

7 Serpentine Galleries

MAP B4, C4 ■ Kensington Gardens W2 ■ Open 10am–6pm Tue–Sun & public hols ■ www .serpentinegalleries.org

Opened in 1970 and 2013, these two contemporary art galleries located on either side of the Serpentine lake have a reputation for promoting avant-garde works. With an extension by the architect Zaha Hadid, the newer Serpentine North hosts temporary exhibitions while the original gallery, Serpentine South, is famous for its summer pavilion installations, in which leading architects design large temporary structures in the gallery's outdoor space. It also has an excellent art bookshop.

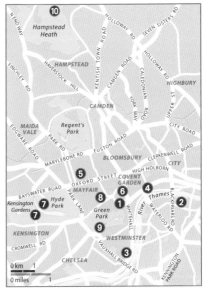

Façade of the Serpentine South

8 Royal Academy of Arts

The Royal Academy's *(see p119)* continual big-name temporary exhibitions draw the crowds, and it is often necessary to reserve a ticket in advance. The traditional Summer Exhibition, which both established and unknown artists can apply to enter, is also extremely popular.

9 Queen's Gallery, Buckingham Palace

Established in 1962, this fascinating gallery showcases the incredible selection of paintings and other pieces collected by British monarchs *(see p24)* over the last 500 years.

10 Kenwood

This majestic mansion with a library designed by Robert Adam has a small but important collection comprising 17th-century Dutch and Flemish works, 18th-century English portraits, and examples of French Rococo. There are statues by Henry Moore and Barbara Hepworth in the landscaped grounds *(see p148)*, which border Hampstead Heath.

Henry Moore sculpture, Kenwood

TOP 10 Literary London

Playwright and poet Oscar Wilde

1 Oscar Wilde

Dublin-born Wilde (1854–1900) dazzled London audiences with his plays and ready wit. Though he never recovered from his conviction for "gross indecency" in 1895, his plays, such as *Lady Windermere's Fan* (1892) and *The Importance of Being Earnest* (1895), are still staged today.

2 Samuel Johnson

Dr Johnson's House: MAP P2; 17 Gough Sq EC4; Open 11am–5:30pm Mon & Thu–Sat; adm; www.drjohnsonshouse.org

"When a man is tired of London, he is tired of life," said Dr Samuel Johnson (1709–84). A towering literary figure, he lived in this house from around 1748 to 1759 and compiled much of his famous dictionary here. His satirical poem, *London* (1738), attacked poverty in the city.

3 Geoffrey Chaucer

Chaucer (c 1343–1400) was a diplomat and son of a London vintner. His *Canterbury Tales* is a classic work of English literature, and follows a group of pilgrims travelling from Southwark to Canterbury. He is buried at Westminster Abbey.

4 Samuel Pepys

The extraordinary diary of Pepys (1633–1703) begins on New Year's Day, 1660, and ends on May 31, 1669. He vividly describes contemporary life, the Plague and the Great Fire, and a naval attack on England by the Dutch. The work was written in shorthand and only deciphered and first published in the 1820s.

5 Virginia Woolf

Woolf (1882–1941) and her sister Vanessa Bell lived in Gordon Square, where the influential pre-war Bloomsbury Group grew from social gatherings. She developed an impressionistic stream of consciousness narrative style in novels such as *Mrs Dalloway* (1925) and *To The Lighthouse* (1927).

6 Alan Bennett

The Yorkshire-born playwright has lived in and around Camden for over 40 years. *The Lady in the Van* is his touching and amusing account of an eccentric elderly woman who spent 15 years living in an old yellow van parked in the author's driveway.

Playwright and author Alan Bennett

Novelist and essayist Zadie Smith

7 Zadie Smith
Her first novel, *White Teeth*, made Smith (b 1975) an overnight sensation in 2000. Wickedly funny, it has remarkably well-drawn portraits of London life.

8 Martin Amis
Darling of the London literary scene in the 1970s and 1980s, Amis (b 1949) had a famous literary father and a precocious talent. His first novel, *The Rachel Papers* (1973), won a prestigious award for young writers and novels such as *Money* (1984) and *London Fields* (1989) are set in London.

9 Charles Dickens
London provided the setting for many of Dickens' novels (1812–70), and his experiences of the city deeply inspired his writing. For instance, working in a factory gave him an insight into London's poverty, and his job in a law firm helped him write *Bleak House* (1853). He also used many familiar places in his works, such as the debtors' prison in *Little Dorrit* (1855).

10 John Betjeman
A devoted Londoner, with a disdain for bureaucracy, mediocrity and hideous architecture, Betjeman (1906–84) was made Poet Laureate in 1972. His poems are full of wit and humour and he remains one of the United Kingdom's favourite poets.

TOP 10 LITERARY SIGHTS

1 Strawberry Hill, Twickenham
The 18th-century home of Horace Walpole that inspired *The Castle of Otranto* (1764).

2 Platform 9¾, King's Cross
Popular with Harry Potter fans for photo opportunities.

3 Russell Square
This square inspired scenes for William Thackeray's *Vanity Fair* (1848) and Virginia Woolf's *Night and Day* (1919).

4 The George Inn, Southwark
Dickens visited this inn and it is also mentioned in *Little Dorrit* (1855).

5 St Giles Cripplegate
This was the parish church of Daniel Defoe and John Bunyan, and the burial place of poet John Milton.

6 Rose Theatre, Bankside
Now partly excavated, this Tudor theatre was where Shakespeare's and Marlowe's plays were staged.

7 Senate House, Bloomsbury
This 1930s building inspired the Ministry of Truth in George Orwell's novel *Nineteen Eighty-Four* (1948).

8 The Criterion, Piccadilly Circus
A plaque commemorates how a meeting here in 1881 led to the introduction of Dr Watson to Holmes.

9 Kensington Park Gardens
Said to be the inspiration for the Darling Family home in J M Barrie's novel *Peter Pan and Wendy* (1911).

10 The Old Curiosity Shop, Portsmouth Street
Claimed to be the subject of Dickens' novel of 1841 and one of the oldest shops in London. It's now an artisan shoe shop.

The Old Curiosity Shop

Famous Residents

① John Keats

The London-born Romantic poet (1795–1821) lived in Hampstead from 1818 to 1820 *(see p147)* before leaving for Italy to try to cure his fatal tuberculosis. After falling in love with his neighbour's daughter, Fanny Brawne, he is said to have written his famous and beautiful *Ode to a Nightingale* in the garden.

② Florence Nightingale

Famously known as the "Lady with the Lamp", Florence Nightingale (1820–1910) tended to wounded soldiers during the Crimean War. After the war, she returned to London and established the first professional nursing school at St Thomas's hospital. The Florence Nightingale Museum *(see p90)* celebrates the life and works of this brilliant nurse and social reformer.

③ Charles Dickens

The great Victorian novelist and social campaigner (1812–70) lived in Doughty Street for two years from 1837 *(see p114)*. The house is his only surviving London home,

and he thought of it as "a frightfully first-class family mansion, involving awful responsibilities".

Statue of Millicent Fawcett

④ Millicent Fawcett

A campaigner for women's suffrage and leader of the National National Union of Women's Suffrage Societies for more than twenty years, Millicent Fawcett (1847–1929) lived in Gower Street for 45 years. There is a statue of her in Parliament Square *(see p36)* holding a banner proclaiming her widely known phrase, "Courage calls to courage everywhere".

⑤ Sigmund Freud

The Viennese founder of psychoanalysis (1856–1939) spent the last year of his life in a north London house *(see p147)*. A Jew, he had fled the Nazis before the onset of World War II, bringing his celebrated couch with him.

⑥ Lord Leighton

Yorkshire-born Frederic Leighton (1830–96) was one of the most successful artists in Victorian London

Charles Dickens

and president of the Royal Academy. He had Leighton House *(see p127)* built for him between 1865 and 1895.

(7) Amy Winehouse
The powerful songwriter with a soulful voice, Amy Winehouse (1983–2011) rose to fame in the 2000s. A bronze statue of her now stands in Stables Market, Camden *(see p147)*, near where she lived.

(8) The Duke of Wellington
Arthur Wellesley, 1st Duke of Wellington (1769–1852), lived at Apsley House *(see p120)*, popularly known as No. 1 London (the actual address is 149 Piccadilly), following his victories in the Napoleonic Wars.

(9) George Frideric Handel
MAP D3 ■ Handel & Hendrix in London, 25 Brook St W1 ■ Check website for opening times ■ Adm ■ www.handelhendrix.org

The great German-born composer settled here in 1712. The attic apartment next door was occupied by Jimi Hendrix in 1968.

Portrait of William Hogarth

(10) William Hogarth
Hogarth's House, Hogarth Lane W4 ■ Open noon–5pm Tue–Sun ■ Closed 1 Jan, Good Fri, Easter Sun, 24–26 Dec ■ www.hogarthshouse.org

The great painter of London life (1697–1764) was used to the gritty life of the city and called his house near Chiswick "a little country box by the Thames".

TOP 10 BLUE PLAQUES

Wax figurine of Mozart

1 Wolfgang Amadeus Mozart
The Austrian composer (1756–91) wrote his first symphony, aged eight, at No 180 Ebury Street.

2 Benjamin Franklin
The US statesman and scientist (1706–90) lived for a time at No 36 Craven Street.

3 Charlie Chaplin
The much-loved movie actor (1889–1977) lived for a period at No 15 Glenshaw Mansions, Brixton.

4 Charles de Gaulle
The exiled general (1890–1970) organized the Free French Forces from No 4 Carlton Gardens.

5 Mary Seacole
Jamaican nurse and heroine of the Crimean War (1805–81) lived at No 14 Soho Square.

6 Virginia Woolf
Before her marriage, the great English novelist (1882–1941) lived at No 29 Fitzroy Square, and later moved to No 34 Paradise Road, Richmond.

7 Mahatma Gandhi
The "father" of India's independence movement (1869–1948) lived as a law student at No 20 Baron's Court Road.

8 Jimi Hendrix
The American guitarist (1942–70) stayed in central London at No 23 Brook Street.

9 Henry James
The American writer (1843–1916) is commemorated with a plaque at De Vere Gardens, Kensington.

10 Emmeline Pankhurst
The leading women's rights activist (1858–1928) lived at No 50 Clarendon Road during World War I.

🔟 River Sights

Morton's Tower, Lambeth Palace

1 Lambeth Palace
MAP F5 ■ Lambeth Palace Rd SE1 ■ Closed for refurbishment until 2024 ■ www.archbishopof canterbury.org

The Archbishop of Canterbury's official London residence is a famous riverside landmark. Part of the palace dates from the 13th century, but it is the red-brick Morton's Tower or Gatehouse (1490) that gives the palace a distinctive appearance.

2 Houses of Parliament
See pp36–7.

3 Millennium Bridge
MAP R3

This blade-like, steel pedestrian-only suspension bridge links Tate Modern on Bankside with St Paul's Cathedral and the City opposite. It was the first central London river crossing to be built in over 100 years.

4 Savoy Hotel
London's first luxury hotel *(see p174)* opened in 1889 on the site of the medieval Savoy Palace. Its Chinese lacquered "ascending rooms" were some of the first lifts in Europe. Oscar Wilde objected to the built-in plumbing: he wanted to ring for his hot water like a gentleman. Take afternoon tea in the Thames Foyer or dine at Michelin-starred chef Gordon Ramsay's Savoy Grill. Attached is the historic Savoy Theatre.

5 Shakespeare's Globe
This modern reconstruction *(see p89)* in oak, thatch and 36,000 handmade bricks is near the site of the original Globe Theatre, which burned down in 1613. The centre of the theatre is uncovered, so performances only happen during part of the year, but there are guided tours all year round, and there is a bar and restaurant with river views *(see p93)*.

6 HMS Belfast
MAP H4 ■ The Queen's Walk SE1 ■ Open 10am–6pm daily (last entry 1 hr before closing) ■ Closed 24–26 Dec ■ Adm ■ www. iwm.org.uk

The last of the big-gun armoured ships, the nine-deck HMS *Belfast*

Millennium Bridge and St Paul's Cathedral at dusk

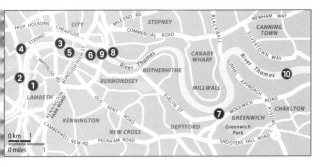

was launched in 1938 and saw active service in World War II and Korea. Retired in 1963, the ship was opened as a floating naval museum in 1971. Visitors can tour the huge engine rooms, the galley and the messdecks, and interactive exhibits make it easy to get an idea of what life must have been like on board.

The hull of the *Cutty Sark*

7 Cutty Sark
King William Walk SE10
■ Train to Greenwich; DLR Cutty Sark ■ Open 10am–5pm daily ■ Closed 24–26 Dec ■ Adm ■ www. rmg.co.uk

Launched in 1869, this is the last of the record-breaking tea-clippers that brought the leaves to thirsty London. Its history and life onboard can be explored inside, and for an additional fee the intrepid can scale the ship's rigging for magnficent views over London.

8 St Katharine Docks
The first piece of modern Docklands development was this handsome dock (see p142) beside Tower Bridge. Designed by Thomas Telford in 1826, it suffered severe bomb damage during World War II and was refurbished between the 1970s and 1990s. The area is now home to luxury apartments, shops and restaurants.

9 Tower Bridge
A magnificent piece of civil engineering, this bridge (see p141) is a Neo-Gothic wonder. It was completed in 1894 with steam pumps to raise its two halves. Tickets include views from the top and the engine room.

10 Thames Barrier
This barrier spanning 520 m (1,700 ft) across the lower reaches of the Thames (see p161), just past Greenwich, was built between 1974 and 1982 to prevent dangerous tidal surges from flooding central London. The Information Centre details historical flooding in London. The barrier has been raised over 200 times since it opened.

🔟 Off the Beaten Track

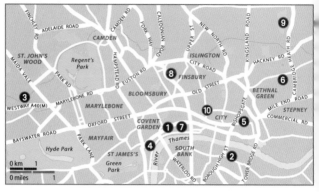

1 St Clement Danes
MAP N2 ▪ **Strand WC2** ▪ **020 7242 8282** ▪ **Open 10am–3:30pm Mon–Fri, 10am–3pm Sat & Sun** ▪ **www.stclementdanesraf.org**

Dating from 1681, this Wren church was rebuilt after bombing in 1941 and became the church of the Royal Air Force. The bells peal out the tune of "Oranges and Lemons".

2 Old Operating Theatre
MAP T4 ▪ **9a St Thomas St SE1** ▪ **020 7188 2679** ▪ **Open 10:30am– 5pm Thu–Sun** ▪ **Adm** ▪ **www. oldoperatingtheatre.com**

Located on the site of the original St Thomas' Hospital, this restored operating theatre is a fascinating window on 19th-century medicine. Housed in the church attic of the old hospital, it is reached by a tightly spiralling staircase. The theatre as

Interior of the Old Operating Theatre

well as the garret is stocked with remedies and surgical implements.

3 Puppet Theatre Barge
MAP B2 ▪ **Little Venice W2** ▪ **020 7249 6876** ▪ **www.puppetbarge.com**

From mid-September to mid-July the narrowboats in the canal quarter of Little Venice include the Puppet Theatre Barge, which puts on shows for children. It moves to the River Thames at Richmond for the summer holidays.

4 Benjamin Franklin House
MAP M4 ▪ **36 Craven St WC2** ▪ **020 7839 2006** ▪ **Architectural Tour: hourly 11am–2pm, 3:15pm & 4:15pm Fri; Historical Experience: same times Sat & Sun** ▪ **Adm** ▪ **www.benjamin franklinhouse.org**

This seemingly modest townhouse was once a hotbed of invention – the great American statesman-scientist lived here from 1757 to 1775, dreaming up the lightning rod and measuring the Gulf Stream. Themed tours explore his story.

5 Leadenhall Market
MAP H3 ▪ **Gracechurch St EC3** ▪ **Open all day, year-round** ▪ **www. leadenhallmarket.co.uk**

Leadenhall was once the site of the Roman forum, and it still dazzles

Crowds dining in Leadenhall Market

today, a warren of cobbled arcades encased in fancy ironwork. Fashion emporia and cheesemongers vie with slick brasseries and bars for patrons.

6 E Pellicci
332 Bethnal Green Rd E2 ■ Tube to Bethnal Green ■ Open 8am–4pm Mon–Sat ■ www.epellicci.co.uk
Lauded as the grandest of all the East End's traditional "greasy spoon" cafés, E Pellicci has been run by the same Italian family for a century. The breakfasts are legendary.

7 Temple
MAP P2–P3
This riverside campus in the heart of the city comprises two of the legal profession's four Inns of Court. A network of alleyways, gardens and medieval buildings make it an alluring spot to escape the West End crowds.

8 The Postal Museum
MAP F2 ■ 15–20 Phoenix Place WC1 ■ 030 0030 0700 ■ Open 10am–5pm Wed–Sun ■ Adm ■ www.postalmuseum.org
Explore the history of the postal service in the UK through interactive displays, interesting exhibits and an exciting ride on the Mail Rail. The miniature train takes you on a short but atmospheric trip along the Post Office's underground railway network.

9 London Fields
E8 ■ Train to London Fields ■ Open all day, year-round ■ www.hackney.gov.uk/london-fields
This very popular park in the heart of trendy Hackney is home to a wildflower meadow, tennis courts and London Fields Lido, an Olympic-sized heated outdoor pool. The nearby Hackney Museum explores the area's rich cultural influences.

10 Postman's Park
MAP R1 ■ EC1 ■ Open 8am–7pm (or dusk if earlier) ■ www.cityoflondon.gov.uk/things-to-do
The name of this picnic-friendly spot derives from its use by workers from the Post Office nearby. It houses the George Frederic Watts Memorial, honouring people who sacrificed their lives saving others'. Each is remembered on a hand-painted tile.

The picnic-friendly Postman's Park

🔟 Children's Attractions

Children looking at infinity mirrors in the Science Museum

1 Science Museum
See pp22–3.

2 Natural History Museum
See pp20–21.

3 Mudchute Park and Farm

City farms are great places for families to enjoy and at 13 ha (32 acres), Mudchute Park and Farm *(see p162)* is one of Europe's largest. This brilliantly conceived place in London's East End is home to more than 100 animals, from llamas and donkeys to pigs and sheep. For the really keen, farm tours are available in the summer holidays. Apart from the animals, the farm also has a range of plants, wetlands and open meadows to be explored. Make for the cracking café, Mudchute Kitchen, when the kids are getting hungry and tired.

A donkey at the Mudchute Farm

4 London Zoo

There's a full day out to be had in this 15-ha (36-acre) zoo *(see p135)*. Home of the Zoological Society of London, the zoo emphasizes its important international role in conservation and research work. Walk-through exhibits include Penguin Beach, Gorilla Kingdom, In With The Lemurs, Monkey Valley and the Land of the Lions enclosure.

Shark tank, Sea Life London Aquarium

5 Sea Life London Aquarium

Located on London's South Bank, the aquarium *(see p90)* is home to thousands of marine creatures. A journey through 14 different zones shows them in all their glory. Sharks, rays, octopuses and penguins are among the sea life to be seen here. For some interactive fun, visit the rock pool to see crabs and starfish, with marine experts on hand.

(6) Diana Memorial Playground

MAP A4 ▪ Kensington Gardens W2 ▪ Open 10am–dusk daily ▪ www. royalparks.org.uk

With its pirate galleon inspired by Peter Pan, the Diana Memorial Playground is the perfect place for imaginations to run wild.

(7) Young V&A

This East End museum (see p161) has one of the world's largest toy collections, and hands-on spaces that encourage children to create.

(8) Coram's Fields

MAP F2 ▪ 93 Guilford St WC1 ▪ Open daily from 8am Mon–Fri, 9am Sat & Sun; closing times vary ▪ www.coramsfields.org

"No adults can enter without a child", says the sign on the gate to this large park for children and young people. There's a paddling pool, sandpits, adventure playground with zipwire and a large slide.

(9) Battersea Park

MAP C6–D6 ▪ Albert Bridge Rd SW11 ▪ Zoo: open Easter–Oct: 10am–5:30pm (winter: until 4:30pm or dusk); adm; www.batterseaparkzoo.co.uk ▪ www.wandsworth.gov.uk/batterseapark

This large south London park (see p156) is ideal for children, with an adventure playground, a boating lake and kids' bikes available to rent. It is also home to a children's zoo, with meerkats, otters, monkeys, pigs and donkeys, among others. Children are allowed to help in feeding some of the animals.

Torture chamber, London Dungeon

(10) London Dungeon

MAP N5 ▪ County Hall, Westminster Bridge Rd SE1 ▪ Open 11am–4pm Mon–Fri, 10am–4pm Sat & Sun (extended opening hours during school hols ▪ Adm ▪ www.thedungeons.com

The scariest experience in town combines history and horror to celebrate an "orgy of grisly entertainment", with death, violence and gore at every turn. Follow in the bloody footsteps of the Victorian serial killer Jack the Ripper, bear witness to Guy Fawkes' Gunpowder Plot or be condemned by Henry VIII on the fast-flowing Tyrant Boat Ride. Be warned that it's not for the faint-hearted.

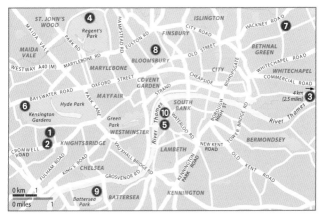

⏍⏍🔟 Performing Arts Venues

Performer at the Royal Opera House

1 Royal Opera House
One of the greatest opera houses in the world, this theatre is home to the Royal Ballet company (see p105), and hosts international opera productions. Apart from the sumptuous main auditorium, there are the Linbury Theatre and the Clore Studio, which stage smaller productions and events. There are regular backstage tours and many performances are broadcast to cinemas worldwide.

2 Southbank Centre
The centre (see p88) contains three concert venues – the Royal Festival Hall, Queen Elizabeth Hall and the Purcell Room – and the Hayward Gallery, Poetry Library, shops and restaurants. It hosts a range of events.

3 Barbican Centre
Home of one of the best music companies in the world – the London Symphony Orchestra – the Barbican (see p141) is the City's most important arts complex. Theatre, cinema, dance concerts and exhibitions can all be seen here, and there are plenty of restaurants, cafés and bars to be enjoyed. The centre also contains a library and convention hall. The Guildhall School of Music and Drama is located nearby.

4 London Coliseum
London's other principal opera house (see p108) stages innovative productions sung in English by the English National Opera. Opened in 1904, it was restored to its Edwardian decor in 2004.

Globe above the London Coliseum

5 National Theatre
MAP N4 ■ South Bank SE1
■ 020 7452 3000 ■ www.national
theatre.org.uk
Seeing a play here takes you to the heart of London's cultural life. Within the concrete blocks of this innovative building, designed by Denys Lasdun and opened in 1976, you can see a musical, a classic play or a new production in one of its three theatres: the Olivier, the Lyttelton or the Dorfman. Guided backstage theatre tours are also available. Reduced price tickets are sold from 10am on the day of the performance.

The National Theatre at night

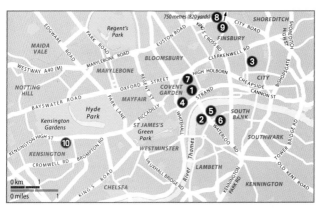

6 Old Vic
MAP P5 ■ The Cut SE1
■ www.oldvictheatre.com
Famed for its associations with
Laurence Olivier and other great
British actors, this historic theatre has
gained new verve in the last decade
with groundbreaking productions
and youth outreach initiatives. The
programme usually includes modern
revivals of neglected classics. A new
wing, housing event spaces and a
café-cum-bar is due to be completed
in 2024.

7 Donmar Warehouse
A little powerhouse, the
intimate Donmar (see p108) has
created some of the most dynamic
productions in London in recent
years, which have gone on to play
in larger theatres and be acclaimed
worldwide. Such is its reputation
that productions often feature star
actors that could fill much larger
performance spaces.

8 Almeida Theatre
MAP F1
One of the most renowned and award-
winning fringe theatres in the city, this
fantastic Islington venue (see p150) is
committed to promoting an innovative
and experimental programme of new
British theatre, reimagined classics,
and up-and-coming talent. This
325-seat theatre has brought to
stage many notable productions.

Dancer at Sadler's Wells

9 Sadler's Wells
Having an unsurpassed
reputation as London's best dance
theatre, Sadler's Wells (see p150) has
programmes for everyone, ranging
from creative re-interpretations of
the classics by Matthew Bourne to
international dance styles and contemporary and hip-hop performances.

10 Royal Albert Hall
This circular building
resembling a Roman amphitheatre,
has a terracotta frieze around the exterior. The atmosphere inside makes it a
treasured venue for every kind of concert, including the eight-week "Proms"
season (see p126), opera, ballet and
Cirque du Soleil performances.

⭑TOP 10 Live Music Venues

Ronnie Scott's, a famous jazz venue bustling with visitors

1 Ronnie Scott's
This legendary London jazz club *(see p99)* was opened by saxophonist Ronnie Scott (1929–96) in Gerrard Street in 1959. It moved to this location in Soho in 1965. Intimate lamplit tables surround a tiny stage that has hosted such stars as Ella Fitzgerald and Dizzy Gillespie, and continues to attract top names from the jazz world.

2 100 Club
MAP K2 ▪ 100 Oxford St W1
▪ www.the100club.co.uk

This atmospheric jazz, blues, rock and pop venue has a legendary heritage – the Rolling Stones played here, as did the Sex Pistols and other punk bands of the 1970s. Today it hosts a range of acts, with an emphasis on rock and indie.

3 The Jazz Café
MAP D1 ▪ 5 Parkway NW1
▪ www.thejazzcafelondon.com

Top performers from diverse genres, as well as great food, make this a popular venue. The best views are to be had from the balcony tables.

4 KOKO
MAP D1 ▪ 1a Camden High St NW1 ▪ www.koko.uk.com

Hosting mainly indie gigs and club nights as well as big names such as Arcade Fire, KOKO reopened in 2022 after a glamorous revamp, which added new performance spaces and a roof terrace.

5 O2 Academy, Brixton
211 Stockwell Rd SW9 ▪ Tube Brixton ▪ www.academymusicgroup.com/o2academybrixton

This is a great place to see acts from across the music spectrum. It holds nearly 5,000 but manages to retain an intimate atmosphere with good views of the performers from across the auditorium.

6 Roundhouse
This place has hosted the Rolling Stones, Jimi Hendrix, Led Zeppelin and other illustrious performers *(see p150)*. Originally a train shed, it was transformed in 2006 into one of the leading performance arts venues of London. Headline acts here include the biggest names in music as well as emerging talent.

7 Eventim Apollo, Hammersmith

45 Queen Caroline St W6 ▪ Tube Hammersmith ▪ www.eventim apollo.com

This giant former cinema remains ever-popular and has hosted many of the city's most memorable gigs.

8 Union Chapel

19b Compton Terrace N1 ▪ Tube Highbury & Islington ▪ www. unionchapel.org.uk

Still a functioning church, this Gothic revival chapel hosts concerts and other live performances, offering one of the most atmospheric gig experiences in London.

9 The O2

Peninsula Sq, North Greenwich SE10 ▪ Tube North Greenwich ▪ www.theo2.co.uk

Built as the Millennium Dome but later converted into a 20,000-seater concert venue in 2007, the O2 hosts some of the biggest names around. The 2,800-capacity indigo at The O2 is more intimate. Arriving via the Thames Clipper or IFS Cloud Cable Car is half the fun.

The O2 arena in Greenwich

10 The Troubadour

MAP A6 ▪ 263–7 Old Brompton Rd SW5 ▪ www.troubadour london.com

A coffee house club devoted to live music. All the great 1960s folk singers played here including Bob Dylan, and today there is a relaxed and enjoyable feel to the regular performance nights.

TOP 10 LONDON MUSICIANS

Stormzy performing at a concert

1 Stormzy
In 2019, the Croydon-born grime superstar became the first black solo artist to headline Glastonbury.

2 David Bowie
Brixton-born Bowie is arguably one of the world's most influential musical artists.

3 Adele
Hailing from Tottenham, Adele is one of the most successful singer/songwriters of the past 15 years.

4 George Michael
Originally part of Wham!, the late Finchley-born singer went on to sell millions as a solo artist.

5 Led Zeppelin
Formed in London in 1968, Led Zep are widely recognized as the progenitors of hard rock.

6 The Kinks
Penned by frontman Ray Davies, the Muswell Hill band's "Waterloo Sunset" is one of London's most enduring anthems.

7 Adam Ant
Lead singer of the new wave group Adam and the Ants who developed a cult following in the 80s.

8 Marc Bolan
From Stoke Newington, Bolan was one of the pioneers of glam rock in the 70s.

9 Sex Pistols
Legendary 70s punk band formed in London in 1975.

10 Amy Winehouse
A statue in Camden honours the late singer, whose soulful voice won her legions of fans.

Best Places to Eat

1 The Barbary

With an informal setting, this restaurant (see p111) set in Neal's Yard in Covent Garden epitomizes all that is exciting about London dining. Enjoy watching the chefs flame the food while eating at the bar. Combining the best of ingredients, the flavours draw inspiration from North Africa and the Middle East.

2 Clarke's

A steady favourite since it opened in 1984, this simple yet elegant restaurant (see p131) serves wonderfully fresh Mediterranean food. The set no-choice lunches that include roasted and baked dishes, are a highlight. There is also a daily changing selection of à la carte dishes and a well-chosen wine list. On most nights the owner, Sally, oversees every part of the operation.

3 Kricket

This modern restaurant (see p101), which originated in a shipping container at a food market in Brixton, now occupies a chic spot in Soho. With a convivial atmosphere, it offers modern Indian cuisine and inventive cocktails. Don't miss out on samphire *pakora* (fritters) or Keralan fried chicken among other highlights.

4 Hakkasan

Alan Yau, the man behind the highly successful Wagamama chain, founded this seriously stylish dining experience (see p117). Michelin-starred Chinese-style food, such as black truffle roasted duck or stir-fry rib black pepper beef with Merlot, along with dim sum specialities, is served in the luxurious surroundings designed by Christian Liaigre. The cocktails are also sublime.

5 J Sheekey

Established in 1896, this legendary restaurant (see p101) still remains head and shoulders above any of the city's other fish and seafood restaurants. Take your seat inside one of the booths, or at the oyster bar, and tuck into tasty morsels such as seared scallops or lobster thermidor.

6 Rules

London's oldest restaurant (see p111), open since 1798, is like a Victorian time capsule. The walls above the velvet seats are covered in hunting trophies and portraits of forgotten figures. Game is a speciality, and this is also the place to go for classic English roast beef.

Fine decor at Rules, London's oldest restaurant

7 The Ledbury

Australian chef Brett Graham is brilliant – make sure you book well in advance for his Notting Hill restaurant (see p131). The six- and eight-course tasting menus served at lunch and dinnertime, while far from cheap, are outstanding.

8 The Wolseley

Although it only opened in 2003, the Wolseley (see p123) has the feel of a 19th-century grand café-brasserie, and Londoners have taken to it as if it has been there forever. It's open from breakfast to dinner, serving finely prepared classic European dishes, and its giant windows offer a great view of Piccadilly.

The elegant interior of The Wolseley

9 Barrafina

One of the coolest tapas bars (see p101) around, using top-quality ingredients to excellent effect. Sit at the bar and watch the experts at work. There are also two branches in Covent Garden, as well as branches in Borough and King's Cross.

10 St John

A great restaurant (see p145) near Smithfield meat market, in a converted smokehouse, the focus here is on nose-to-tail eating. Guests are served a delicious range of high-quality British cuisine, and the bar-menu snacks are not expensive. There's also a sister branch in Commercial Street (see p163).

TOP 10 PLACES TO EAT WITH A VIEW

Seating at Galvin at Windows

1 Galvin at Windows
MAP D4 ▪ 22 Park Lane W1 ▪ 020 7208 4021
Sumptuous cuisine, views of Hyde Park.

2 Hutong
MAP T5 ▪ The Shard, 31 St Thomas St SE1 ▪ 020 3011 1257
On level 33 of the Shard, with great views of the skyline. The speciality is Sichuan and northern Chinese food.

3 Le Pont de la Tour
MAP H4 ▪ 36D Shad Thames SE1 ▪ 020 7403 8403
Modern French cuisine with a view over iconic Tower Bridge.

4 SUSHISAMBA London
MAP H3 ▪ Heron Tower, Bishopsgate EC2 ▪ 0203 640 7330
Inventive menu, served 38 floors up.

5 Portrait Restaurant
MAP L4 ▪ National Portrait Gallery, St Martin's Place WC2 ▪ www.npg.org.uk
Views over Trafalgar Square and Whitehall from this rooftop restaurant.

6 Seabird
MAP Q4 ▪ The Hoxton, 40 Blackfriars Rd SE1 ▪ 020 7903 3050
Fabulous fish on a hotel rooftop.

7 Skylon
MAP N4 ▪ Royal Festival Hall SE1 ▪ 020 7654 7800
One of the finest river views in town.

8 Swan at the Globe
MAP R4 ▪ New Globe Walk SE1 ▪ 020 7928 9444
Look over to the City through mullioned windows.

9 Oxo Tower Restaurant
Terrific river views (see p93) from this South Bank landmark.

10 Coq d'Argent
MAP S2 ▪ 1 Poultry EC2 ▪ 020 7395 5000
Unparalleled views from this rooftop garden bar and French restaurant.

TOP 10 Pubs

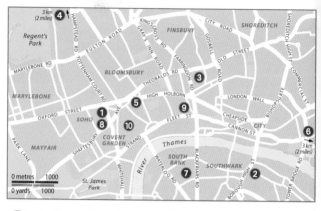

1 The Dog and Duck

Known to have been frequented by noted figures such as George Orwell and Madonna, this tiled Victorian pub *(see p100)* set in Soho. It has a tiny bar, where you might bump into art students and designers, and a blackboard with the latest selection of beers from all corners of Britain.

2 George Inn

Dating back to 1676 in parts, this is the only galleried coaching inn *(see p92)* left in London, and was given to the National Trust in the 1930s. You can enjoy excellent beers in its many old rooms with lattice windows and wooden beams, or in the courtyard.

The galleries of the George Inn

3 Holy Tavern

This delightful and atmospheric little pub *(see p145)* is kitted out in the style of an 18th-century coffee shop. It has a brown wooden interior with tiles, cosy booths and a small bar, and serves a broad range of ales. Note that the pub is closed on the weekend.

4 Spaniards Inn

This lovely 16th-century pub *(see p151)* on the northern edge of Hampstead Heath, with a large, attractive beer garden, is steeped in history and romance: the notorious 18th-century highwayman Dick Turpin is said to have drank here, along with literary luminaries Keats, Shelley and Byron and artist Sir Joshua Reynolds. Although the bar downstairs has been altered frequently over the decades, the small upstairs Turpin Bar is original. The food is generally reliable, too.

5 Princess Louise

The Princess Louise is a beautifully restored 19th-century pub *(see p117)* with stained-glass windows, a mosaic floor, mirrors, nooks and alcoves. A bonus is the Yorkshire-brewed Sam Smiths beer, as well as the delicious pies and puddings that are served here.

Entrance to The Grapes pub

6 The Grapes

This classic East End pub (see p163) has stood here since 1583 – although much of the current building dates from the 1720s – and it features in Charles Dickens' *Our Mutual Friend*. It is now owned by a group that includes actor Sir Ian McKellen They have maintained all its traditional charm, but added a very comfortable, high-quality restaurant on the first floor. It has a heated waterside deck overlooking the Thames.

7 Anchor & Hope

Located close to the Young Vic theatre, this bustling gastropub (see p92) – one of the city's originals – is worth checking out for its excellent food, such as duck confit with hazelnuts and Yorkshire veal milanese. Sunday lunch is very popular, so book well in advance.

8 French House

This was once a meeting place for the French Resistance during World War II – hence the name. Gaining a reputation as a bohemian bolthole, French House (see p100) was also frequented by artists and poets such as Francis Bacon, Brendan Behan and Dylan Thomas. It is now well known for its refreshing Breton cider, fine wines and earthy cooking – meals are served in the upstairs dining room.

9 Ye Olde Cheshire Cheese

In an alley off Fleet Street, this warren of rooms (see p145) still seems as if it should have sawdust scattered on the floors. Rebuilt in 1667, after the Great Fire of London, it was a favourite of Dr Johnson (see p60) and other writers. Never too crowded, its intimate corners make a good meeting place, made cosier with fires in winter. It is an ideal spot for enjoying good pub grub.

Pub sign

10 The Lamb and Flag

This old-world pub (see p110) tucked up an alley looks much as it did in Charles Dickens' day. In the heart of Covent Garden, it can get crowded – during the summer drinkers spill outside into the quiet alley. The 17th-century poet John Dryden was severely beaten up outside this pub, which was known as The Bucket of Blood because of the bareknuckle fights held here.

The Lamb and Flag, Covent Garden

🔟 Shops and Markets

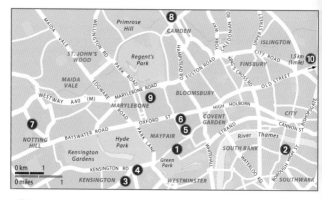

1 Fortnum & Mason

London's most elegant store *(see p122)* has hardly noticed the arrival of the 21st century. The ground-floor food hall is famous for its traditional English produce, and lavish picnic hampers can be found, along with a selection of fine wines, in the basement. The upper floors are good for designer men's and women's fashion and stylish gifts.

2 Borough Market

Nestled alongside Southwark Cathedral, London's oldest food market *(see p91)* is also one of its most atmospheric. It currently boasts over a hundred outlets selling

Artisan bread, Borough Market

high-quality produce from all across the country, as well as exceptional international specialities.

3 Harrods

London's most famous and exclusive department store *(see p129)* is more of an event than a shop. Covering seven floors, it is full of extraordinary things to buy – from pianos to children's racing cars – all with equally extraordinary prices. The children's toy department is excellent, and the store's food hall is rightly famous, with bars selling upmarket ice cream, sushi and countless other treats.

4 Harvey Nichols

With its flagship store in Kinghtsbridge, this is a premium British designer emporium *(see p129)*. There are wall-to-wall designer labels, an extravagant perfume and beauty department and stylish homeware. The fifth floor has a food market and the to-be-seen-in Fifth Floor Café.

5 Hamleys

The seven storeys of London's largest toyshop *(see p98)* contain just about anything a child might want, from traditional puppets and games to giant stuffed toys, models, arts and crafts supplies and all the latest

Hamleys toyshop on Regent Street

electronic gadgets. Of course, there are also many delights here for adults who haven't let go of their childhood.

6 Liberty

This handsome, half-timbered building *(see p98)* dates from 1924 and its fine wood-floored and panelled interior is part of the shopping experience. Long associated with the Arts and Crafts movement, Liberty employed designers such as William Morris to create its fabrics. Great for its own floral fabrics, home furnishings, men's and women's fashions.

7 Portobello Road

West London's liveliest street *(see p126)* sells a mixture of antiques and bric-à-brac. As it heads north, there are food stalls, crafts, clothes and music. Shops and some stalls open daily but the main attraction, the antiques section, is open on Saturday.

8 Camden Market

A great place to spend a Saturday, this rambling market *(see p147)* around Camden Lock takes in several streets and buildings. Street fashion, jewellery and vintage world crafts abound. Do note that weekends are generally very busy.

9 Daunt Books

For all things travel-related – and much more besides – this stunning Edwardian bookshop *(see p138)*, featuring galleried balconies, a conservatory ceiling and a stained glass window, is hard to beat. There are also branches at Cheapside, Hampstead, Belsize Park and Holland Park.

10 Columbia Road Flower Market

A visit to this hugely popular flower and plant market *(see p160)* is one of the most delightful things to do on a Sunday morning in London. With an impressive range on offer, look out for bargains as the day wears on.

The handsome interior of Liberty department store

London for Free

① South Bank Events
MAP P4 ■ www.southbank
centre.co.uk, www.nationaltheatre.
org.uk

Various free events are held along the
entire South Bank – from the National
Theatre (see p70) along to the Royal
Festival Hall (see p88). These include
concerts and shows, art exhibitions
and installations, as well as occasional social dances in the Festival
Hall's Clore ballroom. During
summer many stages and outdoor
bars are set up by the riverside.

② Walking Tours
www.free londonwalking
tours.com

Free London Walking Tours offers
2-hour strolls around the city. Choose
from several tours, including Secrets
of London, Debauched London, Royal
London and the Changing the Guard
tour. There is no upfront charge, but
guides are only paid by tip, so do
leave one.

**③ Museums and
Art Galleries**

Most of London's major public art
galleries and museums are free, and
it's easy to while away a whole day at
Tate Modern (see pp28–9), the British
Museum (see pp12–15) or the Natural
History Museum (see pp20–21). Less
well known are the Wellcome Collection (see p115), with inspiring temporary and permanent exhibitions on
the past, present and future of medicine, and the Wallace Collection (see
p135) and Kenwood House (see p148),
which have impressive collections
displayed in historic home settings.

Pageantry at Horse Guards Parade

④ Changing the Guard
MAP L5 ■ Horse Guards Parade,
Whitehall SW1

This ceremony (see p24) is world-
famous, but it can be tricky to get a
good view at Buckingham Palace.
Horse Guards Parade is more civil-
ized, with guards arriving on horse-
back at 11am (10am on Sundays) for
the mounted changeover ceremony.

⑤ Roman Amphitheatre
At the Guildhall Art Gallery
(see p142), the ruins of the city's
2,000-year-old colosseum lurk in a
dark basement. Built in c 70 AD and
capable of holding over 6,000 spectators, the amphitheatre would have
featured animal fights, executions and
gladiatorial combat. Sound effects
and spotlights bring the arena to life.

⑥ Sky Garden
MAP H3 ■ 20 Fenchurch St EC3
■ www.skygarden.london

A blot on the city skyline for some, the
"Walkie-Talkie" building is home to
London's highest public garden Its
three levels harbour an abundance of
greenery, with plants and herbs from
the Mediterranean to South Africa;
grab a beer or cocktail from one of the
bars and soak up the stunning views.

The Mold Gold Cape, British Museum

7 Nature Watch at St James's Park

www.royalparks.org.uk

Like all the royal parks, St James's (see p119) is full of free entertainment, but the show-stealers are its pelicans. In 1664, the first pelicans arrived as a gift from the Russian ambassador. The birds are fed daily at 2:30pm near Duck Island.

8 Parliamentary Debates

MAP M6 ■ Palace of Westminster, St Margaret St SW1 ■ 020 7219 4114 ■ www. parliament.uk/visiting

You can view debates most days by queuing on Cromwell Green – see the website for details. There are free guided tours of the Palace of Westminster for UK citizens who book ahead by applying to their MP.

Westminster Abbey

9 Evensong

Westminster Abbey (see pp34–5) and St Paul's Cathedral (see pp42–5) are must-visits for many, but the admission fees are steep. Visit for free by attending evensong, and experience London's greatest churches the way they were intended – as places for worship and reflection.

10 Stand-up Comedy

MAP G1 ■ Camden Head, 2 Camden Walk, Islington N1 ■ www. angelcomedy.co.uk

Check out the stars of tomorrow at one of London's free comedy clubs. Angel Comedy at the Camden Head pub runs nightly, with a mix of open-mic sessions and established acts.

TOP 10 BUDGET TIPS

Music at the Southbank Centre

1 Look out for free concerts in churches (see pp50–51), and at various locations in the Southbank Centre.

2 Some museums are free and others have free late-afternoon or evening opening. The London Pass (www. londonpass.com) gives access to more than 90 major sights.

3 There is street entertainment all day at Covent Garden. Leicester Square and the South Bank are also good spots.

4 Cheap theatre tickets (for the same day only) are available at TKTS, a booth on the south side of Leicester Square.

5 You can get standby tickets at many venues by lining up at theatre box offices.

6 London's numerous parks (www. royalparks.org.uk) offer lots of free entertainment, from exhibitions to bandstand concerts.

7 Santander Cycles (www.tfl.gov.uk) are a cheap way to get around the city. Bikes can be hired from as little as £2 – just bring your bank card to any docking station.

8 Check out the capital's plethora of markets for street-food stalls, where you can feast on delicious food at bargain prices.

9 Take advantage of happy hour offers at some of the city's best cocktail bars, usually available on weekdays between 5pm and 7pm.

10 For cheap rooms in London, investigate universities (which rent rooms from June to September) and youth hostels (see pp179–81 and www. lhalondon.com).

Festivals and Events

1 Chinese New Year
MAP L3 ■ Soho W1
■ Late Jan–mid-Feb

Chinatown *(see p95)* is taken over by dancing dragons breathing fire during this colourful festival. Food and craft stalls are authentic.

Fish Figurine, Chinese New Year

2 RHS Chelsea Flower Show
MAP C6 ■ Chelsea Royal Hospital grounds SW3 ■ May ■ Adm

As much a society outing as a horticultural event, this is the Royal Horticultural Society's prestigious annual show. Beautiful and imaginative gardens are created especially for the five-day event.

3 Trooping the Colour
MAP L5 ■ Horse Guards Parade SW1 ■ 2nd or 3rd Sat in Jun

The King celebrates his official birthday on Horse Guards Parade, where troops of the Household Division, in their famous red tunics and bearskin hats, put on an immaculate display of marching and drilling before escorting him to Buckingham Palace.

4 Meltdown Festival
Southbank Centre SE1 ■ Jun ■ Adm for events

The special attraction of this festival of the arts is that each year it is curated by a different guest director. Past curators include David Bowie, Patti Smith, Yoko Ono and Grace Jones.

5 Royal Academy Summer Exhibition
MAP J4 ■ Piccadilly W1 ■ Jun–Aug ■ Adm

Almost 1,500 works are selected from the public as well as Academicians for the art world's most eclectic summer show. Most of the works displayed are for sale.

6 BBC Proms
MAP B5 ■ Royal Albert Hall SW1 ■ Mid-Jul–mid-Sep

This is the most extensive concert series in the world. It culminates in the famous Last Night of the Proms, a patriotic, flag-waving extravaganza, which rocks the Royal Albert Hall *(see p126)* to its foundations.

7 Notting Hill Carnival
MAP A3 ■ Notting Hill W11 ■ Last weekend in Aug

A three-day Caribbean festival, Notting Hill is Europe's largest carnival, with steel bands and DJs playing everything from calypso to house music, street food, brilliant costumes and lively dancing. The children's parade is held on Sunday and the main parade on Monday.

Vibrant costume, Notting Hill Carnival

8 BFI London Film Festival
Various venues ■ Oct ■ www.bfi.org.uk

Hundreds of international films are shown across cinemas, including the BFI Southbank, during this 12-day festival. As well as features, there are short films, talks, immersive art and a free programme of events.

9 Fireworks Night
Around 5 Nov

Traditionally, effigies of Guy Fawkes, who attempted to blow up Parliament in 1605, are burned on bonfires across the country. These days firework displays are the main highlights of this festival. Alexandra Palace (see p150) and other parks host spectacular fireworks shows. Book in advance.

Lord Mayor riding in a gilded coach

10 Lord Mayor's Show
City of London ■ 2nd Sat in Nov

Every year, the City of London elects a Lord Mayor who rides in a procession through the Square Mile in a gilded state coach. This is the world's oldest and longest civic procession and includes military detachments, bands, floats and representatives from the City livery companies in traditional costume. They accompany the Mayor from Mansion House to the Law Courts, via St Paul's. Day-long family entertainment with live music, dance and food is also organized.

TOP 10 SPORTS EVENTS

Rugby at Twickenham Stadium

1 The Six Nations
www.sixnationsrugby.com
Rugby contest between England, France, Ireland, Italy, Scotland and Wales.

2 Oxford and Cambridge Boat Race
www.theboatrace.org
With separate men's and women's races, the two universities' annual contests cover some 6.8 km (4.2 miles).

3 The London Marathon
www.tcslondonmarathon.com
A 42-km (26.2-mile) road race from Greenwich Park to The Mall.

4 FA Cup Final
www.thefa.com
The much-anticipated last match of the Football Association Cup.

5 Test Matches
www.icc-cricket.com
Top-flight international cricket matches, with games lasting up to five days.

6 The Derby
www.thejockeyclub.co.uk
This is the historic highlight of the English flat horse-racing season.

7 Royal Ascot
www.ascot.co.uk
All London Society goes to the races in stylish hats and glamorous clothes.

8 The Wimbledon Championships
www.wimbledon.com
The world's premier grass-court tennis championships.

9 Rugby League Challenge Cup
www.rugby-league.com
The north of England comes to London for this bone-crunching final.

10 The London International Horse Show
www.londonhorseshow.com
Lots of family fun can be found at this Christmas show.

London
Area by Area

Millennium Bridge and St Paul's
Cathedral lit up at night

TOP 10 Westminster, the South Bank and Southwark

Big Ben

This area is rich with sights, cultural institutions and experiences. Attractions range from Westminster Abbey and the Houses of Parliament to the Tate's art institutions, the Southbank Centre and Shakespeare's Globe. In between there are the *Golden Hinde*, the fascinating Imperial War Museum, the London Eye and other attractions around County Hall, former headquarters of the Greater London Council. Two footbridges – the twin Golden Jubilee footbridges and the Millennium Bridge – help to bring together the two sides of the river.

WESTMINSTER, THE SOUTH BANK AND SOUTHWARK

1 Houses of Parliament

The Palace of Westminster (see pp36–7) is the seat of the two Houses of Parliament – the Lords and the Commons. A Union flag flies on the Victoria Tower, replaced by the Royal Standard when the King is present.

2 Tate Modern

One of the great contemporary art galleries in the world, Tate Modern (see pp28–9) is located in the Bankside Power Station and the modern Blavatnik Building extension. River boat services connect Tate Britain and Tate Modern.

3 London Eye

The large and spectacular cantilevered observational wheel offers amazing views of the city (see pp26–7). Close by are the attractions in County Hall – the Sea Life London Aquarium (see p90), London Dungeon (see p69) and Shrek's Adventure.

South façade of Westminster Abbey

4 Westminster Abbey

London's most venerable and most beautiful church (see pp34–5) is the scene of coronations and royal weddings and the final resting place of monarchs.

5 Tate Britain

The best of British art is held at the Tate (see pp30–31), with collections ranging from the 16th century to the present. While the contemporary installations add contrast and dynamism to the elegant spaces, the highlights are the collections of works by Turner and Blake. The atmosphere here is more relaxed than Tate Modern.

1	**Top 10 Sights**	see pp87–9
1	**Restaurants**	see p93
1	**Shopping**	see p91
1	**The Best of the Rest**	see p90
1	**Pubs and Cafés**	see p92

Gallery in the Tate Britain

6 Downing Street
MAP L5 ▪ Downing St
SW1 ▪ Closed to public

The official home and office of the UK's Prime Minister is one of four surviving houses built in the 1680s for Sir George Downing (1623–84) who studied in America as a youth and returned to fight for the Parliamentarians in the English Civil War. The building contains a State Dining Room and the Cabinet Room, where a group of senior government ministers meets regularly to formulate policy. Next door, No. 11, is the traditional residence of the Chancellor of the Exchequer, with numbers 9 and 12 used for other government offices. Downing Street has been closed to the public for security reasons since 1989.

7 Churchill War Rooms
MAP L6 ▪ Clive Steps, King Charles St SW1 ▪ Open 9:30am–6pm daily (last admission 5pm) ▪ Adm ▪ www.iwm.org.uk

During World War II, Winston Churchill and his War Cabinet met in these War Rooms beneath the Treasury building. They remain just as they were left in 1945, with spartan rooms and colour-coded phones. Take an audioguide through the rooms where ministers plotted the course of the war, and visit the Churchill Museum which records the prime minister's life and career.

WHITEHALL AND HORSE GUARD PARADE

The wide street connecting Parliament Square and Trafalgar Square is named after the Palace of Whitehall, the main residence of the Tudor monarchs. The palace was guarded on the north side at what is now Horse Guard Parade, where the guard (**below**) is still mounted daily at 11am (10am on Sundays), with a dismounting inspection at 4pm.

8 Southbank Centre
MAP N4 ▪ South Bank SE1 ▪ www.southbankcentre.co.uk

The most accessible arts centre in London *(see p70)* still has the air of friendly, egalitarian optimism. The Royal Festival Hall, Queen Elizabeth Hall and Purcell Room have diverse programmes, while the Hayward Gallery is a major venue for contemporary art exhibitions. The BFI Southbank, run by the British Film Institute, has a varied programme of films. The National Theatre's three stages (Olivier, Dorfman and Lyttelton)

Map Room at the Churchill War Rooms

are to the east along the river (see p70). Pedestrianized outdoor spaces host free performances, food markets and outdoor bars.

Exterior of Shakespeare's Globe

⑨ Shakespeare's Globe

MAP R4 ▪ 21 New Globe Walk, Bankside SE1 ▪ Performances mid-March to mid-Oct only: 020 7401 9919 ▪ Tours: from 10am daily (check website) ▪ Adm ▪ www.shakespeares globe.com

To see a Shakespeare play at the reconstructed Globe (see p64) is a magical experience. The theatre is open to the skies, with seating in three tiers around the sides and standing in the central courtyard. A second, adjacent indoor venue, the candlelit Sam Wanamaker Playhouse, based on designs of early 17th-century indoor playhouses, has performances year-round. The behind the scenes guided tours are highly worthwhile.

⑩ Imperial War Museum

MAP F5 ▪ Lambeth Rd SE1 ▪ 020 7416 5000 ▪ Open 10am–6pm daily ▪ www.iwm.org.uk

This museum documents the social effects of war as much as the technology. Concerned with conflicts in the 20th and 21st centuries, it will appeal to anyone interested in wartime Britain. Extensive galleries document trench warfare in World War I, life during World War II, and the Holocaust (unsuitable for under 14s).

A DAY BY THE RIVER

▶ MORNING

Start with breakfast at the **Marriott Hotel**, based in the splendid former headquarters of the Greater London Council. Cross Westminster Bridge to visit **Westminster Abbey** (see pp34–5) and the 16th-century **St Margaret's Church** (see p36), located right next to the abbey.

Walk along Abingdon Street and Millbank to Lambeth Bridge and re-cross the river. Have a coffee at the delightful little café at Lambeth Pier, passing **Lambeth Palace** (see p64) on your way. Walk along the Albert Embankment, past the moving **National Covid Memorial Wall**, and take in the stunning view of the **Houses of Parliament** (see pp36–7) across the river.

For lunch, walk along the South Bank and choose whichever eatery takes your fancy.

AFTERNOON

Walk along the river and browse the second-hand book-stalls outside the BFI Southbank. Continue past the craft shops of **Gabriel's Wharf** (see p91) to the **Oxo Tower's** (see p91) designer galleries and take the lift to the tower's viewing platform.

Afterwards, continue along the river to the **Tate Modern** (see pp28–9) – a wonderful place to spend the rest of the afternoon taking in a mind-boggling array of modern art. Further downriver, the **Anchor** pub (see p92) is a good place to stop for a drink, then continue on to Borough, where there are a host of good restaurants for dinner.

The Best of the Rest

① Clink Prison Museum
MAP S4 ■ 1 Clink St SE1
■ Open 10am–6pm daily ■ Adm
■ www.clink.co.uk

On the site of this medieval prison a small exhibition tells the stories of its inmates, and has torture instruments.

② Sea Life London Aquarium
MAP N6 ■ County Hall SE1 ■ Open 10am–4pm Mon–Fri (from 11am Thu); 10am–5pm Sat & Sun; closes 1hr later during school hols ■ Adm ■ www.visitsealife.com/London

See thousands of marine creatures at one of Europe's largest aquariums (see p68), located on the South Bank.

③ The View from the Shard
MAP T5 ■ Joiner St SE1 ■ Open daily; times vary ■ Adm ■ www.theviewfromtheshard.com

At the top of the tallest tower in the city are two viewing galleries. The one on the 72nd floor is open to the sky, and the views stretch beyond the city limits.

④ BFI IMAX
MAP P5 ■ 1 Charlie Chaplin Walk SE1 ■ Open daily (screening times vary) ■ Adm ■ www.bfi.org.uk

Giant-screen cinema that shows the latest movies and documentaries.

BFI IMAX

⑤ London Dungeon
MAP N6 ■ County Hall SE1
■ Open daily (times vary) ■ Adm
■ www.thedungeons.com

This perennial favourite (see p69) illuminates the capital's gory history.

⑥ Florence Nightingale Museum
MAP N6 ■ 2 Lambeth Palace Rd SE1
■ Open 10am–5pm Wed–Sun ■ Adm
■ www.florence-nightingale.co.uk

A fascinating museum devoted to the life and work of revolutionary 19th-century nurse Florence Nightingale.

Florence Nightingale's writing case

⑦ The Golden Hinde
MAP S4 ■ St Mary Overie Dock, Cathedral St SE1 ■ Open 10am–6pm daily (until 5pm Nov–Mar)
■ Adm ■ www.goldenhinde.co.uk

A full-size replica of the ship in which Sir Francis Drake circumnavigated the world from 1577 to 1580.

⑧ Fashion and Textile Museum
MAP H4 ■ 83 Bermondsey St SE1
■ Open 11am–6pm Tue–Sat ■ Adm
■ www.fashiontextilemuseum.org

Founded by Zandra Rhodes, the museum puts on well-curated temporary exhibitions on fashion and textiles.

⑨ Young Vic Theatre
MAP Q5 ■ 66 The Cut SE1
■ www.youngvic.org

This independent theatre company nurtures young thespian talent and attracts diverse audiences with its critically acclaimed productions.

⑩ Oxo Tower Wharf
MAP P4 ■ Bargehouse St SE1
■ Open daily ■ www.oxotower.co.uk

Take a lift to the viewing gallery next to the restaurant (see p93) for great city views.

Shopping

 Houses of Parliament Shop
MAP M6 ▪ 12 Bridge St SW1
Buy political books, homeware and jewellery, plus prints.

 Lower Marsh Market
MAP P6 ▪ Lower Marsh SE1
▪ Open 9am–3pm Mon–Fri ▪ www.lowermarshmarket.com
This market sells vinyl records and crafts and has an array of tempting food stalls.

③ BFI Shop
MAP N4 ▪ South Bank SE1
▪ Open noon–8pm daily
This film shop selling DVDs, books and gifts is a must for movie buffs.

④ Southbank Centre
MAP N4 ▪ South Bank SE1
In addition to concert halls and art galleries (see p88), the Southbank Centre has great shops. The South-bank Centre Shop itself and second-hand book stalls are a must-visit.

Shops in Gabriel's Wharf

⑤ Gabriel's Wharf
MAP P4 ▪ Gabriel's Wharf SE1
Shops in riverside Gabriel's Wharf sell clothing, jewellery and homeware.

 Bermondsey Fayre
MAP H5 ▪ 212 Bermondsey St SE1 ▪ Open 11am–5pm Thu–Sat, noon–5pm Sun ▪ www.bermondsey fayre.com
This gallery and yoga studio sells appealing clothes and accessories made by independent designers.

Food stalls at Borough Market

⑦ Borough Market
MAP S4 ▪ 8 Southwark St SE1 ▪ Open 10am–5pm Mon–Fri, 8am–5pm Sat, 10am–3pm Sun ▪ www.boroughmarket.org.uk
Superb quality produce and hot food stalls come to this incredibly popular traditional market near Southwark Cathedral, from all over the country. Fewer stalls are open for business on Mondays and Tuesdays.

⑧ Bermondsey Antiques Market
MAP H5 ▪ Bermondsey Sq SE1 ▪ Open 6am–2pm Fri ▪ www.bermondseysquare.net
This Friday morning market offers jewellery, glassware, trinkets and all sorts of material curiosities. Get here early in the day for the best finds.

⑨ Oxo Tower Wharf
MAP P4 ▪ Bargehouse St SE1
▪ Opening times vary ▪ www.coinstreet.org/shop-eat-drink
Three floors are given over to designers of fashion, jewellery and interiors. The gallery@oxo regularly showcases cutting-edge photo-graphy, design and architecture.

⑩ Konditor
MAP P5 ▪ 22 Cornwall Rd SE1 ▪ Open 8am–7pm Mon–Fri, 8am–6pm Sat, 10am–5pm Sun
This urban village bakery has a cult following among the cake connois-seurs. Its brownies are legendary.

See map on pp86–7 ←

Pubs and Cafés

The Southwark Tavern
MAP S4 ■ 22 Southwark St SE1

A popular pub with a wide range of food and drink. Upstairs is bright and airy, while the downstairs bar has exposed brick-walled booths.

2 Gentleman Baristas
MAP S5 ■ 63 Union St SE1

All the coffees in this adorable coffee house are named after hats – the bowler hat was invented nearby. The pastries are great, too. Other branches are dotted around town.

3 Anchor & Hope
MAP Q5 ■ 36 The Cut SE1

The food is among the best around. Great British ingredients make dining at this a gastropub (see p77) a wonderful experience.

4 Monmouth Coffee Company
MAP S4 ■ 2 Park St SE1

Serving arguably the best coffee in London, this atmospheric café in the heart of Borough Market also has delicious pastries and snacks.

5 The Anchor at Bankside
MAP Q4 ■ 34 Park St SE1

Snug, old pub close to the Globe Theatre with a large terrace that offers outdoor seating, making it a popular venue in summer. The dining room upstairs serves traditional pub grub.

6 Wheatsheaf
MAP S4 ■ 6 Stoney St SE1

The eclectic selection of craft beers and a menu of burgers and pizzas make this a great choice when exploring Borough Market.

7 The Kings Arms
MAP P5 ■ 25 Roupell St SE1

A deservedly popular real-ale pub, tucked away on a tranquil backstreet lined with beautiful Georgian terraces. It also serves good Thai food.

8 Market Porter
MAP S5 ■ 9 Stoney St SE1

This popular, historic pub overlooks Borough Market and has been serving punters since the late 17th century.

9 Rake
MAP S4 ■ 14a Winchester Walk SE1

A fine selection of beers is on offer at this tiny bar near Borough Market. The outdoor decking area is great for summer drinks.

10 George Inn
MAP S5 ■ 77 Borough High St SE1

London's only surviving galleried coaching inn (see p76) is a maze of plain, wood-panelled rooms and upstairs bars. Food is served throughout the day, all week. The courtyard tables are pleasant in the summer.

A vibrant riverside pub, The Anchor

Restaurants

Tables at the Cinnamon Club

PRICE CATEGORIES

For a three-course meal for one with half a bottle of wine (or equivalent meal), taxes and extra charges.

....

£ under £30   ££ £30–60   £££ over £60

1 The Cinnamon Club
MAP E5 ■ Old Westminster Library, 30–32 Great Smith St SW1 ■ 020 7222 2555 ■ £££

Housed in the Grade II-listed former Westminster Library, the fine-dining Cinnamon Club serves innovative Indian cuisine.

2 Skylon
MAP N4 ■ Royal Festival Hall, Belvedere Rd, Southbank SE1 ■ 020 7654 7800 ■ £££

Named after the symbol of the 1950s Festival of Britain, the Southbank Centre's restaurant is a classy affair. Guests have a fine river view, along with classic British dining.

3 Lupins
MAP S5 ■ 66 Union St SE1 ■ 020 3908 5888 ■ ££

Tasting plates packed with home-grown seasonal ingredients are the order of the day at this relaxed, bare-brick outfit beneath the train tracks.

4 Roast
MAP G4 ■ The Floral Hall, Stoney St SE1 ■ 020 3006 6111 ■ £££

In the middle of Borough Market (see p91) is this handsome restaurant with views of St Paul's. It serves excellent and well-sourced British cooking.

5 The Archduke
MAP N5 ■ 153 Concert Hall Approach SE1 ■ 020 7928 9370 ■ ££

Set in beautifully converted railway arches, this restaurant serves steaks, burgers and cocktails. Open daily with live jazz gigs.

6 50 Kalò di Ciro Salvo
MAP M4 ■ 7 Northumberland Ave WC2 ■ 020 7930 9955 ■ ££

London outpost of a top-flight Neapolitan pizzeria. Bases are thin and light, and toppings are first rate.

7 Pizarro
MAP H5 ■ 194 Bermondsey St SE1 ■ 020 7378 9455 ■ £££

A classic Spanish restaurant serving a small menu of Iberian meat dishes.

Views from Oxo Tower Restaurant

8 Oxo Tower Restaurant, Bar and Brasserie
MAP P4 ■ Oxo Tower Wharf SE1 ■ 020 7803 3888 ■ £££

Delicious modern dishes in the restaurant, and live jazz and a slightly cheaper menu in the Brasserie.

9 Swan at the Globe
MAP R4 ■ 21 New Globe Walk SE1 ■ 020 7928 9444 ■ ££

Next to the Globe, this place has great views of St Paul's and a creative menu.

10 fish!
MAP S4 ■ Cathedral St, Borough Market SE1 ■ 020 7407 3803 ■ ££

Innovative fish dishes are served in this modern, stylish restaurant.

See map on pp86–7

TOP 10 Soho and the West End

London's West End is an eclectic blend of theatre, live entertainment, nightlife, top-notch eating out and shopping. People flock here for the theatres of Shaftesbury Avenue and Charing Cross Road and the cinemas of Leicester Square. At its heart, the atmosphere of Soho is a big draw, its boutique shops and LGBTQ+ bars abuzz with activity as the night wears on. For a taste of East Asia, Chinatown boasts a wealth of restaurants. But this area isn't all about nightlife, Trafalgar Square is home to the National Gallery, the National Portrait Gallery and an excellent series of lunchtime concerts at St Martin-in-the-Fields.

Statue on the Shaftesbury Memorial Fountain

SOHO AND THE WEST END

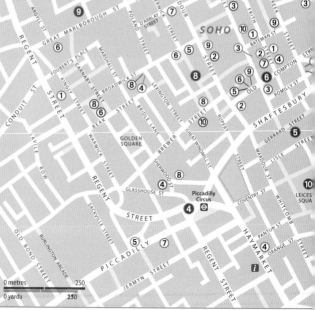

National Gallery
See pp16–17.

National Portrait Gallery
See pp18–19.

Trafalgar Square
MAP L4 ■ WC2

Trafalgar Square is a hub of the West End and a venue for public rallies and events. From the top of a 50-m (165-ft) column, Admiral Lord Nelson, who famously defeated Napoleon's fleet at the Battle of Trafalgar in 1805, looks down Whitehall towards the Houses of Parliament. The column is guarded at its base by four huge lions – the work of Edwin Landseer. At the northwest corner of the square, the Fourth Plinth features temporary artworks by leading national and

National Gallery, Trafalgar Square

international artists. On the north side of the square is the National Gallery *(see pp16–17)* and to the east is St Martin-in-the-Fields church *(see p50)*; to the southwest, Admiralty Arch leads to The Mall, and ultimately to Buckingham Palace.

Piccadilly Circus
MAP K3 ■ W1

Designed by the architect John Nash as a junction in Regent Street, Piccadilly Circus is the endpoint of busy, traffic-choked Piccadilly. Its Anteros statue – often mistakenly called Eros – tops a memorial fountain to the Earl of Shaftesbury that is a familiar London landmark and a popular meeting place. The Circus is renowned for its digital advertising displays and constant crowds. To the south is the Criterion Theatre, next to Lillywhites – a popular sporting-goods store.

Chinatown
MAP L3 ■ Sts around Gerrard St W1 ■ www.chinatown.co.uk

Chinese archways in Gerrard Street mark the entrance to Chinatown, an area of London that has, since the 1960s, been the focus of the capital's Chinese residents. Here you can shop at Chinese supermarkets and gift shops and dine at good-value restaurants. Chinese New Year, which falls between late January and mid-February, is raucously celebrated here with firecrackers and a procession.

1 Top 10 Sights *see pp95–7*
1 Restaurants *see p101*
1 Shopping *see p98*
1 Pubs and Cafés *see p100*
1 Late Night Venues *see p99*

6 Old Compton Street
MAP L2

The main street in Soho is a lively thoroughfare both day and night. It is also the centre of London's LGBTQ+ scene, and the site of the popular gay pubs Comptons of Soho and the Admiral Duncan. Soho's vibrant streetlife spills into Frith, Greek and Wardour streets, where pubs, clubs, restaurants and cafés have pavement tables. Some, like Bar Italia *(see p100)* on Frith Street and Balans No.60 *(see p99)* on Old Compton Street, are open until the early hours. Everywhere fills up when the evening's performance at the Prince Edward Theatre ends. A delicious breakfast is to be had at Café Boheme at No. 13 Old Compton Street, and such long-standing shops as the Italian delicatessen I Camisa & Son *(see p98)*, and the Vintage House (over 1,300 malt whiskeys in stock), give the area its village feel.

LGBTQ+ SOHO

Soho is undoubtedly the heartland of the city's LGBTQ+ community. It's a scene which has its roots at the turn of the 20th century when members of the community would meet in secret in the area's pubs. Today, a plethora of LGBTQ+ bars and clubs, such as Ku Bar **(below)** and Comptons of Soho, testify to the enduring popularity of the area among both residents and visitors.

7 Soho Square
MAP K2

This pleasant square, crossed by footpaths lined with flowerbeds, is popular at lunchtime, after work and at weekends, especially in summer. Many of the buildings in the square have long been occupied by film, TV production and other media companies. On the north side is a church built in 1893 for French Protestants under a charter granted by Edward VI in 1550. The redbrick, Italianate St Patrick's Catholic Church on the east side, dates from 1792. On the corner of Greek Street is the House of St Barnabas, a charitable foundation for the homeless in an 18th-century building, which is occasionally open for cultural events.

Mock-Tudor cottage, Soho Square

Stall at Berwick Street Market

⑧ Berwick Street Market
MAP K2 ■ Open 10am–6pm Mon–Sat

There has been a market on this street since the 18th century, and today the cheap and cheerful fruit and vegetable sellers have been joined by a clutch of excellent street food stalls. Berwick Street has also long had a reputation for its record shops, with Reckless Records at No 30 and Sister Ray at No 75.

⑨ The Photographers' Gallery
MAP J2 ■ 16–18 Ramilies St W1 ■ Open 10am–6pm Mon–Wed & Sat, 10am–8pm Thu & Fri, 11am–6pm Sun ■ Adm (free from 6pm Fri) ■ www.thephotographersgallery.org.uk

Displayed across three floors of exhibition space are works from both emerging global talent and established artists, as well as pieces from the gallery's archives. There are also talks, workshops and courses, plus a bookshop and a café.

⑩ Leicester Square
MAP L3 ■ Leicester Sq W1

This square was originally laid out in the 1670s. Celebrities of the 17th and 18th centuries who lived here included Sir Isaac Newton and the painters Joshua Reynolds and William Hogarth. Today the square forms the heart of London's West End entertainment district and houses the Empire and Art Deco Odeon cinemas. There is also a booth called "TKTS" to the south of the square where cut-price theatre tickets can be bought.

A WALK AROUND THE WEST END

▶ **MORNING**

Start the day in **Trafalgar Square** *(see p95)* at 8:30am when the fountains are switched on and view the latest art on the Fourth Plinth. You could spend a day at the **National Gallery** *(see pp16–17)*, but limit yourself to an hour or two, perhaps just visiting the Impressionist galleries.

For coffee, head next door to the Portrait Café on the ground floor of the **National Portrait Gallery** *(see pp18–19)*. After exploring the gallery, head up Charing Cross Road to Leicester Square. Note the statues of iconic movie characters dotted around the square. Continue towards the bright lights of **Piccadilly Circus** *(see p95)* and the Shaftesbury Memorial Fountain, and then walk up Shaftesbury Avenue, centre of the city's theatre district. Turn off here into bustling **Chinatown** *(see p95)*, with its colourful shops and good-value restaurants.

Lunch in Chinatown is obligatory. Enjoy *xiao long bao* (soup dumplings) at **Dumplings' Legend** *(15–16 Gerrard St)* or piping-hot Beijing dumplings at rough-and-ready **Jen Cafe**, on nearby Newport Place.

AFTERNOON

Spend the afternoon in colourful and lively **Soho**. Buy some fresh fruit from the stall in **Berwick Street Market**, then stroll up Wardour Street, and join in for the free ping-pong on Soho Square. Reward yourself with tea and a slice of cake at the delightful **Maison Bertaux** *(see p100)* in Greek Street.

See map on pp94–5

Shopping

 Hamleys
MAP J3 ■ 188–196 Regent St W1
London's largest toyshop *(see pp78–9)* is worth a visit just to see their fabulous window displays.

2 I Camisa & Son
MAP K3 ■ 61 Old Compton St W1
Established back in 1929, this authentic Italian deli is packed to the ceiling with an awesome selection of Italian foods.

 Foyles
MAP L2 ■ 107 Charing Cross Rd WC2
In a street of bookshops, this grandmother of all bookshops is something of an institution.

4 Dover Street Market
MAP L4 ■ 18–22 Haymarket SW1
Find cutting-edge fashion at this chic retail space offering designer clothing – such as Comme des Garçons – as well as homeware. There is a café on the top floor.

 Milroy's of Soho
MAP L2 ■ 3 Greek St W1
A West End whisky specialist, Milroy's of Soho has a small bar where malts can be sampled.

 Liberty
MAP J2 ■ 210–220 Regent St W1
This is one of London's most appealing department stores

(see p79). Originally founded in 1875, the shop remains famous for its "Liberty Print" fabrics.

 **Waterstones Piccadilly**
MAP K4 ■ 203–206 Piccadilly W1
Housed in an Art Deco building, this flagship store is Europe's largest bookshop, with six floors containing over 200,000 books. The store has cafés as well as a cocktail bar.

8 Lina Stores
MAP K3 ■ 18 Brewer St W1
Named after the Genovese woman who established it, this family-run Italian deli has been operating at this address since 1944. Quality Italian produce is imported and fresh pasta is made on the premises every day.

 Algerian Coffee Stores
MAP K3 ■ 52 Old Compton St W1
Opened in 1887, this is one of the oldest shops in Soho. It sells more than 80 kinds of coffee and exudes a wonderful aroma. Over 120 types of speciality teas and herbal infusions can also be bought here.

10 Goldsboro Books
MAP L3 ■ 23–27 Cecil Court WC2
Long-standing independent bookstore specializing in signed first editions, both fiction and non-fiction.

Liberty department store

Late Night Venues

PizzaExpress Jazz Club
MAP K2 ■ 10 Dean St W1

This Soho branch of the PizzaExpress chain hosts live music every evening, with late shows on Fridays and Saturdays starting from 10pm.

2 **100 Wardour Street**
MAP K3 ■ 100 Wardour St W1

An all-day restaurant serving upmarket global cuisine. Live music and DJs play Thursday to Saturday nights, when the restaurant is open till 3am. There is also a lounge and bar.

3 **Soho Theatre Bar**
MAP K2 ■ 21 Dean St W1

The buzzy bar at this hip comedy and theatre venue is open until midnight at weekends (1am for members and those with a ticket for a performance).

4 **Crazy Coqs**
MAP K3 ■ 20 Sherwood St W1

The Parisian-style Brasserie Zédel hosts comedy, music and magic shows as well as late-night cabaret. The stylish Bar Americain is also open until midnight.

5 **Balans No.60**
MAP L2 ■ 60 Old Compton St W1

This lively restaurant is open until 5am from Wednesday to Saturday nights, making it a great option for a small-hours burger or last drink before bed.

6 **Disrepute**
MAP K3 ■ 4 Kingly Court W1

A dimly lit basement cocktail bar with a cool 1960s vibe. Though technically for members only, it usually takes walk-ins – good thing, too, as it's open till 3am most nights.

7 **Ronnie Scott's**
MAP L2 ■ 47 Frith St W1
■ www.ronniescotts.co.uk

Opened in 1959 by saxophonist Ronnie Scott as a small basement club, this premier jazz venue *(see p72)* is buzzing every night of the week.

The impressive bar at Cahoots

8 **Cahoots**
MAP K3 ■ 13 Kingly Court W1
■ www.cahoots-london.com

Sporting a 1940s theme of a retro underground station, this basement bar hosts live music and mainly focuses on old tunes. Open until 2am Fridays and Saturdays. Book ahead.

9 **Thirst Soho**
MAP L2 ■ 53 Greek St W1

Spilt across two floors and offering an impressive cocktail menu, cosy Thirst is popular for its "Stupid Hour" happy hours. Downstairs, there are DJs and a dance floor that keeps going until 3am from Monday through Saturday.

10 **El Camion**
MAP K3 ■ 25–27 Brewer St W1

As the pubs close, night owls head for El Camion, which serves late-night Mexican food up to 2:30am. The Pink Chihuahua cocktail bar downstairs stays open until 3am Monday to Saturday.

El Camion restaurant

See map on pp94–5

Pubs and Cafés

1 Dog and Duck
MAP L2 ■ 18 Bateman St W1

Mahogany panelling, tiled walls and ornate mirrors make this tiny pub a wonderful slice of Victoriana. George Orwell celebrated the success of *Animal Farm* here and the upstairs dining room is named after the writer.

A taste of Paris at Maison Bertaux

2 Maison Bertaux
MAP L2 ■ 28 Greek St W1

Set in the heart of Soho, this little corner of Paris attracts a faithful clientele, who love its delicious coffee and heavenly cakes.

3 French House
MAP L3 ■ 49 Dean St W1

A small, one-bar establishment (*see p77*) where conversation flows freely among strangers, this Soho pub was once the haunt of the artist Francis Bacon (1909–92).

4 Bar Italia
MAP L2 ■ 22 Frith St W1

Sit at the bar or out on the pavement and enjoy the old-school Soho vibe while having a cup of classic Italian coffee. A huge screen at the back of the bar shows Italian football matches. Open 7am to 5am daily and until midnight on Sundays.

5 My Place Soho
MAP K2 ■ 21 Berwick St W1

This cosy, intimate space has good-value food and is frequented by locals and visitors alike. You'll find top-class coffee, cocktails and an excellent diverse menu served from 8 or 9 in the morning until late every day.

6 The Admiral Duncan
MAP K3 ■ 54 Old Compton St W1

A small, lively bar in Old Compton Street – one of dozens in the area popular with an LGBTQ+ clientele.

7 The Breakfast Club
MAP K2 ■ 33 D'Arblay St W1 ■ 020 7434 2571

One of ten branches across London, this is an excellent all-day breakfast spot. Go for the disco hash.

8 John Snow
MAP K3 ■ 39 Broadwick St W1

Always busy, this Victorian pub with cosy drinking compartments is delightfully atmospheric.

9 The Cork and Bottle
MAP L3 ■ 44–6 Cranbourn St WC2

This basement wine bar is a favourite with connoisseurs due to its exceptional wine list and excellent (if eclectic) food menu.

10 The Coach and Horses
MAP L3 ■ 29 Greek St W1

Long associated with writers and journalists, this old-school pub is a Soho institution, and sometimes hosts boisterous cockney singalongs.

Patrons at The Coach and Horses

Restaurants

PRICE CATEGORIES

For a three-course meal for one with half a bottle of wine (or equivalent meal), taxes and extra charges.

£ under £30   **££** £30–60   **£££** over £60

1 Ceviche
MAP L2 ■ 17 Frith St W1
■ 020 7550 9364 ■ ££

Named after its signature dish of citrus-cured fish, this Peruvian restaurant has been a big hit for more than a decade. The atmosphere is laid-back and the food delicious.

2 Hoppers
MAP L2 ■ 49 Frith St W1
■ www.hopperslondon.com ■ ££

An inviting, down-to-earth Sri Lankan restaurant in Soho where diners mix and match small mouth-watering curries and sides with rice or hoppers (lentil pancakes).

3 Burger and Lobster Soho
MAP K2 ■ 36–8 Dean St W1
■ 020 7432 4800 ■ £££

Offering perfectly cooked, meaty burgers, juicy steamed or char-grilled lobster and buttery lobster rolls with lemon mayo. Service is friendly, quick and polished.

4 BAO
MAP K3 ■ 53 Lexington St W1
■ www.baolondon.com ■ £

Soft, fluffy steamed buns, Taiwanese style, are the order of the day at this casual Soho diner. Try the pork confit *bao*.

5 Restaurant Yoshino
MAP K3 ■ 3 Piccadilly Pl W1
■ 020 7287 6622 ■ ££

Traditional favourites such as sushi, sashimi and tempura are served here. The extensive menu offers set three-course meals as well as à la carte. Try the mouthwatering Japanese barbecue dishes such as Wagyu ox tongue.

6 Yauatcha
MAP K2 ■ 15–17 Broadwick St W1 ■ 020 7494 8888 ■ £££

Book ahead to enjoy steamed scallop *shu mai* or venison in puff pastry at this highly regarded dim sum spot.

7 J Sheekey
MAP L3 ■ 28–32 St Martin's Court WC2 ■ 020 7240 2565 ■ £££

The best fish restaurant in London in a charming setting, with dishes such as Cornish fish stew.

The sleek interior of J Sheekey

8 Kricket
MAP K3 ■ 12 Denman St W1 ■ 0203 019 8120 ■ ££

This busy two-floor restaurant serves imaginative Indian sharing plates.

9 Busaba Eathai
MAP K2 ■ 106–110 Wardour St W1 ■ 020 7255 8686 ■ ££

A reliable Thai restaurant serving a terrific Pad Thai.

10 Barrafina
MAP K2 ■ 26–27 Dean St W1
■ ££

Enjoy quality tapas at the counter in this stylish restaurant. It's extremely popular, so be prepared to queue.

See map on pp94–5

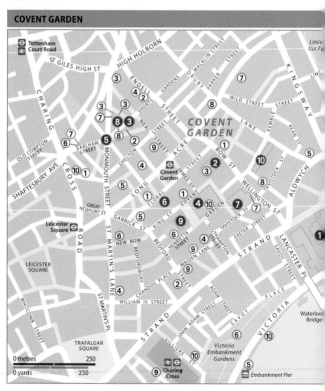 TOP 10 Covent Garden

One of London's most distinct squares and liveliest areas, Covent Garden is a popular destination for Londoners and tourists alike. At its heart is the capital's first planned square, laid out in the 17th century by Inigo Jones and now best known for its central covered Market Building, designed in 1833; here too is the Royal Opera House. While the Piazza is renowned for its luxury stores, nearby Neal Street and Neal's Yard are home to independent boutiques. To the south of Covent Garden, stretching along the river, is imposing Somerset House, home to the Courtauld Gallery and also the setting for outdoor concerts in summer and a superb ice skating rink in winter.

Column at the centre of Seven Dials

Previous pages Ballet at the Royal Opera House

1 Somerset House
MAP N3 ■ Strand WC2 ■ Open 8am–11pm daily (exhibitions from 11am–6pm Sat–Tue, noon–8pm Wed–Fri) ■ www.somersethouse.org.uk

Once a riverside palace, grand Neo-classical Somerset House is best known as the home of the peerless Courtauld Gallery (see p58). Much of the rest of the building is freely open to the public. Other highlights include the Embankment Galleries, with diverse exhibitions.

2 Royal Opera House
MAP M2 ■ Bow St WC2 ■ 020 7304 4000 ■ Open from noon daily; check website for tour times ■ Adm for tours and performances ■ www.roh.org.uk

London's impressive premier music venue is home to both the Royal Opera and Royal Ballet companies (see p70). The present Neo-Classical theatre was designed in 1858 by E M Barry and recycles a portico frieze recovered from the previous building, which was destroyed by fire. The Opera House was expanded in the 1990s to incorporate the old Victorian wrought-iron floral hall, which now houses a restaurant and champagne bar.

3 Seven Dials Market
MAP L2 ■ Earlham St WC2 ■ Open 11am–10am Mon & Tue, 11am–11pm Wed–Sat, 11am–9pm Sun ■ www.sevendialsmarket.com

This food hall, tastefully transformed from a 19th-century former banana warehouse, is the perfect introduction to the city's latest culinary trends. A row of food and wine stalls upstairs and inventive street-food vendors in the atrium offer global specialities. Don't miss the unique cheese conveyer belt that offers tasters the best of British cheeses.

4 The Piazza and Central Market
MAP M3 ■ WC2

For 300 years, Covent Garden was a fruit, vegetable and flower market – immortalized by Lerner and Loewe's hit musical *My Fair Lady*. In the 1970s the market moved and the lovely iron and glass Victorian halls were transformed into a vibrant, modern-day shopping area, surrounded by cafés and bars and enlivened by regular street entertainment.

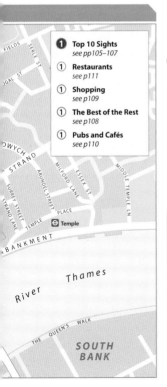

Apple Market, Covent Garden

5 Seven Dials
MAP L2 ■ WC2 ■ www.
sevendials.co.uk

"Covent Garden's hidden village" has an unusual street layout, created by Thomas Neale (1641–99) as a way to increase rents, which were then charged by frontage size rather than interior space. The sundial at the central monument has only six faces. The seven streets leading off it contain a mixture of shops, offices, restaurants and theatres.

6 Floral Street
MAP M3 ■ Floral St WC2

With some of the best shops in the area, this cobbled street is home to stylish British designers such as Ted Baker and Paul Smith. The Floral Court, just off here, is filled with a profusion of foliage and home to a deli and restaurants, including the high-end and elegant Petersham Nurseries.

7 London Transport Museum
MAP M3 ■ Covent Garden Piazza WC2 ■ Open 10am–6pm daily ■ Adm ■ www.ltmuseum.co.uk

This museum (see p57) explores London's transport, and its society and culture along the way, through some 500,000 objects. See vehicles that have served the city for over two centuries. You can

COVENT GARDEN ARCHITECT

Inigo Jones (1573–1652) designed Covent Garden as London's first planned square. The low roofs and classical portico of St Paul's Church **(below)** were influenced by the Italian architect Andrea Palladio (1518–80). As a set designer for royal masques, Jones was responsible for introducing the proscenium arch and moveable scenery to the London stage.

also try your hand at solving engineering conundrums and driving a modern Elizabeth line train.

8 Neal's Yard
MAP L2 ■ Neal St WC2

This delightful enclave is full of colour, with painted shop fronts, flower-filled window boxes and oil drums, and cascades of plants tumbling down the walls. This was once alternative London, with wholefood cafés, though there's now a range of restaurants and wine bars. Visit the now global Neal's Yard Remedies for

Buses on show at the London Transport Museum

Neal's Yard Remedies

Neal's Yard — Monmouth Coffee Company — Opera Tavern — Earlham Street — St Paul's Church — 180 Studios — Leicester Square station — Covent Garden Piazza — Benjamin Pollock's Toyshop — Somerset House

▶ MORNING

Take the Tube to Leicester Square and head up nearby Monmouth Street, where the delicious smell of coffee roasting will lead you to the **Monmouth Coffee Company** *(see p110)* for coffee and a pastry. Continue up Monmouth Street until you reach the small entrance to **Neal's Yard**. Buy some natural soap at Neal's Yard Remedies and check out the cheese in Neal's Yard Dairy round the corner in Shorts Gardens, before exploring the shops in Earlham Street. Visit **Covent Garden Piazza** *(see p105)* for the street entertainers outside Inigo Jones's elegant **St Paul's Church**. Take a look inside before eating lunch at the stylish **Opera Tavern** *(see p111)*.

AFTERNOON

Pop into **Benjamin Pollock's Toyshop** *(see p109)* in the Piazza, then turn down Russell Street and Wellington Street to the Strand. Cross the road and turn left to **Somerset House** *(see p105)*, a palatial Neo-Classical building that is home to numerous organizations. Pause to relax in the café by the courtyard fountains. Next, check out the superb art collection at the **Courtauld Gallery** *(see p58)* and then see what's on at the Embankment Galleries at riverside level. Afterwards, exit Somerset House and continue east along the pedestrianized stretch of the Strand towards **180 Studios** *(180 Strand; entered on Surrey Street)*, home to a maze of gallery spaces, studios and offices.

natural cures and beauty products, or try a variety of British cheeses at Neal's Yard Dairy round the corner in Shorts Gardens. Seek out Homeslice for a pizza or St John Bakery for pastries; either will set you up for an hour or two of shopping.

9 St Paul's Church
MAP M3 ■ Bedford St WC2
■ Open 8:30am–5pm Mon–Fri, 9am–1pm Sun ■ www.actorschurch.org

Inigo Jones built this church (known as "the actors' church") with the main portico facing east, onto the Piazza, and the altar at the west end. Clerics objected to this unorthodox arrangement, so the altar was moved. The entrance is through the garden while the grand east door is essentially a fake.

10 Theatre Royal Drury Lane
MAP M2 ■ Catherine St WC2 ■ Open for guided tours ■ www.thelane.co.uk

Drury Lane is synonymous with the London stage. This theatre has a splendid entrance, with magnificent stairways leading to the circle seats, and has staged some of the biggest musical extravaganzas. Its spaces, including a garden café and a stylish cocktail bar, are open to all-comers during the daytime. The first theatre on this site was built in 1663 for Charles II, whose mistress Nell Gwynne trod the boards.

See map on pp104–5 ←

The Best of the Rest

Bow Street Police Museum
MAP M2 ▪ 28 Bow St WC2 ▪ Adm
▪ www.bowstreetpolicemuseum.org.uk
Trace the story of the Bow Street Runners, London's first police force, in this dinky museum.

2 Donmar Warehouse
MAP L2 ▪ 41 Earlham St WC2
▪ 020 3282 3808 ▪ www.donmarware house.com
This 251-seater venue (see p71) produces theatrical performances. As well as new plays, it also stages at least one classic per season.

3 Backstage tours of the Royal Opera House
Book online in advance for backstage tours of the opera house (see p105). You might catch a dance rehearsal.

4 London Coliseum
MAP L3 ▪ St Martin's Lane WC2
▪ 020 7845 9300 ▪ www.eno.org
Opened in 1904, the home of the English National Opera (see p70) has a distinct Edwardian flavour.

River Cruises
MAP M4 ▪ Embankment WC2
Embankment Pier is a boarding point for a range of trips, from

Riverboat cruising along the Thames

Victoria Embankment Gardens

dining cruises to river boat services down to Greenwich and beyond.

Victoria Embankment Gardens
MAP M4 ▪ WC2
During the summer, outdoor concerts are held in these gardens by the river.

7 Freemasons' Hall
MAP M2 ▪ 60 Great Queen St WC2 ▪ www.ugle.org.uk
Take a free tour of the Grand Temple and ceremonial areas in the headquarters of English freemasonry. Be sure to visit the museum here.

8 St Mary-le-Strand
MAP N3 ▪ Strand WC2
This pleasing church, sitting at the tranquil, pedestrianized east end of the Strand, was consecrated in 1724. It was the first public building by James Gibbs. The interior is richly decorated in white and gold.

9 Benjamin Franklin House
MAP M4 ▪ 36 Craven St WC2 ▪ Adm
The only remaining home of this US founding father (see p66) offers an insight into his life and achievements.

10 Cleopatra's Needle
MAP M4 ▪ Victoria Embankment WC2
This granite obelisk was originally erected in Heliopolis around 1450 BC and transported to London in 1878. Its inscriptions and hieroglyphics document the achievements of the pharaohs of ancient Egypt.

Shopping

1 **The Tintin Shop**
MAP M3 ■ 34 Floral St WC2

Selling everything, from keyrings and Snowy toys to limited edition models, Tintin fans will love this shop.

2 **Whisky Exchange**
MAP M3 ■ 2 Bedford St WC2

The two floors are stacked with spirits from around the world. There's also a fine selection of wines and champagnes.

3 **Neal's Yard Remedies**
MAP L2 ■ 15 Neal's Yard WC2

Remedies, toiletries and make up, all made with purely natural ingredients, have been sold at this shop in pretty Neal's Yard *(see p106)* for more than 40 years.

4 **Stanfords**
MAP L2 ■ 7 Mercer Walk WC2

With an extensive range of travel guides, literature, maps, games and gifts, this shop is a traveller's paradise. There is a small coffee shop, too.

5 **St Martin's Courtyard**
MAP L3 ■ WC2

This new shopping and dining destination is a stylish yet charming urban village enclave, with alfresco tables and top-name stores.

6 **FOPP**
MAP L2 ■ 1 Earlham St WC2

Three storeys of records, DVDs, books, CDs and other media formats that refuse to die out, often at bargain prices: a nostalgist's dream.

7 **Penhaligon's**
MAP M3 ■ 41 Wellington St WC2

In business since the 1870s, this eccentric British perfumery has a glorious range of fragrances and accessories for both men and women. Their luxury candles make elegant gifts.

BOW WOW London

8 **BOW WOW London**
MAP M2 ■ 50A Earlham St WC2

Setting a new standard for the dapper dog-around-town, this dog boutique stocks the finest designer dog products to spoil your pooch with.

9 **Neal's Yard Dairy**
MAP L2 ■ 17 Shorts Gardens WC2

Follow your nose to this famous cheese store, which selects only the best produce from small, artisanal cheesemakers across Britain and Ireland. At Christmas the queues trail down the street.

10 **Benjamin Pollock's Toyshop**
MAP M3 ■ 44 The Market WC2

The place to go for theatrical gifts and traditional toys such as puppets and musical boxes.

Inside Benjamin Pollock's Toyshop

See map on pp104–5

Pubs and Cafés

1 Ladurée
MAP M3 ▪ 1 The Market WC2

This Parisian-style tearoom is known for its delectable macarons, but it also serves other stunning cakes and pastries, as well as champagne.

2 WatchHouse
MAP N3 ▪ Somerset House East Wing WC2

A top choice for recharging your batteries after an exhibition, this artisan Somerset House brew bar serves superb coffee alongside sweet treats, small plates and gut-busting all-day brunches.

3 Freud
MAP L2 ▪ 198 Shaftesbury Ave WC2

With a choice of coffees, cocktails and bottled beers, this basement attracts a designer crowd in the evenings.

4 Covent Garden Grind
MAP M3 ▪ 42 Maiden Lane

As the name suggests, the Grind group offers top-class coffee along with fresh juices and a brunch menu. They serve cocktails and wines, too.

5 The Lamb and Flag
MAP M3 ▪ 33 Rose St WC2

This traditional pub, serving cask bitter, is one of the oldest in the West End (see p77) and was frequented by Charles Dickens. Delicious roasts are served at Sunday lunchtimes.

6 La Gelateria
MAP L3 ▪ 27 New Row WC2

This tiny, artisan *gelateria* on eclectic New Row is among the city's best. Try the tangy honey, rosemary and orange zest variety or choose one of their fabulously rich chocolate creations. They also serve good coffee.

7 Monmouth Coffee Company
MAP L2 ▪ 27 Monmouth St WC2

One of the best places in London to buy and sample really good coffee (see p92). There's also a wonderful small café that serves delicious French pastries.

8 Lowlander
MAP M2 ▪ 36 Drury Lane WC2

Belgian beer and European cuisine served in a relaxed setting attract drinkers and diners alike to this popular spot.

9 Porterhouse
MAP M3 ▪ 21–2 Maiden Lane WC2

There are excellent beers and a great atmosphere to be enjoyed in this pub with three levels.

10 Gordon's Wine Bar
MAP M4 ▪ 47 Villiers St WC2

An ancient and atmospheric candle-lit cellar, where sherries, wines and ports are served, alongside hearty cheese plates.

The cavernous interior of Gordon's Wine Bar

Restaurants

PRICE CATEGORIES
For a three-course meal for one with half
a bottle of wine (or equivalent meal),
taxes and extra charges.

£ under £30   ££ £30–60   £££ over £60

1 The Ivy
MAP L2 ▪ 1–5 West St WC2
▪ 020 7836 4751 ▪ £££

Once London's most fashionable
restaurant, The Ivy these days is
something of a Covent Garden
grande dame. The brasserie-style
food is still as delicious as ever.
Book ahead.

2 The Barbary
MAP L2 ▪ 16 Neal's Yard, WC2
▪ www.thebarbary.co.uk ▪ ££

Sit at the bar of this award-winning
restaurant (see p74) while watching
the chefs at work. The menu combines Middle Eastern and North
African influences.

3 Mon Plaisir
MAP L2 ▪ 19–21 Monmouth St
WC2 ▪ 020 7240 3757 ▪ £££

One of the oldest French restaurants in London, this place has
four rooms, each of a different
size and feel. Daily specials keep
the menu fresh. Set lunch and pre-
theatre menus offer better value
for money.

4 Rock and Sole Plaice
MAP M2 ▪ 47 Endell St WC2
▪ 020 7836 3785 ▪ £

Established in the 1870s, Rock and
Sole Plaice serves excellent traditional English fish and chips.

5 The Delaunay
MAP N2 ▪ 55 Aldwych WC2
▪ 020 7499 8558 ▪ £££

Open from breakfast until late,
this elegant restaurant offers an
extensive à la carte menu inspired by
the grand cafés of Europe. Patrons
can also enjoy breakfast or brunch.
Try the Wiener schnitzel.

Vibrant interior of Cora Pearl

6 Cora Pearl
MAP M3 ▪ 30 Henrietta St WC2
▪ 020 7324 7722 ▪ ££

Occupying two floors, this smart
modern British restaurant with
elegant interiors and vintage lighting
is a delightful addition to Covent
Garden. The varied pre-theatre menu
is good value.

7 Chick 'n' Sours
MAP M3 ▪ 1a Earlham St WC2
▪ 020 3198 4814 ▪ £

Deep-fried chicken, cocktails and
a thumping soundtrack. This is fried
chicken, but not as you know it.

8 Opera Tavern
MAP M3 ▪ 23 Catherine St WC2
▪ 020 7836 3680 ▪ ££

Enjoy scrumptious Italian and
Spanish tapas complemented by
a terrific wine list at this tavern.

9 Rules
MAP M3 ▪ 35 Maiden Lane
WC2 ▪ 020 7836 5314 ▪ £££

London's oldest restaurant (see
p74) has been famed since 1798
for its "oysters, pies and game".

10 Souk
MAP L2 ▪ 27 Litchfield St WC2
▪ 020 7240 1796 ▪ ££

From mint tea to tagines and belly
dancing to Arabic music, this place
offers a real taste of Marrakech.

See map on pp104–5

TOP 10 Bloomsbury and Fitzrovia

Charles Dickens

Literary, legal and scholarly, this is the brainy quarter of London. Dominated by two towering institutions, the British Museum and the University of London, and bolstered by the nearby Inns of Court, it is an area of elegant squares and Georgian façades, of libraries, bookshops and publishing houses. Most famously, the Bloomsbury Group, known for novelist Virginia Woolf, lived here during the early decades of the 20th century. Fitzrovia's reputation as a raffish place was enhanced by the characters who drank at the Fitzroy Tavern, such as Welsh poet Dylan Thomas (1914–53) and the painter Augustus John (1878–1961).

BLOOMSBURY AND FITZROVIA

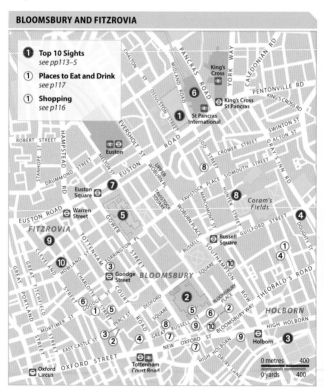

1 Top 10 Sights
see pp113–5

1 Places to Eat and Drink
see p117

1 Shopping
see p116

The red-brick exterior of the British Library

 ### British Library
MAP E2 ▪ 96 Euston Rd NW1
▪ Open 9:30am–8pm Mon–Thu,
9:30am–6pm Fri, 9:30am–5pm Sat,
11am–5pm Sun ▪ Adm for temporary
exhibitions ▪ www.bl.uk

Across its sites in London and York-shire, the British Library holds copies of everything published in the UK and Ireland, as well as many historical publications from around the world. "Readers" have free access to these (you can pre-register for a pass online), while everyone else can enjoy the space and the regular exhibitions. A permanent display in the Treasures of the British Library Gallery includes two out of the four existing editions of Magna Carta (1215), a Gutenberg Bible (1455), Shakespeare's first folio (1623) and many breathtaking illuminated manuscripts. The glass walls in the core of the building reveal the huge leather volumes from the King's Library, donated by George III. There are regular talks and events, a café and a restaurant.

British Museum
See pp12–15.

Sir John Soane's Museum
MAP N1 ▪ 13 Lincoln's Inn Fields WC2
▪ Open 10am–5pm Wed–Sun ▪
Closed 1 week in Jan ▪ www.soane.org

A particular pleasure of this unique museum is watching visitors' faces as they turn a corner and encounter yet another unexpected gem. Sir John Soane, one of Britain's leading 19th-century architects, crammed three adjoining houses with antiques and various other treasures, displayed in the most ingenious of ways. The base-ment crypt, which he designed to resemble a Roman catacomb, is par-ticularly original. *The Rake's Progress* (1753), a series of eight paintings by Hogarth, is another highlight. A highlights tour is run daily at noon, and be sure to ask about the free tours of the upstairs private apart-ments. The houses are situated on the northern side of Lincoln's Inn Fields, the heart of legal London. Lincoln's Inn, located on the east side of the square, is one of the best-preserved Inns of Court, with part of it dating from the 15th century.

Interior of Sir John Soane's Museum

4 Charles Dickens Museum

MAP F2 ■ 48 Doughty St WC1 ■ Open 10am–5pm Wed–Sun ■ Adm ■ www.dickensmuseum.com

Home to Charles Dickens from 1837 to 1839, during which time he completed some of his best work (including *The Pickwick Papers*, *Oliver Twist* and *Nicholas Nickleby*), this five-storey house offers a fascinating glimpse into the life and times of the great Victorian author and social reformer. The rooms are laid out just as they might have been in Dickens' time. Nearby Doughty Mews provides another step back to Victorian times.

5 University College London

MAP E2 ■ Gower St WC1 ■ Museums: open 1–5pm Tue–Fri, 11am–5pm Sat; www.ucl.ac.uk/culture

Founded in 1826, UCL is one of the world's leading multidisciplinary universities and has several fascinating collections of international importance, including the Petrie Museum of Egyptian Archaeology and the Grant Museum of Zoology. The latter houses around 68,000 specimens – animal skeletons, taxidermy, mounted insects and other creatures preserved in jars – making it an atmospheric insight into the world of 19th-century science.

THE BLOOMSBURY GROUP

The Bloomsbury Group was an informal set of writers, artists and intellectuals who lived in and around Bloomsbury at the beginning of the 20th century. The group, with its modern attitudes towards feminism and politics, first gathered at the home of the Stephen sisters, Virginia, later famous as Virginia Woolf (**below**) and Vanessa, later known as Vanessa Bell.

6 St Pancras International Station

MAP E2 ■ Euston Rd NW1

One of the glories of Victorian Gothic architecture, this railway terminus, opened in 1868, was designed by Sir George Gilbert Scott. Eurostar trains depart from here, although most of the frontage is in fact the St Pancras Renaissance Hotel.

St Pancras International Station

(7) Wellcome Collection

MAP E2 ▪ 183 Euston Rd
NW1 ▪ Open 10am–6pm Tue–Sun
(until 8pm Thu) ▪ www.wellcome
collection.org

Home to the medical collection of
businessman and philanthropist
Sir Henry Wellcome (1853–1936),
founder of one of the world's leading
pharmaceutical companies, this
museum explores connections
between medicine, life and art, and
hosts regular temporary exhibitions.
It features a creatively designed
reading room where visitors can
relax and read. There is a café and
an excellent bookshop as well.

(8) Foundling Museum

MAP E2 ▪ 40 Brunswick Sq
WC1 ▪ Open 10am–5pm Tue–Sat,
11am–5pm Sun ▪ Adm ▪ www.
foundlingmuseum.org.uk

Established in 1739 by Thomas Coram,
the Foundling Hospital provided a
refuge for abandoned children until it
closed in 1954. The original interiors
from the hospital are on display, while
the exhibits tell the stories of the thousands of children who were cared for
here. Also on display are paintings
donated by 18th- and 19th-century
artists, alongside more contemporary artworks.

(9) Fitzroy Square

MAP D2 ▪ Fitzroy Sq W1

Much of this square, completed in
1798, was designed by Scottish
architect Robert Adam. Its
many residents have included
Victorian prime minister
Lord Salisbury, who lived
at No 21, the playwright
George Bernard Shaw and
the novelist Virginia Woolf.

(10) BT Tower

MAP D2

At 190 m (620 ft), this was
the tallest building in London
when it opened in 1965. It is
now used as a media and
telecommunications hub
(see p26) and is clo-
sed to the public.   **BT Tower**

BLOOMSBURY AND FITZROVIA ON FOOT

▶ MORNING

Arrive at the **British Museum** (see
pp12–15) at 10am (opening time) so
that you can enjoy the Great Court
in peace. View Norman Foster's
glass dome while having coffee at
the café here, then wander the
museum's extraordinary galleries.
Don't miss the great Assyrian
bas-reliefs on your way out.

Browse the antiquarian book and
print shops, such as **Jarndyce**
(see p116), along Great Russell
and Museum streets. Turn left up
Little Russell Street, noticing the
fine Hawksmoor church of St
George's. Loop around Bloomsbury
Square and check out the list of
Bloomsbury group literary figures
posted here. Head west to Bedford
Square with its Georgian houses.
Cross Tottenham Court Road and
carry on to Charlotte Street.

AFTERNOON

See the photos of literary figures
such as Dylan Thomas in the basement bar of **Fitzroy Tavern** (see
p117) at No 16 Charlotte Street,
while enjoying a pre-lunch drink.
If you fancy something more exotic
than pub grub, try some barbe-
cued Japanese food at **Roka**
(see p117) a little further along
Charlotte Street.

After lunch, head to the **Brunswick
Centre** (1 Byng Place) for shopping, from food to fashion. This
awesome concrete-and-glass
megastructure was a 1960s housing and retail complex. Catch a
film at arthouse cinema **Curzon
Bloomsbury** (Brunswick Centre),
or dine in one of the complex's
many restaurants.

See map on p112 ←

Shopping

 La Fromagerie
MAP F2 ▪ 52 Lamb's Conduit St WC1

Head to the Cheese Room for the best Beaufort Chalet d'Alpage, La Fromagerie's signature cheese.

 Hobgoblin Music
MAP K1 ▪ 24 Rathbone Place WC1

If you're looking for a Chinese flute, mandolin, Irish drum or any other folk instrument, then browse the endlessly fascinating range of this wonderful shop.

 Heals
MAP E2 ▪ 196 Tottenham Court Rd W1

London's leading furniture store is a showcase for the best of British design. There is also a good café.

4 **Maggie Owen**
MAP F2 ▪ 13 Rugby St WC1

This former dairy in the heart of Bloomsbury sells chic, contemporary costume jewellery and accessories from across Europe.

5 **British Museum Shop**
MAP L1 ▪ 22 Great Russell St WC1

Find a wide range of exquisite crafts and jewellery in this museum shop. Everything from a pair of earrings modelled on those of ancient Egypt to contemporary crafts can be found.

Patrons at London Review Bookshop

 Contemporary Ceramics
MAP L1 ▪ 63 Great Russell St WC1

An outstanding gallery that showcases the very best in contemporary studio ceramics, particularly work by British potters.

 James Smith & Sons
MAP L1 ▪ 53 New Oxford St WC1

Established in 1830, James Smith & Sons is a beautiful shop that will meet all your umbrella, parasol, cane and walking-stick needs.

8 **L. Cornelissen & Son**
MAP M1 ▪ 105 Great Russell St WC1

The wooden shelves of this specialist art supplies shop are crammed with rows of glass jars full of pigments.

9 **Jarndyce**
MAP L1 ▪ 46 Great Russell St WC1

This handsome antiquarian bookshop specializes in 18th- and 19th-century British literature.

10 **London Review Bookshop**
MAP M1 ▪ 14 Bury Place WC1

Opened by the literary magazine the *London Review of Books*, this shop is a favourite among readers for its informed staff and richly varied stock. It also regularly hosts readings by a wide range of authors.

Places to Eat and Drink

PRICE CATEGORIES

For a three-course meal for one with half a bottle of wine (or equivalent meal), taxes and extra charges.

£ under £30   **££** £30–60   **£££** over £60

ROKA
MAP K1 ▪ 37 Charlotte St W1 ▪ 020 7580 6464 ▪ £££

Japanese robatayaki cuisine involves slow-cooking the food on skewers over a charcoal grill. At ROKA, this is done at the centrally placed grill, in full view of the customers.

2 Truckles of Pied Bull Yard
MAP M1 ▪ Off Bury Place WC1 ▪ 020 7404 5338 ▪ ££

This wine bar really comes to life in the summertime, when the outdoor terrace is filled with people enjoying chilled rosé and Pimm's on comfortable sofas.

3 The House of Hô
MAP K1 ▪ 1 Percy St W1 ▪ 020 7434 0194 ▪ ££

Set in a lovely four-storey Georgian townhouse and decorated with modern flair, this Pan-Asian restaurant serves traditional meals with a contemporary twist. Enjoy a bowl of pho (Vietnamese noodle soup).

4 Hakkasan
MAP K1 ▪ 8 Hanway Place W1 ▪ 020 7927 7000 ▪ £££

Its location may not be salubrious but this Michelin-starred Chinese restaurant and cocktail bar is superb.

5 Fitzroy Tavern
MAP K1 ▪ 16 Charlotte St W1 ▪ £

This splendidly restored pub, with polished mahogany partitions was once a haunt of London luminaries including George Orwell, Dylan Thomas and Tommy Cooper.

6 Salt Yard
MAP K1 ▪ 54 Goodge St W1 ▪ 020 7637 0657 ▪ ££

Top-notch modern Spanish tapas are served at Salt Yard. Delights on offer include confit *iberico* with whipped manchego and chargrilled octopus.

Outdoor seating at Dalloway Terrace

7 Dalloway Terrace
MAP L1 ▪ 16–22 Great Russell St WC1 ▪ 020 7347 1221 ▪ ££

Pop in for Saturday brunch or afternoon tea at this delightful secret garden terrace (heated in winter).

8 Norfolk Arms
MAP E2 ▪ 28 Leigh St WC1 ▪ 020 7388 3937 ▪ ££

This gastropub serves food influenced by the Mediterranean, both à la carte and as tapas. It's a local favourite.

9 Princess Louise
MAP M1 ▪ 20 High Holborn WC1

A beautifully restored Victorian pub *(see p76)* with carved mahogany partitions separating the drinking areas.

10 Cosmoba
MAP E2 ▪ 9 Cosmo Place WC1 ▪ 020 7837 0904 ▪ ££

This authentic, family-run restaurant has an extensive menu of classic Italian dishes.

See map on p112

🔟 Mayfair and St James's

These exclusive districts are home to some of London's wealthiest individuals. Many of the wonderful shops here were established to serve the royal court. Piccadilly – named after the fancy collars called "piccadills" that were popular in the 17th century – divides St James's to the south from Mayfair to the north, where shops continue up Bond Street, Cork Street and Savile Row to Oxford Street. The Royal Academy of Arts was established here in 1868, and the area retains its reputation as a top destination for art lovers, with some of the best commercial galleries in town.

Guard at Buckingham Palace

MAYFAIR AND ST JAMES'S

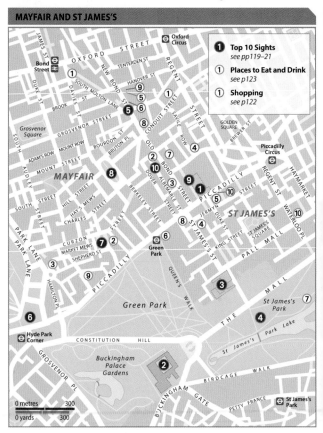

1	Top 10 Sights	see pp119–21
①	Places to Eat and Drink	see p123
①	Shopping	see p122

The Royal Academy of Arts

1 Royal Academy of Arts
MAP J4 ■ Burlington House, Piccadilly W1 ■ Open 10am–6pm Tue–Sun (until 9pm Fri) ■ Adm for temporary exhibitions ■ www.royalacademy.org.uk

Major temporary art exhibitions are staged at the Royal Academy, home to Britain's most prestigious fine arts institution. It holds one of the country's finest collections of British art, displayed across two Italianate buildings – palatial Burlington House and Burlington Gardens – linked by a bridge.Displays include Michelangelo's *Virgin and Child with the Infant St John*, known as the

Taddei Tondo, and J M W Turner's atmospheric and bleak *Dolbadern Castle, North Wales* (1800). In the Royal Academy's popular annual summer exhibition (see p59), around 1,500 new works by both established and unknown artists are displayed.

2 Buckingham Palace
See pp24–5.

3 St James's Palace
MAP K5 ■ The Mall SW1 ■ Closed to public

Built by Henry VIII (see p52), on the site of the former Hospital of St James, the palace's redbrick Tudor gatehouse is a familiar landmark.

4 St James's Park
MAP K5–L5 ■ SW1 ■ Open 5am–midnight daily

Originally a marsh, drained by Henry VIII and incorporated into his hunting grounds, this is undoubtedly London's most elegant park, with dazzling flower beds, exotic wildfowl on the lake and the lovely view from the lakeside St James's Café (see p123). The bridge over the lake has a good view of Buckingham Palace to the west and, to the east, of Whitehall's rooftops.

Buckingham Palace as seen from St James's Park

5 Bond Street
MAP J3–J4

London's most exclusive shopping street, Bond Street (which is known as New Bond Street to the north and Old Bond Street to the south) has long been the place for high society to promenade: many of its establishments have been here for over 100 years. The street is home to top fashion houses, elegant galleries such as Halcyon, Sotheby's auction rooms and jewellers such as Tiffany and Asprey. Where Old and New Bond Street meet, there is a delightful sculpture of wartime leaders Franklin D Roosevelt and Winston Churchill on a bench – it's well worth a photograph.

6 Apsley House
MAP D4 ■ 149 Piccadilly, Hyde Park Corner W1 ■ Open 11am–5pm Wed–Sun (Jan–Mar Sat & Sun only) ■ Adm

Originally designed by Robert Adam in the 1770s, Apsley House was expanded and altered in 1819 for the Duke of Wellington (see p63). Today it is given over to the paintings and memorabilia of the military leader, and is still partly occupied by the family. The paintings include *The Waterseller of Seville* by Diego Velázquez. The nude statue of Napoleon by Antonio Canova has special poignancy.

HANDEL IN MAYFAIR

The great composer (see p63), George Frideric Handel (**below**) arrived in London in 1710 to have his operas staged at the capital's reputed venues. In 1723, he was appointed Composer to the Chapel Royal and moved to Mayfair. He lived there until his death in 1759. By the end of his life, he had written 31 operas for London audiences.

7 Shepherd Market
MAP D4

This square was named after Edward Shepherd who developed the area from 1735 to 1746. Today, this pedestrianized area in the heart of Mayfair, between Piccadilly and Curzon Street is a good place on a summer evening for a drink or dinner. Ye Grapes, dating from 1882, is the principal pub (see p123), while local restaurants include Titu, Misto, Le Boudin Blanc and Iran. Until the

The imposing façade of Apsley House

Ye Grapes in Shepherd Market

1760s, an annual May Fair was held here, giving the wider area its name.

8 Berkeley Square
MAP D4

This pocket of green in the middle of Mayfair was planted in 1789 and its 30 huge plane trees may be the oldest in London. Famous residents include Clive of India at No. 45 and Winston Churchill, who lived at No. 48 as a child. Memorial benches in the square bear moving inscriptions, many from Americans billeted here during World War II. It was the London base of P G Wodehouse's Bertie Wooster and Jeeves.

9 Burlington Arcade
MAP J4 ■ 51 Piccadilly W1
■ Open 9am–7pm Mon–Sat, 11am–6pm Sun.

This arcade of bijou shops was built in 1819 for Lord George Cavendish of Burlington House (see p119) to prevent people from throwing rubbish into his gardens. The arcade of luxury stores is patrolled by uniformed beadles who control unseemly behaviour.

10 Royal Institution
MAP J3 ■ 21 Albemarle St W1
■ Museum: open 9am–5pm Mon–Fri
■ www.rigb.org

The Royal Institution was founded in 1799 to encourage the practical application of scientific knowledge. Its most influential member was Michael Faraday (1791–1867), a pioneer of electro-technology. The three floors of the Faraday Museum explore science, the highlight being Faraday's 1850s magnetic laboratory.

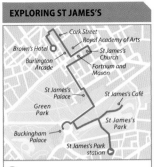

EXPLORING ST JAMES'S

▶ **MORNING**

Starting from St James's Park Tube, walk up through Queen Anne's Gate, noting the lovely 18th-century houses. Pass through the alley in the corner into Birdcage Walk, then **St James's Park** (see p119). Get a coffee from **St James's Café** (see p123), admire the floral displays and watch the pelicans before heading to **Buckingham Palace** (see pp24–5) for the Changing the Guard at 11am. Afterwards, head up The Mall past **St James's Palace** (see p119) into St James's Street. Turn into Jermyn Street, and check out such shops as Hawes & Curtis, for classic fashions, perfumery Floris and cheeseseller Paxton & Whitfield. Walk through St James's Church, leaving by the north exit onto Piccadilly. Head west down Piccadilly, perhaps pausing to browse the books at Hatchards (see p119), and then to Fortnum & Mason.

AFTERNOON

Fortnum & Mason (see p78) is the perfect place to have lunch at one of the store's several restaurants, where the dieter's choice is caviar and half a bottle of champagne. Cross Piccadilly to the **Royal Academy of Arts** (see p119) and enjoy their permanent collection, including Michelangelo's *Taddei Tondo*. Window-shop along Burlington Arcade and the **Cork Street** galleries (see p122). Turn into Bond Street, heading for **Brown's Hotel** (see p174) to relax over afternoon tea.

See map on p118

Shopping

 Browns
MAP D3 ▪ 23–27 South Molton St W1

London's most famous designer clothing store stocks pieces by Burberry, Balenciaga, Alexander McQueen and Valentino among many others.

2 Asprey
MAP J3 ▪ 167 New Bond St W1

The UK royal family have bought jewels here for more than a century. Other luxury items to be found here include exquisite vases, handbags and silver gifts.

3 Charbonnel et Walker
MAP J4 ▪ 1 The Royal Arcade, 28 Old Bond St W1

One of the best chocolate shops in town with a tempting array of hand-made goodies. Fill one of the pretty boxes with your choice of treats.

4 Gieves and Hawkes
MAP J3 ▪ 1 Savile Row W1

Purveyors of fine, handmade suits and shirts to the gentry since 1785, this shop is one of the best known in a street of expert tailors. Off-the-rack clothes are also available.

5 Fortnum & Mason
MAP K4 ▪ 181 Piccadilly W1

Famous for its food hall and restaurants, this elegant department store *(see p78)* still has male staff who wear coat-tails.

Try the extravagant ice creams in the Parlour restaurant or enjoy their afternoon tea.

 Mulberry
MAP J3 ▪ 50 New Bond St W1

Come here for must-have leather handbags, purses and other luxurious accessories and shoes.

7 Cork Street Galleries
MAP J3

Cork Street is famous for its art galleries. You can view or purchase works by the best artists here and check out the special exhibitions.

8 Sotheby's
MAP J3 ▪ 34–35 New Bond St W1

View anything from pop star memorabilia to Old Master paintings at this venerable fine arts auction house founded in 1744.

9 Fenwick
MAP J3 ▪ 63 New Bond St W1

A small, upmarket department store with designer labels, accessories and expensive lingerie.

10 Hatchards
MAP K4 ▪ 187 Piccadilly W1

Established in 1797 and now owned by Waterstones, this delightful bookshop claims to be the oldest in the UK. It is the official supplier of books to the King.

Fortnum & Mason, the iconic department store on Piccadilly

Places to Eat and Drink

PRICE CATEGORIES
For a three-course meal for one with half
a bottle of wine (or equivalent meal),
taxes and extra charges.
....
£ under £30 ■ ££ £30–60 ■ £££ over £60

1 Sketch
MAP J3 ■ 9 Conduit St W1
■ 020 7659 4500 ■ £££

Culinary genius is to be found in the
arty surroundings at Sketch. The
Gallery is informal and features
British artist Yinka Shonibare's work.
The three-Michelin-starred Lecture
Room attracts fashionable and
famous people.

2 Ye Grapes
MAP D4 ■ 16 Shepherd Market
W1 ■ 020 7493 4216 ■ £

This convivial pub spills out onto the
street on sunny days. The food
offering includes Thai classics.

3 Galvin at Windows
MAP D4 ■ 22 Park Lane W1
■ www.galvinatwindows.com ■ £££

At the top of the Hilton, this restaurant
has fine London views and superb
French-influenced cuisine.

4 Cafe Murano
MAP J4 ■ 33 St James's St SW1
■ 020 3371 5559 ■ ££

The simple pasta dishes burst with
freshness and flavour at Angela
Hartnett's informal but classy Italian.

5 Bond Street Kitchen
MAP J3 ■ Fenwick, 63 New
Bond St W1 ■ www.fenwick.co.uk
■ ££

The modern British cuisine upstages
the department store setting. A variety
of small plates, mains and salads are
offered here.

6 The Ritz
MAP J4 ■ 150 Piccadilly W1
■ 020 7300 2345 ■ £££

The poshest afternoon tea in town,
accompanied by a pianist and harpist.

Verandah seating at St James's Café

7 St James's Café
MAP L5 ■ St James's Park SW1
■ 020 839 1149 ■ £

This café serves breakfasts and hearty
mains in the leafy surroundings of St
James's Park. Watch the world go by
through the large glass windows.

8 The Wolseley
MAP J4 ■ 160 Piccadilly W1
■ 020 7499 6996 ■ £££

The Art Deco interior gives this
famous brasserie (see p75) an
air of glamour. You need to book
ahead, especially for dinner.

9 El Pirata
MAP D4 ■ 5–6 Down St W1
■ 020 7491 3810 ■ Closed Sun & Mon
■ ££

A lively, casual and enticing tapas
restaurant which excels at the
Spanish classics.

10 Wild Honey
MAP K4 ■ 8 Pall Mall W1
■ 020 7389 7820 ■ ££

Michelin-starred modern European
food with the finest seasonal produce
is on offer at this beautifully designed
restaurant. It is located within the
Sofitel Hotel.

See map on p118

🔟 Kensington and Knightsbridge

The heart of affluent and cultural London life, this is where wealthy visitors come to shop, not least because it's home to Harrods. It's also the location of Kensington Palace, its place in history once intertwined with the life of Princess Diana, and the great Victorian museums of South Kensington. Some of the best antique shops can be found on Kensington Church Street but for a better bargain try Portobello Road – a lively place to be on a Saturday.

Gate detail, Kensington Palace

KENSINGTON AND KNIGHTSBRIDGE

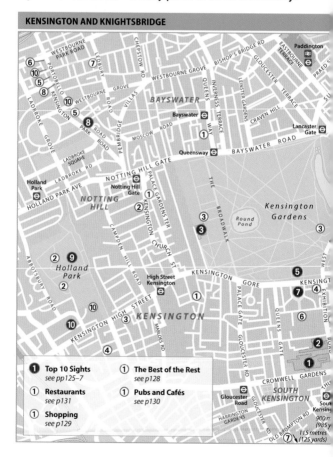

① **Top 10 Sights** see pp125–7	① **The Best of the Rest** see p128	
① **Restaurants** see p131	① **Pubs and Cafés** see p130	
① **Shopping** see p129		

1 Natural History Museum
From earthquakes to blue whales, the natural world is explored in this museum (see pp20–21).

2 Science Museum
The scientific achievements on show at this museum (see pp22–3) are truly awe-inspiring.

3 Kensington Palace
MAP A4 ■ Kensington Palace Gardens W8 ■ Open 10am–4pm Wed–Sun (Apr–Oct: until 6pm) ■ Adm ■ www.hrp.org.uk

This delightful royal residence, which used to be the residence of Diana,

The elegant Kensington Palace

Princess of Wales (see p52) as well as of Princess Margaret, is still in use by members of the royal family. Exhibitions offer glimpses into both the public and the private lives of some of the palace's most illustrious former residents. A highlight of the grand State Apartments built for William and Mary is the King's Gallery, hung with paintings from the Royal Collection.

4 Victoria and Albert Museum
MAP B5–C5 ■ Cromwell Rd SW7 ■ Open 10am–5:45pm daily (until 10pm every Fri) ■ www.vam.ac.uk

A cornucopia of treasures is housed in this museum named after the devoted royal couple and affectionately known as the V&A. Fine and applied arts from all over the world, from ancient China to contemporary Africa, are on display here. In total, there are 7 miles (11 km) of galleries. The stunning Britain Galleries display more than 3,000 objects illustrating the best of British art and design from 1500 to 1900. Highlights include The Great Bed of Ware (1590s), mentioned in Shakespeare's *Twelfth Night*.

5 Albert Memorial
MAP B4 ■ Kensington Gardens SW7

This edifice is a fitting tribute to Prince Albert, Queen Victoria's beloved consort, who played a large part in establishing the South Kensington museums. Located opposite the Royal Albert Hall, the memorial was designed by George Gilbert Scott and completed in 1876. At its four corners are marble statues representing the four continents: Europe, Asia, Africa and America.

6 Harrods
MAP C5 ▪ 87–135 Brompton Rd SW1

No backpacks, no torn jeans – the staff on the door at Harrods ensure that even people in the store are dressed tastefully. This famous emporium (see p78) began life in 1849 as a small, impeccable grocer's, and the present terracotta building was built in 1905. It is most striking at night, when it is illuminated by 12,000 lights. The store has more than 300 departments and you should not miss the wonderfully tiled and decorated food halls (see p129), which are great for picnic foods as much as for exotic specialities.

7 Royal Albert Hall
MAP B5 ▪ Kensington Gore SW7 ▪ Open for performances and tours ▪ www.royalalberthall.com

When Queen Victoria laid the foundation stone for The Hall of Arts and Sciences, to everyone's astonishment she put the words "Royal Albert" before its name, and today it is usually just referred to as the Albert Hall. This huge, nearly circular building, modelled on Roman amphitheatres (see p71), seats 5,000. Circuses, sport, dance and all manner of musical entertainments are held here, notably the Sir Henry Wood Promenade Concerts, familiarly known as the Proms.

PRINCE ALBERT

Queen Victoria and her first cousin Prince Albert of Saxe-Coburg-Gotha (below) were both 20 when they married in 1840. Albert was a Victorian in every sense, and his interest in the arts and sciences led to the founding of the great institutions of South Kensington. He died at the age of 41, and the queen mourned him for the rest of her life. They had nine children.

8 Portobello Road
MAP A3–A4

Running through the centre of the decidedly fashionable Notting Hill, and with a bustling, cheerful atmosphere, Portobello Road is a great place to spend some time. Though Saturday's antiques market is the biggest draw, other markets run along the street on different days, starting just beyond Westbourne Grove and offering fruit and vegetables, sausages, bread and cheeses, then music, clothes and bric-à-brac. Under the railway bridge at Portobello Green, vintage and new

The red brick and terracotta exterior of the Royal Albert Hall

fashions are on offer (Friday to Sunday). Take a seat by the window at GAIL's Bakery (No. 138) and enjoy coffee and a sandwich while watching the world go by. Street food is also widely available.

A formal garden in Holland Park

9 Holland Park
MAP A4–A5 ■ Ilchester Place W8

There is a great deal of charm about Holland Park, where enclosed gardens are laid out like rooms in an open-air house. At its centre is Holland House, a beautiful Jacobean mansion, which was largely destroyed in a bombing raid in 1941. What remains is used as a wedding venue and the backdrop for summer concerts. Peacocks roam in the woods and in the gardens, including the beautiful Kyoto Garden, which has a waterfall and koi carp pond.

10 Leighton House
MAP A5 ■ 12 Holland Park Rd W14 ■ Open 10am–5:30pm Wed–Mon ■ Adm

All the themes of the Victorian Aesthetic movement can be found in the extraordinary Leighton House. It was designed by Lord Leighton (see p62) and his friend George Aitchison in the 1860s. Its high point is the fabulous Arab Hall, with a fountain and gilded cupola. Some of the oil paintings in the collection are from Leighton himself, such as *The Death of Brunelleschi* (1852). Other artists such as Tintoretto and John Everett Millais are also represented.

KENSINGTON ON FOOT

▶ MORNING

Start at the South Kensington Tube station, and follow the signs to the **Victoria & Albert Museum,** (see p125). Spend a delightful hour wandering in the Medieval and Renaissance Galleries. Pause for coffee at the beautiful museum café that has rooms adorned with original Victorian decor. Then, follow Old Brompton Road to the **Brompton Oratory** (see p51), and take a look at its grand Italianate interior, with 12 marble Apostles.

Cross the road and turn right into Beauchamp Place, where shops such as Caroline Charles and Lalage Beaumont display crea-tions by British designers. Con-tinue down into Pont Street, and turn left up Sloane Street. Check out Hermès, Chanel and Dolce & Gabbana before walking up towards Knightsbridge Tube, turning left into Brompton Road for **Harrods**.

It has an impressive choice of cafés and restaurants, including the Garden Terrace and the Harr-ods Tea Rooms on the fourth floor.

AFTERNOON

Five minutes north of Harrods, **Hyde Park** (see p54) offers a peaceful walk along the south bank of the Serpentine. Heading for **Kensington Palace** (see p125), you pass the famous statue of J M Barrie's *Peter Pan* and the Round Pond. West of here, explore the palace, then visit the Sunken Garden opposite, where The **Kensington Palace Pavilion** (see p130) provides traditional afternoon tea.

See map on pp124–5 ←

The Best of the Rest

1 Queens Ice and Bowl
MAP A3 ■ 17 Queensway W2 ■ Bowling: 10am–11pm Sun–Thu (until midnight Fri & Sat); skating day and evening sessions daily ■ Adm ■ www.queens.london

Enjoy ten-pin bowling and ice-skating all year round here – but try to avoid the after-school crowd.

2 Holland Park Opera
MAP A4–A5 ■ Ilchester Pl W8 ■ Adm ■ www.operahollandpark.com

The open-air theatre in the park (see p127) hosts an annual summer season of opera, against the stunning backdrop of Holland House.

3 Serpentine Galleries
MAP B4, C4 ■ Kensington Gardens W2 ■ Open 10am–6pm Tue–Sun plus public hols ■ www.serpentinegalleries.org

On the eastern side of the gardens, these galleries (see p59) host short-term contemporary art exhibitions.

4 Royal Geographical Society
MAP B4 ■ 1 Kensington Gore ■ Open 10am–5pm Mon–Fri ■ www.rgs.org

Founded in 1830, this learned society hosts exhibitions of maps, photographs and much more in its Pavilion.

5 Electric Cinema
191 Portobello Rd W11 ■ Tube Ladbroke Grove ■ www.electriccinema.co.uk

London's oldest purpose-built movie theatre is also one of its prettiest.

It offers luxury seats including sofas and double beds. There is also a bar and diner here.

Exterior of the Royal College of Music

6 Royal College of Music
MAP B5 ■ Prince Consort Rd SW7 ■ Museum: open 10:15am–5:45pm Tue–Fri, 11am–6pm Sat & Sun ■ www.rcm.ac.uk

This beautiful 1894 building houses UK's leading music college and an excellent museum. During term-time there are weekly student-led tours.

7 Royal Court Theatre
MAP C5 ■ Sloane Sq SW1 ■ www.royalcourttheatre.com

Pre-eminent since the 1960s, this theatre produces work by both established and emerging playwrights.

8 The LookOut
MAP C4 ■ Hyde Park W2

Escape the crowds and connect with nature in this eco-friendly space.

9 Speakers' Corner
MAP C3 ■ Hyde Park W2

This corner of Hyde Park attracts public speakers, especially on Sundays.

10 Design Museum
MAP A5 ■ 224–238 Kensington High St W8 ■ Open 10am–6pm daily ■ Adm for temporary exhibitions ■ www.designmuseum.org

Spectacular building displaying the finest contemporary design, including architecture, fashion and furniture.

Swanky interior of Electric Cinema

Shopping

 Rigby & Peller
MAP C5 ■ 2 Hans Rd SW3

This company is famous for its high-quality lingerie, swimwear and corsetry, and superb bra fitting service. Lady Gaga, Scarlett Johansson and Princesses Beatrice and Eugenie are among the famous people who have shopped here.

 Harvey Nichols
MAP C4 ■ 109–125 Knightsbridge SW1

This is another top London store (see p78). There are six glorious floors of fashion, beauty and home collections alongside one floor dedicated to high-quality food.

Burberry
MAP C4 ■ 1 Sloane St SW1

Iconic British brand Burberry has traded since 1856. It sells all its latest must-have seasonal collection items here, as well as its timeless trenchcoats, checked clothing and distinctive luggage.

The Burberry store in Knightsbridge

 Sloane Street
MAP C4–C5

A dazzling concentration of luxury and designer shops extends along the street south of the vast Harvey Nichols department store.

Artisan du Chocolat
MAP C6 ■ 89 Lower Sloane St SW1

Combining extraordinary craftsmanship and artistry, this store creates some of London's most innovative chocolates.

The iconic Harrods building

 Harrods
London's most famous store (see p78) is full of the finest goods that money can buy. Specialities here (see p126) include food, fashion, china, glass and kitchenware.

Designers Guild
MAP B6 ■ 267–277 King's Rd SW3

Designers Guild's fabrics and wallcoverings have a fresh, vibrant style all of their own. The variety on show is stunning.

 Cutler and Gross
MAP C5 ■ 16 Knightsbridge Green SW1

Treat yourself to the latest eyewear and browse the superb collection of retro classics.

John Sandoe Books
MAP C5 ■ 10 Blacklands Terrace SW3

An unmissable experience for the discerning bibliophile, this bookshop is crammed to the rafters with a wonderful selection of volumes.

Ceramica Blue
10 Blenheim Crescent W11
■ Tube Ladbroke Grove

This delightful little Notting Hill shop stocks a unique, highly eclectic range of ceramics, glassware, fabrics and other household accessories.

See map on pp124–5

Pubs and Cafés

1 Montparnasse Café
MAP A5 ▪ 22 Thackeray St W8

This homely café and pâtisserie offers a real taste of France, with croques, galettes, salads and a whole range of sweet treats. It's a good choice for breakfast, too.

Flower-bedecked exterior of Churchill Arms

2 Churchill Arms
MAP A4 ▪ 119 Kensington Church St W8

Filled with intriguing bric-à-brac and Churchill memorabilia, this is a large, friendly Victorian pub. Inexpensive Thai food is served in the conservatory at lunchtime and for dinner until 9:30pm.

3 Kensington Palace Pavilion
MAP A4 ▪ Kensington Palace W8

With views overlooking the Sunken Garden, the elegant restaurants and tearooms here (see p127) are open for breakfast and lunch. This is the only place in London that allows you to enjoy afternoon tea inside a royal palace.

4 The Scarsdale Tavern
MAP A5 ▪ 23a Edwardes Sq W8

Just a couple of blocks from Kensington High Street, this cosy and popular neighbourhood pub serves decent food and a variety of good ales.

5 Nags Head
MAP C4 ▪ 53 Kinnerton St SW1

A short walk from Hyde Park is this little gem serving Adnams beer. The low ceilings and wood panelling add to the cosy, village-like atmosphere here. Mobile phones are not allowed.

6 The Castle
MAP A3 ▪ 225 Portobello Rd W11

This busy gastropub in Portobello market is a great spot for craft beer as well as for people-watching.

7 The Anglesea Arms
MAP B6 ▪ 15 Selwood Terrace SW7

Lovely, traditional local pub with a worn yet handsome darkwood interior. It offers excellent seasonal dishes, pub classics and a top selection of ales.

8 Trailer Happiness
MAP A3 ▪ 177 Portobello Rd W11

This kitsch but cosy bar is a lively place to enjoy some of the best rum cocktails in town.

9 Paxtons Head
MAP C4 ▪ 153 Knightsbridge SW1

A popular watering-hole for both locals and visitors, this old Victorian pub has a classic menu of traditional pub grub, alongside ales and a selection of wines.

10 Portobello Stalls
Portobello Rd W11 ▪ Tube Westbourne Park

Lined along the market here are stalls offering cuisines from all over the world. Visit the Acklam Village Market for live music and delicious street food.

Restaurants

PRICE CATEGORIES
For a three-course meal for one with half a bottle of wine (or equivalent meal), taxes and extra charges.
....
£ under £30   ££ £30–60   £££ over £60

1 Clarke's
MAP A4 ■ 124 Kensington Church St W8 ■ Closed Sun, Mon ■ 020 7221 9225 ■ £££

The menu consists of whatever chef Sally Clarke decides to cook for the evening meal. No matter what it is, it will be excellent.

2 Belvedere
MAP A4 ■ Holland Park W8 ■ 020 8191 1407 ■ £££

The restaurant's charming setting in Holland Park is enhanced by its good European food. From the patio in summer, you may hear distant opera from the park's open-air theatre.

3 Kitchen W8
MAP A5 ■ 11–13 Abingdon Rd W8 ■ 020 7937 0120 ■ £££

A satisfying blend of British and French cuisine characterizes this chic but comfortable restaurant, perfect for a romantic dinner.

4 Amaya
MAP C5 ■ Halkin Arcade, Lowndes St SW1 ■ 020 7823 1166 ■ £££

Michelin-starred Amaya's dishes take modern Indian cuisine to a new level. Tandoori wild prawns, spinach and fig tikkis, and tapas-style Indian food are served up in a stylish rosewood-panelled dining room.

5 Core by Clare Smyth
MAP A3 ■ 92 Kensington Park Rd W11 ■ 020 3937 5086 ■ £££

With extraordinary attention to detail and a dedication to UK produce, this three Michelin-starred restaurant is run by the brilliant chef Clare Smyth and her team. You have a great choice of tasting menus or à la carte.

6 Mari Vanna
MAP C4 ■ 116 Knightsbridge SW1 ■ 020 7225 3122 ■ ££

Classic Russian cooking, served with style, in a homely and rustic setting adorned with trinkets.

7 The Ledbury
MAP A3 ■ 127 Ledbury Rd W11 ■ 020 7792 9090 ■ £££

Praise has been heaped on chef Brett Graham's food, which bursts with exciting, original flavours.

8 Claude Bosi at Bibendum
MAP C5 ■ 81 Fulham Rd SW3 ■ 020 7581 5817 ■ £££

In a former Michelin tyre factory, this restaurant and oyster bar is adorned with tiles and stained glass.

Interior of Claude Bosi at Bibendum

9 Ognisko
MAP B5 ■ 55 Prince's Gate, Exhibition Rd SW7 ■ 020 7589 0101 ■ ££

Polish cuisine is served in an elegant dining room. There's an alfresco terrace for warmer nights.

10 Dinner by Heston Blumenthal
MAP C4 ■ 66 Knightsbridge ■ www.dinnerbyheston.co.uk ■ £££

This restaurant serves imaginative dishes inspired by historic Tudor feasts. Try the "meat fruit".

See map on pp124–5

🔟 Regent's Park and Marylebone

Ceramic plate, Wallace Collection

Once a medieval village surrounded by fields, Marylebone is now one of the city's most elegant neighbourhoods. In the 19th century, the area's grand mansion blocks were used by doctors to see wealthy clients. The medical connection continues today in the discreet Harley Street consulting rooms of private medical specialists. Encircled by John Nash's magnificent terraces is Regent's Park, where office workers, kids and dog walkers enjoy the inviting lawns and fabulous flowers.

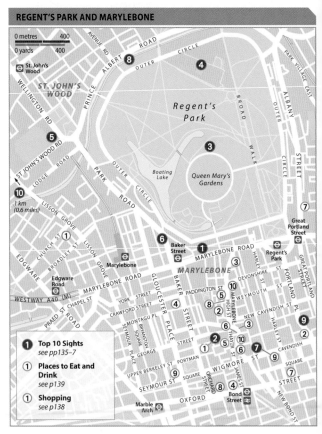

REGENT'S PARK AND MARYLEBONE

0 metres 400
0 yards 400

1 km
(0.6 miles)

1 Top 10 Sights
see pp135–7

1 Places to Eat and Drink
see p139

1 Shopping
see p138

1 Madame Tussauds

MAP C2 ■ Marylebone Rd NW1
■ Opening times vary, check website
■ Adm ■ www.madametussauds.com

This, the very first museum of wax-work models of the famous, has long been one of London's major attractions. In "Spirit of London" you can travel in stylized London taxi-cabs through events such as the Great Fire of 1666 and 1960s Swinging London. Book in advance for slight reductions.

2 Wallace Collection

MAP D3 ■ Manchester Sq W1 ■ Open 10am–5pm daily
■ www.wallacecollection.org

"The finest private collection of art ever assembled by one family," is the claim of the Wallace Collection, and it is hard to disagree. Sir Richard Wallace, who left this collection to the nation in 1897 (see p58), was not only outrageously rich but a man of great taste. As well as many galleries of fine Sèvres porcelain and an unrivalled collection of armour and furniture, there are a number of exceptional old master paintings by English, French and Dutch artists, including Frans Hals' *The Laughing Cavalier*.

3 Regent's Park

MAP C1–D2 ■ NW1
■ Open 5am–dusk daily

The best part of Regent's Park (see p54) is the Inner Circle. Here are Queen Mary's Gardens, with beds of nearly 12,000 wonderfully fragrant roses; the Open Air Theatre, which stages summer shows; and the Regent's Bar & Kitchen, one of the

Fountain in Regent's Park

best of the park's five cafés. Boats, tennis courts and deck chairs can be rented and on summer Sundays musical performances take place on the bandstand.

4 London Zoo

MAP C1–D1 ■ Regent's Park NW1 ■ Open Apr–Aug: 10am–6pm; Sep, Oct & Mar: 10am–5pm; Nov–Feb: 10am–4pm ■ Adm ■ www.zsl.org

Lying on the northern side of Regent's Park, London Zoo (see p68) is home to over 750 different animal species. One of the most breathtaking enclosures is the imaginative Land of the Lions, where Asiatic lions roam around a recreation of the Gir Forest, skirted by a miniature Indian village. The Rain-forest Life and In with the Lemurs walk-through exhibits, let you get close to some adorable creatures.

A tigress and her cub taking an afternoon nap at London Zoo

5 Marylebone Cricket Club Museum

MAP B2 ▪ St John's Wood NW8
▪ Open daily (book a tour in advance)
▪ Adm ▪ www.lords.org

Founded in 1787, the MCC was once the governing body of the global game, and its home ground, Lord's, remains the sport's most iconic venue. The world's oldest sporting museum is only accessible via guided tours of the ground , which also lead visitors through the famous Long Room, the players' dressing rooms and the Media Centre. Its star exhibit is the tiny trophy known as The Ashes.

6 Sherlock Holmes Museum

MAP C2 ▪ 221b Baker St NW1
▪ Open 9:30am–6pm daily ▪ Adm
▪ www.sherlock-holmes.co.uk

This museum is small but great fun. Take a camera when you visit and get your picture taken sitting by the fire in the great detective's front room, wearing a deerstalker hat and smoking a pipe. A Victorian policeman stands guard outside and upstairs, wax dummies re-enact moments from Holmes's most famous cases.

7 Wigmore Hall

MAP D3 ▪ 36 Wigmore St W1
▪ www.wigmore-hall.org.uk

One of the world's most renowned recital venues presents more than 460 events a year, featuring song,

REGENCY LONDON

Regent's Park was named after the Prince Regent (the future George IV), who employed John Nash in 1812 to lay out the park on the royal estate of Marylebone Farm. Nash was given a free hand and the result is a delight. Encircling the park are sumptuous Neo-Classical terraces, including Cumberland Terrace (**above**), named after the Duke of Cumberland.

early music, chamber music and new commissions as well as a diverse education programme. This hall, built in 1901, is reputedly one of the best acoustic spaces in the world.

8 Regent's Canal

MAP C1

John Nash wanted the canal to go through the centre of his new Regent's Park, but objections from neighbours, who were concerned about smelly canal boats and foul-mouthed crews, resulted in it being sited on the northern side of the

Canal boats moored along Regent's Canal

park. In 1874, a cargo of explosives demolished the Macclesfield Bridge beside London Zoo.

9 BBC Broadcasting House

MAP D3 ■ Portland Place W1
■ www.bbc.co.uk/showsandtours

The first radio broadcast was made from here in 1932, two months before the Art Deco building was officially opened. Redevelopment has now turned it into a state-of-the-art digital centre for BBC Radio and BBC News TV programmes and online services. The only way to visit "the Beeb" beyond the handsome Art Deco foyer is to apply for audience-member tickets, available for a range of shows. Tours of the grounds have been prohibited for security reasons.

BBC Broadcasting House

10 Abbey Road Studios

MAP B1 ■ 3 Abbey Rd NW8
■ www.abbeyroad.com

An iconic landmark in the capital, these studios are a must for Beatles aficionados, as is the nearby zebra crossing shown on the *Abbey Road* (1969) album cover. Have a picture taken as you re-enact the "fab four" crossing the road. The studios are not open to the public, other than the occasional event, but there is a gift shop where you can buy souvenirs.

EXPLORING MARYLEBONE

▶ MORNING

Before setting out for the day, reserve a ticket for **Madame Tussauds** *(see p135)* for the afternoon. Start at **Bond Street Tube**, exiting on Oxford Street. Opposite is St Christopher's Place, a narrow lane with charming shops, which opens into a pedestrian square. Stop for a coffee at one of the pavement tables at **Sofra** *(1 St Christopher's Place).*

Continue into Marylebone Lane, a pleasant side street of small shops, which leads to **Marylebone High Street** and its wide choice of designer shops. Stop for a bit in the peaceful memorial garden next to **St Marylebone Parish Church**, on the site of an old church. Methodist minister and hymn-writer Charles Wesley (1707–88) has a memorial here.

AFTERNOON

For lunch, buy some delicious fish and chips from the **Golden Hind** *(see p139)* or head to Caldesi in Marylebone *(see p.139)* for fresh homemade pasta.

After lunch, bypass the infamous lines of people outside **Madame Tussauds** with your booking and spend an hour and a half checking out the celebrity wax figures.

Cross Marylebone Road to Baker Street, for tea and a sandwich at **Reubens** *(see p139)*, before heading for the charming **Sherlock Holmes Museum** at No. 221b, a faithful reconstruction of the fictional detective's home.

See map on p134 ←

Shopping

 Alfie's Antique Market
MAP C2 ■ 13–25 Church St NW8

Vintage jewellery, fashion, Middle Eastern antiques, art and furniture are all under one roof, plus there is a café for when you're all shopped out.

2 Marylebone Farmers' Market
MAP D3 ■ Aybrook, St Vincent St & Moxon St W1 ■ Open 10am–2pm Sun

With dozens of producers, this is one of London's best and biggest farmers' markets.

3 The Conran Shop
MAP D2 ■ 55 Marylebone High St W1

Set in an old stable building, Conran sells the best of modern British and classic mainland European designs in homeware and furniture, such as a Mies van der Rohe reclining chair.

 Dr. Martens
MAP D3 ■ 386 Oxford St W1

Showcasing distinctive shoes and boots, this shop is continually favoured by Britain's youth subcultures.

5 Daunt Books
MAP D3 ■ 83–84 Marylebone High St W1

All kinds of travel books and literature, plus much more besides, are arranged along oak galleries in this atmospheric Edwardian bookshop.

 Marylebone Lane
MAP D3 ■ Off Marylebone High St W1

This charming lane off Marylebone High Street still has plenty of quirky gems to tempt the shopper.

7 John Lewis
MAP D3 ■ 300 Oxford St W1

There's not much that you can't buy from this sophisticated department store. The vast collection of John Lewis ranges from clothes and furniture to electronics and stationery. It also has a gifts department, and the staff are both helpful and knowledgeable.

 Selfridges & Co
MAP D3 ■ 400 Oxford St W1

Opened in 1909, this store has a handsome Neo-Classical façade. A London institution, Selfridges is great for designer fashion for women. Its award-winning food hall is wonderful.

 Margaret Howell
MAP D3 ■ 34 Wigmore St W1

Classic elegance for both men and women from one of Britain's top designers at her flagship store.

10 Le Labo
MAP D2 ■ 28A Devonshire St W1

A luxury perfumery where the fragrances can be made to order with a personalized label.

Long oak galleries in the Edwardian interiors of Daunt Books

Places to Eat and Drink

PRICE CATEGORIES

For a three-course meal for one with half
a bottle of wine (or equivalent meal),
taxes and extra charges.

£ under £30   ££ £30–60   £££ over £60

 The Wallace Restaurant
MAP D3 ▪ Hertford House,
Manchester Sq W1 ▪ 020 7563 9505
▪ ££

Located in the courtyard of the
Wallace Collection *(see p135)*,
this smart brasserie serves delicious
lunches and afternoon teas. The
menu changes regularly.

2 Artesian
MAP J1 ▪ 1C Portland Place
W1 ▪ 020 7636 1000 ▪ £££

A sophisticated bar, Artesian offers
a small menu of classics and
cocktails to die for.

3 Caldesi in Marylebone
MAP D3 ▪ 118 Marylebone
Lane W1 ▪ 020 7487 0754 ▪ £££

This light and airy Italian eaterie
offers classic dishes and a good
wine list. The upstairs restaurant
is slightly more formal.

 Reubens
MAP C3 ▪ 79 Baker St W1
▪ 020 7486 0035 ▪ ££

One of the best kosher restaurants
in London, Reubens offers classic
deli sandwiches such as salt beef.

5 Pachamama
MAP D3 ▪ 18 Thayer St W1
▪ 020 7935 9393 ▪ £££

This lively spot is one of the city's
most popular Peruvian restaurants.
It offers pisco-heavy cocktails and
tapas with distinctive flavours.

 Golden Hind
MAP D3 ▪ 71a–73 Marylebone
Lane W1 ▪ 020 7486 3644 ▪ ££

Serving Londoners since 1914,
this no-nonsense little place is
popular with locals, and offers

customers fish cakes and calamari
as well as traditional English
fish and chips.

7 Queen's Head & Artichoke
MAP D2 ▪ 30–32 Albany St NW1
▪ 020 7916 6206 ▪ ££

A snug upstairs dining room and
bustling bar downstairs offer a wide
range of good international food.

A range of cheeses at La Fromagerie

8 La Fromagerie
MAP D3 ▪ 2–6 Moxon St W1
▪ 020 7935 0341 ▪ ££

Sample the fine cheese and
charcuterie plates here, along
with delicious seasonal dishes.

9 Locanda Locatelli
MAP C3 ▪ 8 Seymour St W1
▪ 020 7935 9088 ▪ £££

Georgio Locatelli is one of the finest
Italian chefs in the UK. Dishes are
presented with great skill and care.

10 The Ivy Café
MAP D3 ▪ 96 Marylebone Lane
W1 ▪ theivycafemarylebone.com ▪ ££

A more casual spin-off from the
well-known Ivy restaurant, this bistro
offers an appetizing all-day menu
that includes brunches, sandwiches,
as well as classic mains.

See map on p134 ←

🔟 The City

The ancient square mile of London, defined roughly by the walls of the Roman city, is a curious mixture of streets with medieval names, state-of-the-art finance houses and no fewer than 38 Grade 1-listed churches, many of them, including St Paul's Cathedral, designed by Sir Christopher Wren. Don't miss the City's old markets: Smithfield still operates as a meat market, Leadenhall *(see p66)* is in many ways more attractive than Covent Garden, and the old Billingsgate fish market offers a great view of the once busy Pool of London.

Bust of William Shakespeare, Guildhall Art Gallery

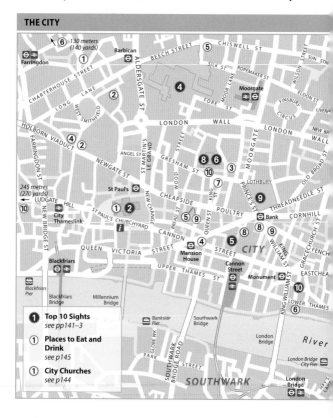

THE CITY

1 **Top 10 Sights**
see pp141–3

1 **Places to Eat and Drink**
see p145

1 **City Churches**
see p144

Tower of London
See pp38–41.

St Paul's Cathedral
See pp42–5.

Tower Bridge
MAP H4 ▪ 020 7403 3761
▪ Open 9:30am–6pm daily ▪ Adm
▪ www.towerbridge.org.uk

When the Pool of London (the stretch of the Thames between Limehouse and London Bridge) was the gateway to the city, this bridge (see p65) was constantly being raised and lowered for sail and steam ships bringing their cargoes from all over the world. Pedestrians who needed to cross the river when the bridge was open had to climb up the 200 steps of

The majestic Tower Bridge

the towers to the walkway. Today, visitors can enjoy panoramic views from the 33.5-m- (109-ft-) high glass-floored walkways, accessed via the north tower, which has an exhibition. You descend to street level via the south tower, and then explore the Victorian Engine Rooms, exiting via a shop on the south bank.

Barbican Centre
MAP G2–G3 ▪ Silk St EC2
▪ 020 7870 2500 ▪ www.barbican.
org.uk

This centre (see p70) plays host to music, dance, theatre, film and art events with top visiting performers and artists. There is also an excellent library, cafés and restaurants. Opened in 1982, the centre is part of the Barbican Estate, which houses over 4,000 people and also contains the Guildhall School of Music. There is also the Conservatory (check opening days and book online) with tropical fish and around 1,500 species of plants and trees. The centre looks across a lake to St Giles' Cripplegate church.

The Brutalist-style Barbican Centre

5 London Mithraeum

MAP S3 ▪ 12 Walbrook EC4
EC4 ▪ Open 10am–6pm Tue–Sat,
noon–5pm Sun ▪ www.london
mithraeum.com

Beneath Bloomberg's headquarters,
the London Mithraeum preserves the
remains of a 3rd century temple built
by followers of a bizarre Roman god
cult. A sound-and-light show brings
one of the secret ceremonies to life.

6 Guildhall

MAP S2 ▪ Great Hall: Guildhall
Yard, Gresham St EC2; open for
monthly tours (book in advance);
check website for times ▪ Adm
▪ www.cityoflondon.gov.uk/
things-to-do

For around 900 years the Guildhall
has been the administrative centre
of London. For centuries, its
magnificent medieval Great Hall
was used for trials, and many
important people were sentenced
to death here, including Lady Jane
Grey, who reigned as queen in
1553 for just nine days

7 St Katharine Docks

MAP H4 ▪ E1 ▪ www.sk
docks.co.uk

Located near Tower Bridge and the
Tower of London, this is the place
(see p65) to come and relax, to watch
the rich on their yachts and enjoy
the unique experience of sailing
up the river from nearby Tower

Boats docked in St Katharine Docks

DICK WHITTINGTON

A stained-glass window (**below**) in
St Michael, Paternoster Royal, depicts
Dick Whittington (and his cat) – the
hero of a well-known London rags-
to-riches fairy tale. In fact, Richard
Whittington, who was Lord Mayor
of London four times between 1397
and 1420, was a wealthy merchant and
the City's first major benefactor. He
pioneered public lavatories, building
them to overhang the Thames.

Bridge Quay. There are several cafés
as well as a number of popular bars
and restaurants.

8 Guildhall Art Gallery and Roman Amphitheatre

MAP S2 ▪ Gresham St EC2 ▪ Open
10:30am–4pm daily

On the east side of Guildhall Yard
is the Guildhall Art Gallery, containing two floors of paintings that
cover more than 400 years of art.
Many works of art are associated
with the City, and there is a rich
collection of 19th-century paintings,
including some pre-Raphaelite
works. Accessed via the gallery,
you can also visit the remains of
London's only Roman amphitheatre,
built in AD 70 and with a capacity of
6,000 spectators. It was discovered in
1988 during an archaeological dig.

⑨ Bank of England Museum

MAP T2 ■ Bartholomew Lane EC2 ■ Open 10am–5pm Mon–Fri ■ www.bankofengland.co.uk

This fascinating museum, located within the impressive walls of the Bank of England, tells the history of the bank from its foundation in 1694 to the present day. Its unique collections of coins, banknotes and artifacts are supplemented by interactive displays. Visitors can even handle a real gold bar.

⑩ Monument

MAP T3 ■ Monument St EC3 ■ Open 9:30am–1pm & 2–6pm Sat, Sun and school hols ■ Adm ■ www.themonument.org.uk

Standing at 61.5 m (202 ft), this monument by Sir Christopher Wren offers panoramic views of the City of London. Commemorating the Great Fire of London, the height of this free-standing stone column is equal to its distance from the baker's shop in Pudding Lane where the fire started in 1666. Inside, 311 stairs spiral up to a viewing platform; when you return to the entrance, you will receive a certificate to say that you have made the climb.

The Monument, completed in 1677

THE CITY ON FOOT

▶ **MORNING**

Start with a brisk trot up the 311 steps of the **Monument** and see how the surrounding narrow streets all slope down towards the Thames. Descend and carry on down Fish Street Hill across Lower Thames Street to the historic church of **St Magnus the Martyr** *(see p144)*, where a model of the former London Bridge shows the city's great landmark as it was until the 18th century.

Return up Fish Street Hill and Philpot Lane to Lime Street to check out the Lloyd's of London building and "The Gherkin", 30 St Mary Axe. Enter the ornate, 1881 **Leadenhall Market** building *(see p66)* for trendy shops, restaurants and bars, and a delicious lunch at **Luc's Brasserie** *(22 Leadenhall Market)* in the market.

AFTERNOON

After lunch, see the City's historic financial buildings along Cornhill. Notice the Royal Exchange's grand Corinthian portico, behind which is a high-end shopping centre. Opposite is the Mansion House, official residence of London's Lord Mayor and a very familiar City landmark. To the north, across Threadneedle Street, is the **Bank of England**. Continue into Lothbury and along Gresham Street to Guildhall.

Head up Wood Street to the **Barbican Centre** *(see p141)* for a cocktail or the pre-theatre menu at the Osteria overlooking the lake. Check the programme for the day's events and attend a performance.

See map on pp140–41

City Churches

1 St Paul's Cathedral
See pp42–5.

2 St Bartholomew-the-Great
MAP R1 ■ West Smithfield EC1
■ Open 10am–5pm Mon–Sat,
8:30am–6:30pm Sun

This is one of London's oldest
churches *(see p51)*, built in the
12th century. Some Norman architectural details may be seen.

3 St Katharine Cree
MAP H3 ■ 86 Leadenhall St EC3
■ Check website for opening times

One of eight churches to survive
the Great Fire of London in 1666,
this building dates from about 1630.
Both Purcell and Handel played
its organ.

4 St Sepulchre-without-Newgate
MAP Q1 ■ Holborn Viaduct EC1
■ Open 11am–3pm Mon, 8:30am–
2:30pm Tue–Thu

The City's largest post-Fire church
after St Paul's, St Sepulchre
is famous for its peal of
12 bells. Recitals are held
on Thursdays at lunchtime
and in the early evening.

5 St Mary-le-Bow
MAP S2 ■ Cheapside
EC2 ■ Open 7:30am–
6pm Mon–Fri

St Mary-le-Bow
was rebuilt by
Christopher Wren
after its destruction
in the 1666 Great
Fire of London.

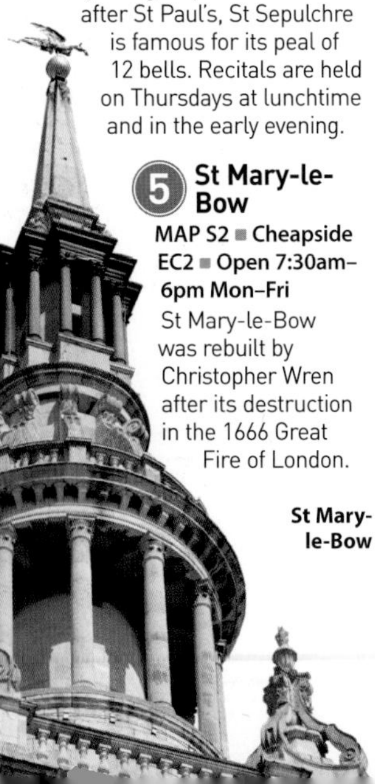

St Mary-
le-Bow

6 St Magnus the Martyr
MAP H4 ■ Lower Thames St
EC3 ■ Open 10am–4pm Tue–Fri,
10am–1pm Sun

Designed by Wren in the 1670s, the
splendid church retains its elegant
pulpit. Celebrated choral recitals
take place throughout the year.

7 All Hallows by the Tower
MAP H3 ■ Byward St EC3
■ Open 8am–5pm Mon–Fri, 10am–
5pm Sat & Sun

Take a guided tour of this church,
which dates from Saxon times.

The dome of St Stephen Walbrook

8 St Stephen Walbrook
MAP S3 ■ 39 Walbrook EC4
■ Open 10am–3:30pm Mon–Fri

A forerunner to St Paul's Cathedral,
the Lord Mayor's parish church is
considered to be one of Wren's finest.

9 St Mary Woolnoth
MAP T2 ■ Lombard St EC3
■ Open 7am–4pm Mon–Fri

One of Nicolas Hawksmoor's six
surviving London churches, this was
built in his typically bold Baroque
style and completed in 1727.

10 St Lawrence Jewry
MAP S2 ■ Guildhall EC2
■ Open 9:30am–5:30pm Mon–Fri

Beautiful stained-glass windows of
historic figures are the highlight here.

Places to Eat and Drink

PRICE CATEGORIES

For a three-course meal for one with half a bottle of wine (or equivalent meal), taxes and extra charges.

£ under £30   **££** £30–60   **£££** over £60

1 St John Smithfield
MAP G2 ■ 26 St John St EC1
■ 020 7251 0848 ■ £££

Sister restaurant of St John Bread & Wine (*see p163*), this delightful British place is famous for "nose-to-tail" dining with bold flavours and a focus on offal. Delicious light bar meals available.

2 Viaduct Tavern
MAP Q1 ■ 126 Newgate St EC1
■ 020 7600 1863 ■ Closed Sun ■ £

Built on the site of a former jail, this former Victorian gin palace has a unique period atmosphere thanks to its ornate wall paintings and other original fittings. Sandwiches and snacks are served all week.

3 Hawksmoor Guildhall
MAP S2 ■ 10 Basinghall St EC2
■ 020 7397 8120 ■ £££

Huge and bustling, Hawksmoor has revived the old London tradition of the steakhouse, with a variety of cuts, all cooked perfectly to order. One of several branches around the city.

4 Sweetings
MAP S3 ■ 39 Queen Victoria St EC4 ■ Open 11:30am–3pm Mon–Fri ■ No reservations ■ ££

This is a weekday lunchtime haven for fish lovers. Starters such as potted shrimps are followed by plaice and Dover sole.

5 The Jugged Hare
MAP G2 ■ 49 Chiswell St EC1
■ 020 8161 0190 ■ £££

This upmarket gastropub near the Barbican is well known for its excellent game dishes and first-rate Sunday roasts.

6 Holy Tavern
MAP G2 ■ 55 Britton St EC1

Snug and rustic, with delft tiles and box pews, this tiny pub oozes charm.

7 City Càphê
MAP S2 ■ 17 Ironmonger Lane EC2 ■ Open 11:30am–3pm Mon–Fri ■ £

Pork *banh mi* is the speciality at this small Vietnamese café in the heart of the City. It gets pretty busy so you may need to queue, but it's well worth the wait.

8 1 Lombard Street
MAP S2 ■ 1 Lombard St EC3
■ 020 7929 6611 ■ Closed Sat & Sun ■ £££

Enjoy top-class British dining in the striking setting of a former banking hall.

9 Café Below
MAP S2 ■ Cheapside EC2
■ 020 7329 0789 ■ ££

This popular café in the crypt of St Mary-le-Bow church serves breakfast and lunch on weekdays.

10 Ye Olde Cheshire Cheese
MAP Q2 ■ 145 Fleet St EC4

One of London's most famous pubs (*see p77*), this 17th-century establishment has served luminaries such as Samuel Johnson and Charles Dickens.

Interior of Ye Olde Cheshire Cheese

See map on pp140–41

 North London

Beyond Regent's Park, London drifts up into areas that were once distant villages where the rich built their country mansions. Parts of their extensive grounds now make up the wild and lofty expanse of Hampstead Heath. Some of the "villages", such as

Karl Marx's tombstone, Highgate Cemetery

Hampstead and Highgate, are still distinct from the urban sprawl that surrounds them, with attractive streets full of well-preserved architecture. Other parts of north London have different flavours – from bustling Camden, with its canalside market and lively pubs, to fashionable Islington, with its clothes and antique shops and smart bars.

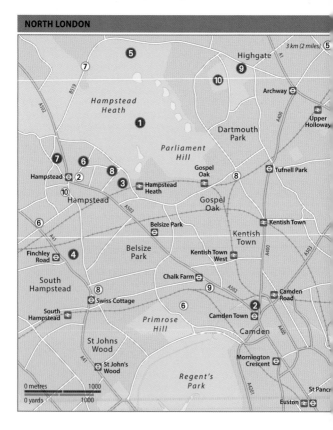

1 Hampstead Heath and Parliament Hill

NW3, NW5 ▪ Tube Hampstead or Golders Green, train to Hampstead Heath or Gospel Oak

A welcome retreat from the city, this large, open area is one of the best places in London for walking. Covering miles of countryside, it contains ancient woodlands and ponds for swimming and fishing. The top of Parliament Hill has great city views and is a popular place for kite-flying.

2 Camden Markets

Camden High St and Chalk Farm Rd NW1 ▪ Tube Camden Town ▪ Open 10am–late daily

The most exciting north London markets (see p79) are linked by the busy and colourful Camden High Street. Camden Market (see p79), near the Tube station, has stalls selling clothes, shoes and jewellery. Further up the road, by the canal, both Camden Lock Market and Stables Market sell an eclectic mix of arts and crafts, vintage and street fashions. There are plenty of bars and cafés, plus street food stalls.

The 19th-century Keats House

3 Keats House

10 Keats Grove NW3 ▪ Train to Hampstead Heath, Tube Hampstead or Belsize Park ▪ Open 11am–1pm & 2–5pm Wed–Fri & Sun (winter closes 4pm and on Wed) ▪ Adm ▪ www.cityoflondon.gov.uk/keats

Keats Grove, off Downshire Hill, is one of the loveliest streets in Hampstead. The house where the poet John Keats (see p62) wrote much of his work contains facsimiles of his fragile manuscripts and letters, and personal possessions. It also hosts poetry readings and talks.

4 Freud Museum

20 Maresfield Gardens NW3 ▪ Tube Finchley Rd ▪ Open 10:30am–5pm Wed–Sun ▪ Adm ▪ www.freud.org.uk

Sigmund Freud (see p62), the founder of psychoanalysis, came to live here when his family fled Nazi-occupied Vienna in 1938. Looking much as it did in his day, the house contains Freud's collection of antiques, his library (including first editions of his own works) and the couch on which his patients related their dreams.

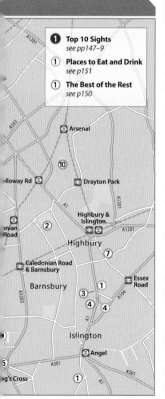

Arsenal

Drayton Park

lloway Rd

Highbury & Islington

onian Road

Highbury

Caledonian Road & Barnsbury

Barnsbury

Essex Road

Islington

Angel

g's Cross

Eighteenth-century Kenwood, Hampstead Heath

(5) Kenwood

Hampstead Lane NW3 ■ Tube Golders Green or Archway then bus 210 ■ Open 10am– 5pm daily (Nov–Mar: until 4pm) ■ Tours available ■ www.english-heritage.org.uk/visit/places/kenwood

This mansion *(see p59)*, filled with Old Masters, is set in an estate on the edge of Hampstead Heath. Vermeer's *The Guitar Player* and a self-portrait by Rembrandt are among the star attractions. Tours are run on Wednesday, Friday and Saturday, and the house has a tearoom and café with a delightful garden seating area.

(6) Burgh House

New End Sq NW3 ■ Tube Hampstead ■ Open 10am–4pm Wed–Fri & Sun ■ www.burghhouse.org.uk

Built in 1704 and housing Hampstead Museum, this grand house has a significant art collection, along with furniture and archive material on the area. The panelled music room is used for concerts and meetings, the Peggy Jay Gallery has contemporary art exhibitions, and the café has a terrace and a cosy indoor space.

(7) Fenton House

Hampstead Grove NW3 ■ Tube Hampstead ■ Open Mar–Oct: 11am–4pm Fri, Sun & bank hols ■ Adm ■ www.nationaltrust.org.uk/fenton-house-and-garden

This 17th-century mansion is the oldest in Hampstead. Its exceptional collection of Chinese and European

HAMPSTEAD WELLS

Hampstead's heyday began in the early 18th century, when a spring in Well Walk **(below)** was recognized as having medicinal properties. This brought Londoners flocking to take the waters from the Pump Room within the Great Room at Well Walk, which also housed an Assembly Room for dances and concerts. The spa gradually fell into disrepute, but Hampstead retained its fashionable status.

porcelain, furniture and needlework was bequeathed to the National Trust with the house in 1952. A formal walled garden contains an orchard. Pre-booking is required.

(8) 2 Willow Road

2 Willow Rd NW3 ■ Train to Hampstead Heath ■ Open Mar–Oct: 11am–4:30pm Thu, Sat & public hols ■ Adm ■ www.nationaltrust.org.uk/2-willow-road

Designed in 1939 by the architect Ernö Goldfinger for himself and his wife, artist Ursula Blackwell, this is a fine example of modern architecture in the UK. Goldfinger designed all the furniture and collected works by Henry Moore, Max Ernst and Marcel Duchamp. Admission 11am–3pm is strictly limited to hourly tours and must be pre-booked.

9 Lauderdale House
Waterlow Park, Highgate Hill N6 ■ Tube Archway ■ Opening times vary; check website ■ www.lauder dalehouse.org.uk

Dating from the late 16th century, Lauderdale House is said to have been home for a brief period to Charles II's mistress Nell Gwynne. It now houses a popular arts and cultural centre, with regular concerts and exhibitions.

10 Highgate Cemetery
Swain's Lane N6 ■ Tube Archway ■ Open 10am–5pm (Nov–Feb: until 4pm) ■ Tours of West Cemetery available (book online) ■ Adm ■ www.highgatecemetery.org

Across the heath from Hampstead, Highgate developed as a healthy, countrified place for the nobility, who built large mansions here in the 18th and 19th centuries. Many well-off Victorians chose to be buried in the two leafy sections of Highgate Cemetery. Opened in 1839, its Victorian architecture and fine views soon made it a very popular outing for Londoners. Karl Marx and novelist George Eliot are buried in the East Cemetery, though the overgrown West Cemetery is the more atmospheric and architectually interesting of the two.

Grave markers in Highgate Cemetery

EXPLORING NORTH LONDON

▶ MORNING

Starting at **Hampstead Tube station**, head left down pretty Flask Walk (the Flask pub once sold spa water) to the local museum in **Burgh House** for some background on the area. Then spend some time exploring the many attractive back streets, most of which are lined with expensive Georgian houses and mansions. Visit **Well Walk**, fashionable in the days of the Hampstead spa (a fountain in Well Passage on the left still remains).

Stop for a coffee at one of the many cafés along Hampstead High Street and then make your way to **Keats House** *(see p147)*, spending half an hour looking around. Afterwards, a stroll across **Hampstead Heath** to **Kenwood** will prepare you for lunch.

AFTERNOON

The Brew House at Kenwood serves excellent light meals and has a fine position beside the house, overlooking the lake. After lunch, visit the house itself.

Leave the Heath by the nearby East Lodge and catch a No. 210 bus back towards Hampstead. The bus passes the **Spaniards Inn** *(see p76)* and Whitestone Pond, the Heath's highest point. Alight at the pond and walk to the Tube station, taking a train to Camden Town. Spend the rest of the afternoon in lively Camden Lock Market *(see p147)*, ending the day on the Lockside terrace.

See map on pp146–7

The Best of the Rest

 Sadler's Wells
MAP F2 ▪ Rosebery Ave EC1
▪ www.sadlerswells.com
London's premier venue for dance (see p71) attracts internationally renowned artists and companies from around the world.

② Freightliners City Farm
Sheringham Rd N7 ▪ Tube Highbury & Islington or Caledonian Rd ▪ Closed Tue ▪ www.freightliners farm.org.uk
A little bit of the countryside in the city with animals, produce, gardens and a vegetarian café.

③ Almeida Theatre
MAP F1 ▪ Almeida St N1
▪ www.almeida.co.uk
This famous local theatre attracts top actors and directors from the UK and the US.

④ King's Head Theatre
MAP F1 ▪ 115 Upper St N1
▪ www.kingsheadtheatre.com
This busy Victorian pub has a 110-seat theatre. It hosts an eclectic programme of works by new and emerging talent, including drama, comedy, opera and musicals, with an emphasis on LGBTQ+ works. There's also a wide selection of wines and ale.

⑤ Alexandra Palace
Alexandra Palace Way N22
▪ Tube Wood Green, then bus W3
▪ www.alexandrapalace.com
Set in the 196 acres of Alexandra Park, this restored 1873 exhibition centre is principally used as an ice-skating rink and concert venue.

Alexandra Palace

⑥ Camden Art Centre
Arkwright Rd NW3 ▪ Tube Finchley Road or Hampstead
▪ www.camdenartcentre.org
This place is known for its fascinating contemporary art exhibitions and excellent art book shop.

⑦ Estorick Collection
39A Canonbury Sq N1
▪ Tube Highbury and Islington
▪ Adm ▪ www.estorickcollection.com
Elegant Georgian house with a superb collection of 20th-century Italian art, including works by Amedeo Modigliani and Emilio Greco. There's a delightful garden with an inviting café.

⑧ Hampstead Theatre
Eton Ave NW3 ▪ Tube Swiss Cottage ▪ www.hampsteadtheatre. com
This important fringe theatre is a venue for ambitious new writing, and has produced plays by innovative English writers such as Harold Pinter, Michael Frayn and Mike Leigh.

⑨ Roundhouse
Chalk Farm Rd NW1 ▪ Tube Chalk Farm ▪ www.roundhouse.org.uk
This former Victorian railway shed is now an exciting venue for both theatre and music.

⑩ Emirates Stadium Tours
Hornsey Rd, Highbury N7
▪ Tube Arsenal ▪ Adm ▪ www. arsenaldirect.arsenal.com
The tour of the stadium – home to Arsenal Football Club – covers the directors' box, home and away changing rooms, players' tunnel and free access to the Arsenal Museum.

Places to Eat and Drink

PRICE CATEGORIES
For a three-course meal for one with
half a bottle of wine (or equivalent meal),
taxes and extra charges.

£ under £30 **££** £30–60 **£££** over £60

① Ottolenghi
MAP G1 ■ 287 Upper St N1
■ 020 7288 1454 ■ ££

Yotam Ottolenghi has revitalized London's approach to Middle Eastern food with his flavourful dishes based on the finest – and sometimes unusual – ingredients.

② The Flask
14 Flask Walk NW3 ■ Tube Hampstead ■ 020 7435 4580 ■ ££

Dating from 1700, this pub has a country atmosphere, good cask beer and homemade pub food.

③ Dishoom
MAP E1 ■ 5 Stable St N1 ■ 020 7420 9321 ■ ££

With decor inspired by Bombay Irani cafés, Dishoom offers a stylish take on Indian cuisine. Don't miss the signature black daal, or the cocktails.

④ Gallipoli Again
MAP G1 ■ 120 Upper St N1
■ 020 7359 1578 ■ ££

Good quality Turkish cuisine with an emphasis on mezze in a busy, bois-terous and friendly bistro. The walls are adorned with small portraits.

⑤ Camino
MAP E1 ■ 3 Varnishers Yard N1
■ 020 7841 7330 ■ ££

Enjoy tapas and great cocktails as well as Spanish wines and sherries in a relaxed atmosphere.

⑥ Lemonia
89 Regent's Park Rd NW1
■ Tube Chalk Farm ■ 020 7586 7454
■ ££

Traditional and modern Greek dishes served in a brasserie-style setting. There is an attractive conservatory.

Spaniards Inn, Hampstead Heath

⑦ Spaniards Inn
Spaniards Rd NW3 ■ 020 8731 8406 ■ Tube Hampstead or East Finchley ■ ££

One of London's most famous old pubs, this offers traditional English pub food and good Sunday roasts.

⑧ Southampton Arms
139 Highgate Rd NW5 ■ Train to Gospel Oak

A laidback traditional boozer close to Hampstead Heath with a dinky beer garden, offering a superb range of ales and ciders from independent brewers and producers. Bar food is basic but tasty, revolving almost exclusively around pork.

⑨ Rotunda
MAP E1 ■ 90 York Way N1
■ 020 7014 2840 ■ ££

A classy restaurant with fine views of the Battlebridge Basin. The menu changes regularly and uses seasonal ingredients; the meat is sourced from the restaurant's own farm.

⑩ 28 Church Row
28 Church Row ■ Tube Hampstead ■ 020 7993 2062 ■ ££

Quality ingredients go into simple Spanish and Italian cuisine served here in small, shareable plates. The restaurant is located in a Georgian building on one of the prettiest streets in the area.

See map on pp146–7

🔟 South and West London

The palaces that once graced London's river to the south and west of the city centre were built in places that remain popular today, from Hampton Court and Richmond in the west, downriver to Greenwich. There, on a deep meander in the Thames, a vast Tudor palace was the dramatic first sight of the city for anyone arriving by ship. It has been replaced by Wren's handsome Old Royal Naval College, a stunning building that is the high point of this UNESCO World Heritage Site and the start of the many delights of Greenwich, home of Greenwich Mean Time and the *Cutty Sark*, the world's last surviving tea clipper.

Richmond's palace has also disappeared, but nearby lies Kew Palace in the grounds of the incomparable Kew Gardens. Chiswick House, Ham House and Syon House are the best of a number of palatial mansions near Richmond, while culture is catered for in the Dulwich Picture Gallery and the Horniman Museum.

Shepherd Gate Clock, Greenwich

SOUTH AND WEST LONDON

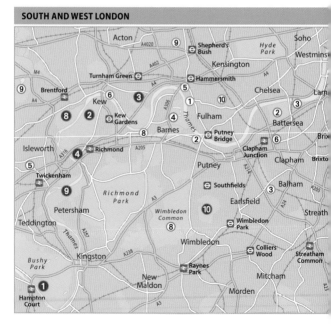

Palm House, Kew Gardens

1 Hampton Court
East Molesey, Surrey KT8
■ Train Hampton Court ■ Open Apr–
Oct: 10am–5:30pm Wed–Sun; Nov–
Mar: 10am–4pm Wed–Sun; open daily
in school hols ■ Adm ■ www.hrp.org.uk

Originally leased in 1514 by Cardinal
Wolsey, who substantially enlarged it,
Hampton Court *(see p52)* was handed
over to Henry VIII in 1528. Visiting
this historic palace, with its grand
Tudor and Baroque apartments and
extensive grounds, is a popular day
out from London. Enlightening audio
tours are available and at weekends
costumed interpreters bring the
Tudor world to life. Events held
through the year include a three-
week-long music festival in June,
which regularly attracts big-name
performers. In July, the grounds are
filled by the world's largest flower
show, organized by the Royal
Horticultural Society. Trains from
Waterloo take about half an hour but
for a delightfully leisurely trip, catch
a boat from Westminster Pier, which
takes about four hours.

2 Kew Gardens
**Richmond TW9 ■ Train to Kew
Bridge or tube Kew Gardens ■ Open
10am daily (closing times vary between 3 and 6pm in winter and 6 and
9pm in summer); check website
■ Adm ■ www.kew.org**

A UNESCO World Heritage site,
these former royal gardens hold a
collection of around 50,000 living
plants. A highlight is the magnificent
Temperate House, the world's largest Victorian-era glasshouse, which
showcases over 1,500 rare or
endangered plant species from
around the world. Kew Palace *(see
p52)* was used as a residence by
George III, whose parents, Prince
Frederick and Princess Augusta, laid
the first garden here. Take a Kew
Explorer land train tour of the gardens
– you can get on and off it any time.

3 Chiswick House and Gardens
**Burlington Lane, Chiswick W4
■ Tube Turnham Green ■ House:
open end May to Sept: 11am–4pm
Thu–Sun; adm ■ Gardens: open 7am–
dusk all year ■ www.chiswickhouse
andgardens.org.uk**

This piece of Italy in London is a
high spot of English 18th-century
architecture. A fine example of a
Palladian villa, with its dome, portico
and painted interiors, it was built for
Lord Burlington by architect William
Kent. The house is packed with
references to ancient Rome and
Renaissance Italy. The Italianate
gardens are complemented with
temples, statues and a lake.

The Thames riverfront at Richmond

4 Richmond
Train or tube to Richmond

This attractive, wealthy riverside suburb, with its quaint shops, pubs and pretty lanes, is worth visiting to join the delightful riverside path, which you can follow to Ham House. Its vast royal park *(see p55)* is home to red and fallow deer. There is also a spacious green, where cricket is played in summer. It is overlooked by the lovely restored Richmond Theatre and the early 18th-century Maids of Honour Row, which stands next to the last vestiges of an enormous Tudor palace.

5 Dulwich Picture Gallery
Gallery Rd SE21 ■ Train to North or West Dulwich ■ Open 10am–5pm Tue–Sun & bank hols ■ Adm ■ www.dulwichpicturegallery.org.uk

The oldest purpose-built public art space in England, this gallery *(see p58)* is located opposite the main entrance to Dulwich Park and is well worth the journey from central London. Apart from the stunning collection, including the exquisite *Girl at a Window* by Rembrandt (1645) and fine portraits by Gainsborough, there are regular exhibitions, lectures and other events, as well as over 1.2 hectares (3 acres) of lawns on which to relax.

6 Greenwich
Greenwich SE10 ■ Train to Greenwich; DLR Cutty Sark, Greenwich ■ Old Royal Naval College and Royal Observatory: open 10am–5pm daily; adm ■ www.ornc.org, www.rmg.co.uk

The World Heritage Site of Greenwich includes Sir Christopher Wren's Old Royal Naval College, Greenwich Park *(see p55)* and the historic Royal Observatory Greenwich where the Prime Meridian was established. Bordering the park are the Queen's House *(see p53)* and the National Maritime Museum *(see p56)*. The Greenwich Market and nearby *Cutty Sark (see p65)* are also must-sees.

7 Horniman Museum
100 London Rd SE23 ■ Train to Forest Hill ■ Open 10am–5:30pm daily ■ Aquarium: adm ■ www.horniman.ac.uk

Built in 1901 by Frederick Horniman, this museum appeals to both adults and children. It has a superb

> **GREENWICH PALACE**
>
> The ruins of this enormous royal riverside palace lie beneath the Old Royal Naval College. Many of the Tudor monarchs lived here, including Henry VII and Henry VIII who was born here. Abandoned under the Commonwealth in 1652, it was eventually demolished for Wren's present buildings.

anthropological collection, along with galleries on natural history. There is also an aquarium, a café overlooking the gardens and a small petting zoo.

⑧ Syon House and Park
Brentford, Middlesex ▪ Train to Syon Lane ▪ House: open mid-Mar–Oct: 10:30am–4:30pm Wed, Thu & Sun ▪ Gardens: open 10:30am–4:30pm Wed–Sun ▪ Adm ▪ www.syonpark.co.uk

This Neo-Classical villa is home to the Duke of Northumberland. It has fine Robert Adam interiors and a 16-hectare (40-acre) garden landscaped by Capability Brown.

⑨ Ham House and Garden
Ham, Richmond ▪ Train to Richmond , then bus 65 or 371 ▪ House: open noon–4pm daily ▪ Garden: 10am–5pm daily (Nov–Feb to 4pm) ▪ Adm ▪ www.nationaltrust.org.uk/ham-house-and-garden

This 17th-century house and garden was at the centre of court intrigue during Charles II's reign. It is richly furnished and there is a fine picture collection. The Orangery café serves dishes made from its garden produce.

The façade of Ham House

⑩ Wimbledon Lawn Tennis Museum
Church Road SW19 ▪ Tube Southfields ▪ Open 10am–5:30pm daily (winter: to 5pm) ▪ Adm ▪ www.wimbledon.com

With a view of the famous Centre Court, the museum tells the story of tennis, from its gentle, amateur beginnings to its professional status today. Guided tours are available, which must be booked ahead.

A DAY EXPLORING MARITIME GREENWICH

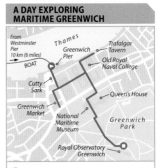

▶ MORNING

Start the day from **Westminster Pier**, because the best way to arrive at Greenwich *(see p153)* is by boat. The journey takes 40–50 minutes and there are terrific river sights on the way *(see pp64–5)*. Visit the historic tea clipper **Cutty Sark** *(see p65)* where you can walk beneath the impressive copper hull.

Behind is Greenwich Market, liveliest on weekends. Grab a coffee here, and then explore the surrounding streets, full of antique and other charming shops. Turn into Wren's **Old Royal Naval College** *(see p154)*, visit the magnificent Painted Hall and admire its murals, then walk around the Grand Square and down to the river. Stop for some lunch and a pint at the old **Trafalgar Tavern** *(see p157)*, on the far side of the Naval College overlooking the river.

AFTERNOON

After lunch, explore the fascinating **National Maritime Museum** *(see p56)*, the largest of its kind in the world, and the **Queen's House** *(see p53)* next door, and then make your way to the **Royal Observatory Greenwich** *(see p154)*, which is on the hill behind. This is the home of world time, and stands on the 0° longitude Prime Meridian. You can be photographed with one foot in the eastern hemisphere and one in the west. Return to central London by boat, DLR or rail from Greenwich.

See map on pp152–3 ←

The Best of the Rest

 Brixton Market
Electric Avenue to Brixton Station Rd SW9 ▪ Tube Brixton ▪ www.brixtonmarket.net
This lively market lies at the heart of London's Caribbean community. Shop for fresh produce and bargain fabrics, and enjoy street food in nearby Brixton Village and Market Row.

2 Battersea Park
The park (see p69) includes a boating lake, a children's zoo, sports facilities, and a gallery. There is also a woodland walk, the Peace Pagoda, as well as sculptures by Henry Moore and Barbara Hepworth.

The Peace Pagoda, Battersea Park

3 Battersea Power Station
MAP D6 ▪ SW8 ▪ Open 10am–9pm Mon–Sat, noon–6pm Sun ▪ www.batterseapowerstation.co.uk
Long derelict, this gargantuan icon of the riverside skyline opened to the public in 2022 after a £9 billion restoration. Its lower levels house three floors of shops and restaurants.

 WWT London Wetland Centre
Queen Elizabeth Walk SW13 ▪ Train to Barnes ▪ Open from 9:30am daily; closing times vary (check website) ▪ Adm ▪ www.wwt.org.uk
Managed by the Wildfowl & Wetlands Trust, this haven for nature is one of the best urban wildlife sites in Europe.

5 World Rugby Museum
Twickenham Stadium, Whitton Rd ▪ Train to Twickenham ▪ Open 10am–5pm Tue–Sat, 11am–5pm Sun ▪ Adm (no tours on match days) ▪ www.worldrugbymuseum.com
Tour the impressive stadium, home of England rugby, before visiting the museum.

6 Battersea Arts Centre
Lavender Hill SW11 ▪ Train to Clapham Junction ▪ www.bac.org.uk
One of the main fringe theatre venues, with a huge programme of activities.

7 Peckham
Train to Peckham Rye
Peckham is one of London's latest hotspots, with hip arts spaces and trendy bars and restaurants. Peckham Levels is a multi-storey car park turned into a cultural and creative space.

8 Wimbledon Common
Wimbledon Common SW19 ▪ Train to Wimbledon ▪ www.wpcc.org.uk
Visit the windmill then enjoy a walk. Head for southside pubs the Crooked Billet and the Hand in Hand.

9 Osterley Park and House
Jersey Rd, Isleworth ▪ Train to Isleworth ▪ House: open mid-Mar–Oct 11am–3:30pm Wed–Sun ▪ Adm ▪ www.nationaltrust.org.uk
A large Georgian mansion on a country estate on the outskirts of west London.

10 IFS Cloud Cable Car
27 Western Gateway Royal Docks E16 and Greenwich Peninsula SE10 ▪ Opening times vary, check website ▪ Adm ▪ www.ifscloudcablecar.co.uk
This cable car links Docklands with Greenwich Peninsula, offering great views of the city and river.

Places to Eat and Drink

PRICE CATEGORIES
For a three-course meal for one with half
a bottle of wine (or equivalent meal),
taxes and extra charges.

£ under £30   **££** £30–60   **£££** over £60

1 The River Café
Thames Wharf, Rainville Rd
W6 ▪ Tube Hammersmith ▪ 020
7386 4200 ▪ £££

This imaginative Hammersmith
restaurant, housed in a converted
warehouse with a river terrace, is
considered to be the "one of the
best Italian restaurants outside
Italy" by many.

2 Thai Square Putney Bridge
2–4 Lower Richmond Rd SW15 ▪ Tube
Putney Bridge ▪ 020 8780 1811 ▪ ££

A brilliant view of the river from this
smart, innovative glass restaurant
makes it a good spot year-round,
and the Thai menu is excellent.

3 Chez Bruce
2 Bellevue Rd SW17 ▪ Train
to Wandsworth Common ▪ 020
8672 0114 ▪ £££

Stylish yet relaxed, Michelin-starred
Chez Bruce serves excellent modern
French and Mediterranean food next
to leafy Wandsworth Common. Service
is impeccable and booking is essential.

4 Trafalgar Tavern
Park Row SE10 ▪ DLR Cutty
Sark ▪ 020 3887 9886 ▪ ££

Visitors flock in droves to this riverside pub, scattered with images of
Greenwich's maritime heritage.

5 The Gate
51 Queen Caroline St W6
▪ Tube Hammersmith ▪ 020 7833
0401 ▪ ££

Perhaps the best vegetarian
restaurant in London, The Gate is
worth hunting out. The gourmet
menu changes regularly, and the
meals are hearty and inventive.

The City Barge pub at Chiswick

6 The City Barge
27 Strand-on-the-Green W6
▪ Train to Kew Bridge ▪ 020 8994
2148 ▪ ££

Set in a delightful enclave of
18th-century Thames-side London,
this appealing pub serves hearty food.

7 Peckham Bazaar
119 Consort Rd, SE15
▪ 020 7732 2525 ▪ ££

This restaurant serves pan-Balkan
food cooked on the outdoor grill. Mari-
nated octopus and quail often make
an appearance on the rotating menu.

8 The Brown Dog
28 Cross St SW13 ▪ Train
Barnes Bridge ▪ 020 8392 2200 ▪ ££

With its warm atmosphere, this
gastropub feels like a real discovery.
Beer is sourced locally and in the
summer you can eat in the garden.

9 Esarn Kheaw
314 Uxbridge Rd W12 ▪ Tube
Shepherd's Bush ▪ 020 8743 8930
▪ ££

Authentic food from Thailand's Isaan
region, with familiar favourites as
well as more unusual dishes such
as spiced catfish.

10 The Harwood Arms
Walham Grove SW6 ▪ Tube
Fulham Broadway ▪ 020 7386 1847
▪ £££

The first gastropub to be awarded
a Michelin star, the Harwood Arms
offers delicious Sunday roasts and
an inventive British menu.

See map on pp152–3

🔟 East London

Traditionally a working-class area, the vibrant East End has over the centuries provided refuge for successive generations of immigrants, from French silk weavers to Jewish and Bangladeshi garment workers. Today, the media and finance worlds occupy stylish developments in the Docklands, galleries and trendy restaurants thrive in Hoxton, and lively markets draw visitors who marvel at the area's unspoiled 18th- and 19th-century architecture.

Rugs, Spitalfields Market

EAST LONDON

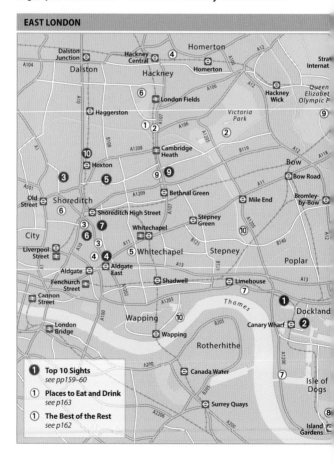

① **Top 10 Sights**
see pp159–60

① **Places to Eat and Drink**
see p163

① **The Best of the Rest**
see p162

1 Museum of London Docklands

West India Quay E14 ■ Tube & DLR Canary Wharf, DLR West India Quay ■ Open 10am–5pm daily ■ www. museumoflondon.org.uk

Set in a historic warehouse, this museum explores the history of London's river, port and people with a wealth of objects on display. Don't miss Mudlarks, an interactive area for kids; Sailortown, an atmospheric recreation of 19th-century riverside Wapping; and London, Sugar & Slavery, which reveals the city's involvement in the transatlantic trade in enslaved Africans.

The towers of Canary Wharf

2 Canary Wharf

E14 ■ Tube & DLR Canary Wharf

The centrepiece of the Docklands development is Canary Wharf, home to many of London's tallest sky-scrapers. Loftiest of all is 235-m (770-ft) One Canada Square. The tower is not open to the public but the complex has a mall with shops, restaurants and bars. The area's architecture includes the stunning Canary Wharf tube station, designed by Norman Foster, and an enclosed rooftop garden above at Crossrail Place.

3 Hoxton and Shoreditch

MAP G2 ■ N1/EC1

Once renowned as a hub for British contemporary art (thanks in large part to the now-closed White Cube art gallery on Hoxton Square), this trendy area is now home to a tech community around the junction of Old Street and City Road, dubbed "Silicon Roundabout". Lively at night, bars, pubs and restaurants here include The Three Crowns, The Fox (see p163) and the Queen of Hoxton.

4 Whitechapel Gallery

MAP H3 ■ 77–82 Whitechapel High St E1 ■ Open 11am–6pm Tue–Sun (until 9pm Thu) ■ www.white chapelgallery.org

This excellent gallery has a reputation for showing cutting-edge contemporary art from around the world. The gallery has launched the careers of David Hockney, Gilbert and George and Anthony Caro. Behind the distinctive 1901 Arts and Crafts façade there is a bookshop, café and restaurant.

THE HUGUENOTS IN LONDON

Driven from France in 1685, the Huguenots were Protestants fleeing religious persecution by Catholics. Many were silk weavers, whose masters and merchants settled in Spitalfields and built the beautiful Georgian houses (**below**) around Fournier, Princelet and Elder streets. Spitalfields silk was famous for its fine quality, but by the mid-19th century the industry had declined.

Spitalfields
MAP H2–H3 ■ Old Spitalfields Market: 16 Horner Square E1; market stalls open 10am–6pm daily (to 5pm Sun), 8am–6pm Thu; www.old spitalfieldsmarket.com

Streets such as Fournier Street, lined with 18th-century Huguenot silk weavers' houses remind that this area, just east of the City, has provided a refuge for immigrant populations for centuries. On the site of London's oldest market, the covered Victorian Old Spitalfields Market draws shoppers and diners to its craft, clothing and food stalls. Thursdays are good for antiques and every other Friday for vinyl records. Opposite is one of Europe's great Baroque churches. Christ Church, completed in 1729, was designed by Nicholas Hawksmoor.

⑤ Columbia Road Market
MAP H2 ■ Columbia Rd E2
■ Open 8am–3pm Sun

A ten-minute walk from the north end of Brick Lane, Columbia Road comes alive on Sunday mornings, as it fills with stalls teeming with plants and flowers. It is a delightful cornucopia of all things horticultural at wholesale prices. The street is also home to some charming restaurants, bars and stores selling, among other things, homemade bread and farmhouse cheeses through the week.

⑦ Brick Lane
MAP H2 ■ E1

Once the centre of London's Jewish population, this street is now the heart of London's Bangladeshi community. Some of the city's best bagels are available from the 24-hour Brick Lane Beigel Bake, a famous dawn haunt for late-night revellers. There are inexpensive restaurants, vintage and designer shops and a lively flea market on Sundays. Towards the street's northern end, the Old Truman Brewery is home to a mix of bars, shops and stalls.

Crowds exploring Brick Lane

The silver fins of the Thames Barrier

8 Thames Barrier
Information Centre 1 Unity Way SE18 ▪ Train to Charlton or Woolwich Dockyard ▪ Visitor Centre: open for group guided tours only ▪ Adm

With its 10 curved gates rising like shark fins from the river, this barrier (see p65) is a magnificent sight. There is a small visitor centre on the south side.

9 Young V&A
Cambridge Heath Rd E2 ▪ Tube Bethnal Green ▪ Check website for opening times ▪ www.vam.ac.uk/young

The former Museum of Childhood showcases 2,000 amazing objects from the UK's National Childhood Collection. Its three immersive galleries, called Imagine, Play and Design, are designed to spark youngsters' creativity, and there are play areas, multi-sensory exhibits and a gaming space.

10 Museum of the Home
MAP H2 ▪ 136 Kingsland Rd E2 ▪ Open 10am–5pm Tue–Sun ▪ www.museumofthehome.org.uk

Set in a beautiful 18th-century almshouse, this fascinating museum explores the evolution of the home and home life from 1630 to the present day. A series of rooms are decorated in distinct period style, reflecting changes in society, behaviour, style and taste. The rooms change through the year, restyled with different objects, and are based on real Londoners' homes.

A DAY AROUND THE EAST END

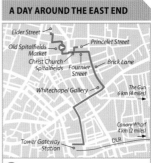

▶ MORNING

Start at **Old Spitalfields Market**, home to a mixture of stalls selling clothes, food and crafts. Grab a coffee and pastry from one of the street food stalls for breakfast.

Exit onto Commercial Street, cross the road and slip past **Christ Church Spitalfields** (see p160) into Fournier Street, where the gallery at No. 5 retains the panelling of the 18th-century silk weavers' houses. Stroll along Princelet and Elder streets, just off Fournier, for a taste of historic London.

Head into **Brick Lane** to browse among the numerous sari and Bangladeshi gift shops and then stop for lunch at one of the many curry houses.

AFTERNOON

After lunch head to Whitechapel Road. Notice the Arts and Crafts façade of the **Whitechapel Gallery** (see p159). Pop into the gallery's stunning two-floor exhibition space dedicated to contemporary and modern art.

Finally, take a ride on the driverless Docklands Light Railway from Tower Gateway, for some of the best views of East London. Emerge at **Canary Wharf** (see p159) to see some impressive architecture around Cabot Square, and end the day with a drink at **The Gun** (see p163) on Coldharbour.

Canary Wharf clock

The Best of the Rest

1 Theatre Royal Stratford East

Gerry Raffles Sq E15 ■ Train, Tube & DLR Stratford ■ www.stratfordeast.com

This local theatre with an international reputation was established by the director Joan Littlewood in 1953.

2 Victoria Park

Bow E9 ■ Tube Bethnal Green

One of East London's largest parks, with a boating lake, sculptures, skatepark and pretty gardens.

3 Dennis Severs' House

MAP H2 ■ 18 Folgate St E1 ■ Check website for times; book in advance ■ Adm ■ www.dennis severshouse.co.uk

Artist Dennis Severs created a theatrical experience in this 18th-century silk-weaver's home (see p160). Each room appears as if the inhabitants have just left it – dinner is half-eaten and cooking smells emanate from the kitchen.

4 Sutton House

2–4 Homerton High St E9 ■ Train Hackney Central ■ Check website for times ■ Adm ■ www. nationaltrust.org.uk/sutton-house

This Tudor merchant's house dates from 1535 and is one of the oldest in the East End.

5 House Mill

Three Mill Lane E3 ■ Tube Bromley-by-Bow ■ Open May–Nov: 11am–4pm Sun (plus 1st Sun in Mar, Apr & Dec) ■ Guided tours only ■ Adm ■ www.housemill.org.uk

Built in 1776, this tidal mill was once the country's largest. Today it is a working museum.

6 London Fields Lido

London Fields West Side E8 ■ Train Hackney Central ■ Adm ■ www.better.org.uk

Amidst the greenery of London Fields is an Olympic-sized, Art Deco heated outdoor swimming pool.

7 Docklands Sailing & Watersports Centre

Millwall Dock, 235a Westferry Rd E14 ■ DLR Crossharbour ■ www.dswc.org

Enjoy sailing, kayaking, windsurfing and paddleboarding facilities here.

8 Mudchute Park and Farm

Pier St E14 ■ Open 9am–5pm daily ■ DLR Mudchute ■ www.mudchute. org

Britain's largest city farm (see p68) has a fine collection of animals.

The futuristic ArcelorMittal Orbit

9 ArcelorMittal Orbit

Queen Elizabeth Olympic Park E20 ■ Train, Tube & DLR Stratford ■ Open noon–5pm Mon–Thu, 10am–6pm Fri–Sun ■ Adm ■ www.arcelor mittalorbit.com

Designed for the 2012 London Olympics, this 114.5-m- (376-ft-) tall sculpture offers great views of the city and the world's highest tunnel slide. Advance booking is advised.

10 Mile End Park

Mile End Rd E3 ■ Tube Mile End

One of London's most unusual parks with an Art Pavilion, Ecology Pavilion, sports centre and a go-kart track.

Places to Eat and Drink

PRICE CATEGORIES
For a three-course meal for one with half
a bottle of wine (or equivalent meal),
taxes and extra charges.
....
£ under £30 ■ ££ £30–60 ■ £££ over £60

1 Buen Ayre
50 Broadway Market E8
■ Train to London Fields ■ 020 7275
9900 ■ ££
Located in Hackney, this restaurant
specializes in authentic Argentinian
food and steaks.

2 Bright
Netil House, 1 Westgate St E8
■ Train to London Fields ■ 020 3095
9407 ■ ££
It's all about the food at this cool,
stripped-back restaurant, where
diners sit at scrubbed-oak tables.
Menu comprises of a mix of classic
Italian and modern European dishes.

3 St John Bread & Wine
MAP H2 ■ 94–96 Commercial
St E1 ■ 020 7251 0848 ■ £££
This sister restaurant of St John (see
p145) is a much-loved local haunt.

4 Som Saa
MAP H3 ■ 43a Commercial St
E1 ■ 020 7324 7790 ■ ££
Originally a "pop-up" eatery, Som
Saa has grown into a stylish restau-
rant. It offers innovative Thai dishes
including deep-fried whole seabass,
as well as curries and salads.

Façade of the Prospect of Whitby

5 Tayyabs
83–89 Fieldgate St E1 ■ Tube
Whitechapel ■ 020 7247 9543 ■ £
A longstanding institution, this buzzy,
labyrinthine Punjabi restaurant is
the place to go for succulent grilled
meats. The lamb chops are legendary. It's BYOB.

6 The Fox
MAP H2 ■ 28 Paul St EC2
■ 020 7729 5708 ■ £
The menu in this lovely refurbished
pub celebrates fried chicken. There's
also a decent range of ales and wines.

7 The Grapes
76 Narrow St E14 ■ DLR West
Ferry ■ 020 7987 4396 ■ ££
It is said that Charles Dickens danced
on the tables at this pub (see p77).
The heated terrace and upstairs
dining room have Thames views, and
the menu is classic pub grub.

8 The Gun
27 Coldharbour E14 ■ DLR
South Quay/Blackwall ■ 020 7519
0075 ■ ££
This swish Docklands operation
overlooking the Thames serves
up quality gastropub food.

9 Mother Kelly's
251 Paradise Road E2 ■ Tube
Bethnal Green ■ 020 7012 1244
Fabulous craft beer tap room in a
converted railway arch. For food,
cheese and meat boards are available or take your pick
from the eateries nearby.

**10 Prospect of
Whitby**
57 Wapping Wall E1
■ Tube Wapping
■ 020 7481 1095 ■ ££
East London's oldest
riverside pub dates
to 1520, and has old
beams, a pewter bar,
great river views and
decent pub food.

See map on pp158–9

Streetsmart

**Modern interior of St Pancras
International Station**

Getting Around

Arriving by Air

Heathrow, Gatwick, Stansted, Luton and City. airports serve London.

Heathrow, London's main airport, is 24 km (15 miles) west of central London. The Heathrow Express to Paddington is a quick but pricey way into the centre, taking 15 minutes. A cheaper alternative is the Elizabeth line, which takes 35–40 minutes into central London. Cheaper still is the Tube, which takes an hour or so to the centre. National Express runs a coach service from Heathrow's bus station to Victoria Coach Station.

Gatwick airport is 45 km (28 miles) south of London. Expensive Gatwick Express trains run non-stop to Victoria railway station every 30 minutes, taking 30 minutes. The regular stopping services to Victoria and London Bridge are a cheaper alternative.

Stansted, London's third busiest airport, is 56 km (35 miles) northeast of London. The Stansted Express train to Liverpool Street takes 50 minutes and runs every 30 minutes or so. National Express provides 24-hour coaches to Victoria, taking just under 2 hours.

From **Luton Airport**, 50 km (31 miles) north of the city, the Luton DART takes passengers to Luton Airport Parkway station, from which trains go to St Pancras, taking 20–30 minutes. **London City Airport** is 14 km (9 miles) from the centre. It is served by Docklands Light Railway (DLR) trains from Bank station.

International Train Travel

St Pancras International is the London terminus for **Eurostar**, the high-speed train linking the UK with the Continent.

You can buy tickets and passes for multiple international journeys via **Eurail** or **Interrail**; reservations for high-speed trains are usually mandatory. Check that your pass is valid on the service on which you wish to travel before attempting to board.

Eurostar runs regular services from Paris, Brussels, Amsterdam and Rotterdam to London via the Channel Tunnel.

Eurotunnel operates a drive-on-drive-off train service between Calais and Folkestone, in southeast England.

Domestic Train Travel

The UK's railway system is complicated and can be confusing. Lines are run by several different companies, but they are coordinated by **National Rail**, which operates a joint information service.

London has 14 railway termini serving different parts of Britain (the main ones are Charing Cross, Euston, King's Cross, London Bridge, St Pancras, Paddington, Waterloo and Victoria). There are also over 300 smaller London stations.

Each main terminus is the starting point for local and suburban lines that cover the whole of southeast England.

London's local and suburban train lines are used by commuters every day. For visitors, rail services are most useful for trips to the outskirts of London and areas of the city without nearby Underground connections (especially in south London). If you are planning to travel outside of the capital, always try to book rail tickets in advance.

Long-Distance Bus Travel

Coaches from European and UK destinations arrive at Victoria Coach Station. The biggest operator in the UK is **National Express**. Various European operators offer cheap travel to London from other European cities. Book in advance.

Public Transport

Transport for London (**TFL**) is London's main public transport authority. Safety and hygiene measures, timetables, ticket information, transport maps and more can be found on their website.

TFL divides the city into nine charging zones for Underground, Elizabeth line, DLR, Overground and National Rail services, radiating out from Zone 1 in the centre. On buses, there is a flat fare for each trip, no matter how far you travel.

Tickets

Tube and rail fares are expensive, especially individual tickets. The cheapest and most flexible way to travel is to purchase a Visitor Oyster Card online or (slightly more expensive) an Oyster pay as you go card from stations, "ticket stops" and newsagents in the city. These are smart-cards, which you can preload and top up with credit, and are valid for all zones, as well as on trains from Gatwick Airport. You will need one card per person. You can also use contactless credit or debit cards in the same way as the Oyster card. Fares are subject to daily and weekly caps.

When using public transport, you "touch in" with your card on a yellow card reader, and the corresponding amount is deducted. On Under-ground, Elizabeth line, DLR and Overground trains, you must also remember to "touch out" where you finish your journey, or you will be charged a maximum fare, though the excess can usually be reclaimed via the website if you forget. Prices rise during peak times: 6:30–9:30am and 4–7pm Mon–Fri.

Paper tickets are also available, though usually work out more expensive. A paper Day Travelcard gives unlimited travel on all systems after 9:30am on weekdays (or any time on weekends and public holidays) until 4:30am the next morning for a flat fee. Make sure it covers all the zones you're travelling through.

The Underground

The London Underground (commonly referred to as "the Tube") has 11 lines, all named and colour-coded, which intersect at various stations.

Some lines, like the Jubilee, have a single branch; others, like the Northern, have more than one, so it is important to check the digital boards on the platform and the destination on the front of the train.

Trains run every few minutes 7:30–9:30am and 4–7pm, and every 5–10 minutes at all other times. The Jubilee, Northern, Central, Victoria and Piccadilly lines offer a 24-hour service on selected routes on Fridays and Saturday nights. All other lines operate roughly 5am–12:15am Mon–Sat, with reduced hours on Sun.

Around 90 Tube stations offers step-free access. These are marked on Tube maps, which are located on all trains and at every station.

The DLR

The DLR (Docklands Light Railway) is a mostly over-ground network of trains that run from the City to stops in east and south-east London, including City Airport and Green-wich. It operates roughly 5:30–12:30am Mon–Sat, 7am–11:30pm Sun.

The whole of the DLR offers step-free access from street to platform.

The Overground

Marked on Tube maps by an orange line, the Overground connects with the Underground and main railway stations at various points across the city. It operates in much the same way as the Underground, and covers most areas of the city without nearby Under-ground connections. The line between Highbury & Islington and New Cross Gate runs 24 hours on Friday and Saturday nights.

The Elizabeth Line

Finally opened after many setbacks and delays in 2022, the Elizabeth line is a new railway running through central London from Reading and Heathrow in the west to Shenfield and Abbey Wood in the east. With several key stops in the city centre (including Paddington and Liverpool Street), it has sped up journey times into and between popular destinations in the capital.

Up to 22 trains run an hour on the busiest section between Paddington and Whitechapel, operating between roughly 5:30am and 12:30am Mon–Sat, with reduced hours and frequency on Sun.

Bus

Slower but cheaper than the Tube, buses are also a good way of seeing the city as you travel.

Bus routes are displayed on the TFL website and on maps at bus stops. The destination and route number is indicated on the front of the bus and the stops are announced on board.

Buses do not accept cash so an Oyster card, Travelcard or contactless payment is required.

A single fare costs £1.65, while unlimited bus travel caps out at £4.95 – just use the same card each time you use the bus to reach the daily cap.

The hopper fare lets you make unlimited bus journeys for free within an hour of touching in. Travel is free on buses for under-11s, and for those aged 11–15 as long as they carry a Zip Oyster photocard; apply online well in advance.

Some routes run 24 hours, supplemented by Night buses (indicated by the letter "N" added before the route number), which run from around midnight until 6am, generally 2–3 times per hour.

Taxis

London's iconic black cabs can be hailed on the street, booked online or over the phone, or picked up at taxi ranks throughout the city. The yellow "Taxi" sign is lit up when the taxi is free. The driver's cab licence number should be displayed in the back of the taxi.

All taxis are metered, and fares start from £3.80. Taxi apps such as Uber also operate in London. **Licensed London Taxi** is one of numerous services that can be booked by phone or online.

Driving

Holders of non-UK licences do not need an international driving licence to drive a car or motorcycle in the UK for stays of less than a year, but if you bring your own vehicle make sure you have a green card or proof of insurance.

Driving in London

Driving in London is not recommended. Traffic is slow-moving, parking is scarce and expensive, and in central London there is the added cost of the

Congestion Charge – a £15 daily charge for driving in central London 7am–6pm Mon–Fri, and noon–6pm Sat, Sun and public holidays. Older vehicles may also incur the £12.50 Ultra Low Emission Zone (ULEZ) charge; check the TFL website for details.

In the event of an accident, contact the **AA** for roadside assistance.

Parking

Parking is prohibited at all times wherever the street is marked with double yellow or red lines by the kerb.

If there is a single yellow line, parking is normally allowed from 6:30pm–8am Mon–Sat and all day Sun, but exact hours vary, so always check the signs along each street before leaving your vehicle. Where there is no line at all, parking is free at all times, but this is rare in central London. Rental car drivers are still liable for parking fines.

Car Rental

To rent a car in the UK you must be 21 or over (or in some cases, 25) and have held a valid driver's licence for at least a year.

Driving out of central London will take about an hour in any direction, more during rush hours; if you want to tour the countryside, it can be easier to take a train to a town or city outside London and rent a car from there. Airports tend to offer cheaper car rental.

Rules of the Road

Drive on the left. Seat belts must be worn at all times by the driver and all passengers. Children up to 135 cm tall or the age of 12 or under must travel with the correct child seat for their weight and size.

Mobile phones may not be used while driving except with a "hands-free" system. Third-party insurance is required by law.

Overtake on the outside or right-hand lane. When approaching a roundabout, give priority to traffic approaching from the right, unless indicated otherwise. All vehicles must give way to emergency services vehicles.

It is illegal to drive in bus lanes during certain hours. See roadside signs for restrictions.

The drink-driving legal limit (p170) is strictly enforced and penalties upon conviction can be severe.

Cycling

Provision for cyclists in London has improved greatly in recent years, and cycling can be a great way to see the city. There are dedicated Cycleways linking destinations across London. These offer a mix of protected cycling on main roads and routes through quieter backstreets and green spaces.

Santander Cycles, London's self-service cycle and e-bike hire service, has docking stations in central London. Bikes can also be rented from the **London Bicycle Tour Company** and other rental companies throughout the city. Be aware that drink-drive limits (p170) also apply to cyclists.

Walking

Walking is a rewarding way to get around in London. The centre is not large, and you will be surprised at how short the distance is between places that seem far apart on the Tube.

Guided walking tours abound, with themes including Jack the Ripper, ghosts and hauntings and Shakespeare's London. The longest established operator, **London Walks**, offers a wide choice.

Boats and Ferries

Car ferries departing from Calais and Dunkirk arrive in Dover or Folkestone, around 2 hours' drive from London.

Passenger and car-ferry services also sail from other ports in northern France to the south of England, as well as from Bilbao and Santander in Spain.

Ferry services also run to other ports around the country from the Netherlands and the Republic of Ireland.

London by Boat

Some of London's most spectacular views can be seen from the Thames. **Uber Boat by Thames Clippers** runs river services every 15–30 minutes on catamarans between Battersea Power Station or Embankment/ the London Eye and North Greenwich in both directions, via Bankside and Tower Bridge. Some commuter services start in Putney, in the west, and Barking, in east London.

Standard tickets cost £9.50 in the central zone, but discounted fares apply if bought online, via the Thames Clippers app or when using a Travelcard, contactless or Oyster card.

A number of providers offer **river tours** and experiences on the Thames, with numerous options available, from dining experiences to hop-on-hop-off services.

Practical Information

Passports and Visas

For entry requirements, including visas, consult your nearest British embassy or check the **UK Government** website. Visitors from the EU, the United States, Canada, Australia and New Zealand do not require a visa to enter the country, for stays of, in most cases, up to six months.

Government Advice

It is important to consult your government's advice before travelling. The **US Department of State**, **Global Affairs Canada** and the **Australian Department of Foreign Affairs and Trade** offer the latest information on security, health and regulations.

Customs Information

You can find information on the laws relating to goods and currency taken in or out of the UK on the **UK Government** website.

Insurance

We recommend that you take out a comprehensive insurance policy covering theft, loss of belongings, medical care, cancellations and delays, and read the small print carefully. Emergency treatment is usually free from the National Health Service, and there are reciprocal healthcare arrangements with EU member states, Australia, New Zealand and some other countries (check the NHS website for details). Visitors from EU or EFTA countries should ensure they bring a valid European Health Insurance Card (EHIC) in order to access healthcare.

Health

The UK has a world-class healthcare system. Emergency medical care in the UK is generally free. It is important to arrange comprehensive medical insurance before travelling. If you have an EHIC card, be sure to present this as soon as possible. You may have to pay after treatment and reclaim the money later. Those without an EHIC may have to pay upfront for medical treatment and reclaim on insurance at a later date; check the NHS website for details of reciprocal agreements in place for treatment between your home country and the UK.

No vaccinations are needed before visiting the UK. Tap water in the UK is safe to drink, unless otherwise stated.

For minor ailments go to a pharmacy or chemist. These are plentiful throughout the city; chains such as Boots and Superdrug have branches in almost every shopping district. If you have an accident or medical problem requiring non-urgent medical attention, you can find details of your nearest non-emergency medical service on the NHS website. Alternatively, you can contact **NHS 111** (the NHS emergency care service) at any hour online or by calling 111, or go to your nearest Accident and Emergency (A&E) department.

You may need a doctor's prescription to obtain certain pharmaceuticals; the pharmacist can inform you of the closest doctor's surgery or medical centre where you can be seen by a GP (general practitioner).

Smoking, Alcohol and Drugs

The UK has a smoking ban in all enclosed public places, including bars, cafés, restaurants, public transport, train stations and hotels. The ban doesn't cover vaping, though in general it is prohibited by local laws, including on public transport and in stations.

The legal limit for drivers in England is 80 mg of alcohol per 100 ml of blood, or 0.08 per cent BAC (blood alcohol content). This is roughly equivalent to one small glass of wine or a pint of regular-strength beer; however, it is best to avoid drinking altogether if you plan to drive.

The possession of controlled drugs is prohibited and could result in a prison sentence.

ID

Visitors to the UK are not required to carry ID on their person. Anyone who looks under 18 may be asked for photo ID to prove their age when buying alcohol.

Personal Security

London is a relatively safe city to visit. Pickpocketing is less of a problem than in many other capitals. Keep your belongings in a safe place and with you at all times, use your common sense and be alert to your surroundings. Use only licensed black cabs and private hire vehicles displaying an identification disc.

Make sure possessions are insured, and if possible leave passports and tickets in the hotel safe. If you have anything stolen, report the crime as soon as possible to the nearest police station. Get a copy of the crime report in order to claim on your insurance

Contact your embassy if you have your passport stolen, or in the event of a serious crime or accident

For emergency **police**, **fire** or **ambulance** services dial 999 or 112 – the operator will ask which service you require; For medical help, dial the NHS 111 service unless it's an emergency.

Anything found on the Tube, buses, trains or black cabs is sent to the **TFL Lost Property** office. Allow three to five days for items to get there; property is held for three months.

As a rule, Londoners are very accepting of all people, regardless of their race, gender or sexuality. Homosexuality was legalized in England in 1967 and in 2004, the UK recognized the right to legally change your gender. If you do feel unsafe, the **Safe Space Alliance** pinpoints your nearest place of refuge.

Travellers with Specific Requirements

Accessibility information, braille maps, apps and audio guides for public transport are available from the **TFL** website. The Tube and Overground have many stations with step-free access and all Elizabeth line and DLR stations are step-free. The city's bus fleet is wheelchair-accessible.

The nationwide Blue Badge scheme offers parking provision for people with mobility issues, though note that special rules apply in parts of central London. The Visit London website offers handy tips on the city's accessibility provisions. **AccessAble** has a useful searchable online directory.

Most large hotels and attractions have wheelchair access, but make sure you check before booking. Even if a restaurant has wheelchair access, the dining area and toilet may be on different floors, so check when booking.

Museums and galleries offer audio tours, which are useful to those with impaired vision. The **RNID** (Royal National Institute for Deaf People) and the **RNIB** (Royal National Institute of Blind People) can also offer useful information and advice. Call theatres and cinemas in advance to ask about disabled seating. Many offer audio-described performances and have hearing loop or infrared systems. Some also offer British Sign Language-interpreted performances.

DIRECTORY

PASSPORTS AND VISAS

UK Government
w gov.uk/check-uk-visa

GOVERNMENT ADVICE

Australian Department of Foreign Affairs and Trade
w smartraveller.gov.au

Global Affairs Canada
w travel.gc.ca

US Department of State
w travel.state.gov

CUSTOMS INFORMATION

UK Government
w gov.uk/duty-free-goods

INSURANCE

NHS
w nhs.uk

HEALTH

NHS 111
w 111.nhs.uk

PERSONAL SECURITY

Police, Fire, Ambulance
999 or 112

Safe Space Alliance
w safespacealliance.com

TFL Lost Property
w tfl.gov.uk/help-and-contact/lost-property

TRAVELLERS WITH SPECIFIC REQUIREMENTS

AccessAble
w accessable.co.uk

RNID
w actiononhearingloss.org.uk

RNIB
w rnib.org.uk

TFL
w tfl.gov.uk/transport-accessibility

Time Zone

London operates on Coordinated Universal Time (UTC), known locally as Greenwich Mean Time (GMT), which is one hour behind Continental European Time and five hours ahead of US Eastern Standard Time. The clock advances one hour during "British Summer Time", spanning the last Sunday in March until the last Sunday in October.

Money

The UK's currency is the pound sterling. One pound sterling (£1) is divided into 100 pence (100p). Paper notes are in denominations of £5, £10, £20 and £50. Coins are £2, £1, 50p, 20p, 10p, 5p, 2p and 1p. Major credit, debit and prepaid cards are accepted, and contactless payment is almost universal, including on public transport. However, it is worth carrying some cash, as some smaller businesses and markets still operate a cash-only policy. Cash machines (ATMs) are conveniently located at banks, train stations, shopping areas and main streets.

Tipping in London is discretionary. In restaurants it's customary to tip 10–12.5 per cent for good service. It is usual to tip taxi drivers 10 per cent and hotel porters, concierge and housekeeping £1–2 per bag or day.

Electrical Appliances

The electricity supply is 240 volts AC. Plugs are of a three-square-pin type.

Most hotels have shaver sockets in the bathrooms.

Mobile Phones and Wi-Fi

Most visitors travelling to the UK with EU tariffs are not affected by data roaming charges but check with your local provider.

Internet access is very easy to find in London. Free Wi-Fi hotspots are widely available in the city centre. Cafés and restaurants will usually give you their Wi-Fi password, though you should make a purchase beforehand. **O2** offers Wi-Fi across central London, though you will need to register to access their hotspots. Wi-Fi is available at most Tube stations via the **Virgin Media** portal. By the end of 2024, 4G mobile coverage should be available in all Underground stations and tunnels.

Postal Services

Standard post in the UK is handled by the **Royal Mail**. There are post office branches throughout London, generally open 9am–5:30pm Monday to Friday and until 12:30pm on Saturday.

You can buy 1st-class, 2nd-class and international stamps in post offices, shops and supermarkets. Distinctive red post boxes are located on main streets throughout the city.

Weather

London's weather is very unpredictable. Daytime highs average 22°C (75°F) in summer. Winter can be cold and icy.

The heaviest rainfall is in October and November, but showers occur all year round: an umbrella and raincoat are advisable. To check ahead, visit the **Met Office** website, which carries detailed forecasts for the next seven days.

Opening Hours

Shops generally open 9am–6pm Monday to Saturday; bigger stores and supermarkets usually stay open later. Sunday has limited trading hours: these vary but many stores open 11am–5pm.

Museum and gallery times vary widely. Some museums and attractions are closed on Mondays, and since the COVID-19 pandemic many have operated shorter opening hours and close on other days, too: it's best to check before starting out. Last admission to many attractions is 30 minutes or an hour before closing.

On public holidays, public services are closed and some shops, museums and attractions either close or operate shorter hours.

The COVID-19 pandemic proved that situations can change suddenly. Always check before visiting attractions and hospitality venues for up-to-date hours and booking requirements.

Visitor Information

Visit London is the official tourist organization for London; its website includes a what's on guide, maps, event calendars, offers on theatre tickets and attractions, and an accommodation booking service. Major visitor centres include the **City Information Centre**, right by St Paul's from where the walking tours of the city depart, and **Greenwich Tourist Information**, which offers local advice on places to stay, what to see, guided tours and much more. Visitor Centres run by TFL are located in the Tube stations at Piccadilly Circus, Victoria, Kings Cross St Pancras and Liverpool Street, as well as at Heathrow Airport.

London can be an expensive city, but there are a number of ways in which costs can be reduced, and many museums are free. Students and under-18s pay lower admission to many exhibitions, and holders of an ISIC (International Student Identity Card) or IYTC (International Youth Travel Card) are eligible for a range of other discounts.

A number of visitor passes and discount cards are available online. These cards are not free, so consider carefully how many of the offers you are likely to take advantage of before buying one. For a full list of the options available, consult the Visit London website.

One such card is the **London Pass**, which offers free entry to more than 80 of the city's top attractions, fast-track entry to some busier sights, money off selected tours and discounts in participating shops, with the option of adding a Visitor Oyster card.

Local Customs

Always stand to the right on escalators or stairwells. Allow passengers to exit before you board public transport. On the Tube, it is customary to offer your seat to passengers who are less able-bodied, pregnant or elderly.

Visiting Places of Worship

Dress respectfully when entering places of worship: cover your torso and upper arms. Ensure shorts and skirts cover your knees.

Language

English is the official language spoken in London. However, it is a multicultural city, in which you will hear many languages spoken. Numerous attractions and tour companies offer foreign language tours.

Taxes and Refunds

VAT (Value Added Tax) is charged at 20 per cent and almost always included in the marked price. Post-Brexit, visitors to Britain are only able to buy tax-free items in shops and ask them to be shipped to an address outside the UK; check with the retailer if they offer this service.

Accommodation

London offers a huge variety of accommodation to suit any budget, including luxury five-star hotels, family-run B&Bs and budget hostels.

Lodgings can fill up and prices become inflated during the summer, so it's worth booking well in advance. Hotels usually quote room rates rather than prices per person and include VAT in their published rates. Look for special offer deals. The best deals are usually to be had online and well in advance but do consider calling to request last-minute deals, too. Note that some hotels and B&Bs require a minimum stay of two or more nights, especially at weekends.

A comprehensive list of accommodation to suit all needs can be found via Visit London.

DIRECTORY

POSTAL SERVICES
W postoffice.co.uk

Royal Mail
W royalmail.com

MOBILE PHONES AND WI-FI

O2
W o2.co.uk/connectivity

Virgin Media
W my.virginmedia.com/wifi/faqs.html

WEATHER

Met Office
W metoffice.gov.uk

VISITOR INFORMATION

City Information Centre
MAP R2 ■ St Paul's Churchyard EC4
cityoflondon.gov.uk/things-to-do

Greenwich Tourist Information
Old Royal Navy College SE10
C 020 8305 5235
W visitgreenwich.org.uk

London Pass
W londonpass.com

Visit London
W visitlondon.com

Places to Stay

Luxury Hotels

Brown's Hotel
MAP J4 ■ Albemarle St W1
■ 020 7493 6020 ■ www.
roccofortehotels.com ■ £££
Founded in 1837 by James Brown, valet to Lord Byron, this Mayfair hotel has accommodated many a celebrity staying in London. With 115 rooms set across 11 Georgian townhouses, it is decorated with contemporary as well as antique art, while retaining its intimacy and charm. It is renowned for its afternoon teas in the Drawing Room.

Claridge's
MAP D3 ■ 49 Brook St W1
■ 020 7629 8860 ■ www.
claridges.co.uk ■ £££
This historic hotel established a reputation for glamour and style following its Art Deco makeover in 1929–31 and has maintained it ever since. A stunning renovation, completed in 2021, has added a spa and pool; a stay here is guaranteed to make you feel pampered.

The Connaught
MAP D3 ■ Carlos Place W1 ■ 020 7499 7070
■ www.the-connaught.
co.uk ■ £££
Tucked away in a quiet corner of Mayfair, the Connaught is more discreet than other grand hotels in London. With three Michelin stars, its Hélène Darroze restaurant is one of the finest in London. The hotel also has small spa with a black granite pool.

The Lanesborough
MAP D4 ■ 1 Hyde Park Corner SW1 ■ 020 7259 5599 ■ www.oetker collection.com/hotels/ the-lanesborough ■ £££
Offering a butler service in every room, this opulent hotel is one of London's most decadent hotels. There is a sense of theatre at its richly decorated restaurant, The Lanesborough Grill, which focuses on sophisticated modern British cuisine.

Mandarin Oriental
MAP C4 ■ 66 Knightsbridge SW1 ■ 020 7235 2000
■ www.mandarinoriental.
com ■ £££
Overlooking Hyde Park, the Edwardian-style Mandarin Oriental is home to three restaurants, including the world-renowned, two-Michelin-starred Dinner, the creation of celebrity chef Heston Blumenthal. Following a £130 million refurbishment, every part of this hotel is stunning, from the rooms to the lobby.

The Ritz
MAP J4 ■ 150 Piccadilly W1 ■ 020 7300 2222
■ www.theritzlondon.
com ■ £££
One of London's most glamorous hotels, the Ritz features Louis XVI style, with shades of blue, yellow, pink and peach, gold and silk trimmings, chandeliers and period furniture. Afternoon tea in the Palm Court is popular and the elegant, Michelin-starred restaurant has a garden terrace.

The Savoy
MAP M3 ■ Strand WC2
■ 020 7836 4343 ■ www.
thesavoylondon.com
■ £££
In a lovely riverside setting, the Savoy is London's top traditional hotel and has been restored to its original Art Deco splendour. Leisure facilities include a private pool and gym.

Shangri-La at The Shard
MAP T5 ■ 31 St Thomas St SE1 ■ 020 7234 8000
■ www.shangri-la.com/
london/shangrila ■ £££
Occupying floors 34 to 52 of the city's highest skyscraper, The Shard, this is the London outpost of one of Asia's top hotel chains. The rooms here are spacious and the service attentive but it is the views that make the stay a memorable experience. The swimming pool on the 52nd floor is also one of the highest in London.

The Waldorf Hilton
MAP N3 ■ Aldwych WC2
■ 020 7836 2400 ■ www.
hilton.com ■ £££
This is one of London's great Edwardian hotels, located a stone's throw from theatres and shopping districts. The leisure facilities are excellent.

Character Hotels

Portobello Hotel
22 Stanley Gardens W11
▪ **Tube** Notting Hill Gate
▪ 020 7727 2777 ▪ www.
portobellohotel.com ▪ ££
Brimming with character,
each of the 21 rooms in
this boutique hotel is
individually decorated –
some with wall-to-wall
murals – and tastefully
furnished. This is exactly
the kind of hotel you
would hope to find near
London's great antiques
market. A light snack
menu accompanies an
honesty bar.

The Rookery
MAP G2 ▪ 12 Peter's
Lane, Cowcross St EC1
▪ 020 7336 0931 ▪ www.
rookeryhotel.com ▪ ££
Located at a short distance
from St Paul's Cathedral,
the hotel takes its name
from a former term for a
slum – this area, around
Smithfield market, was
once a den of vice. An
atmospheric warren of
rooms has been linked
together to create a brilliant hotel that evokes
Victorian London, with
a touch of the Gothic.

York & Albany
MAP D1 ▪ 127–29
Parkway, NW1 ▪ 020 7387
5700 ▪ www.gordonram
sayrestaurants.com/york-
and-albany ▪ £££
Situated between Regent's
Park and Camden, this
is chef Gordon Ramsay's
take on the gastropub,
with deliciously inventive
cuisine. Above it is the
surprisingly secluded
townhouse, with eight
beautiful, luxurious
rooms and suites combin-
ing period fittings and
electronic gadgets.

Durrants Hotel
MAP D3 ▪ George St W1
▪ 020 7935 8131 ▪ www.
durrantshotel.co.uk ▪ £££
Set close to Marylebone
High Street and Bond
Street, this Georgian hotel
has been in business since
1790. It has a comfort-
able, old-fashioned style,
with antique furniture
and modern bathrooms.

The Chesterfield Mayfair
MAP D4 ▪ 35 Charles St
W1 ▪ 020 7491 2622
▪ www.chesterfield
mayfair.com ▪ £££
Set in the heart of Mayfair,
just off Berkeley Square,
this 4-star luxury hotel is
full of British old-world
charm. The honey served at
breakfast comes directly
from the beehives on the
hotel's rooftop. The fine
dining restaurant serves
excellent British food.

The Gore
MAP B5 ▪ 190 Queen's
Gate SW7 ▪ 020 7584
6601 ▪ www.collezione.
starhotels.com ▪ £££
Built in 1892 under
the patronage of Prince
Albert, consort of Queen
Victoria, this hotel retains
a relaxed, fin-de-siècle
feel. Its Persian rugs,
period photos and paint-
ings are in keeping with
the elegance of the
building, and rooms are
furnished with antiques.
The restaurant, 190
Queen's Gate, is recom-
mended as well.

Hazlitt's
MAP L2 ▪ 6 Frith St W1
▪ 020 7434 1771 ▪ www.
hazlittshotel.com ▪ £££
A literary event as much
as a hotel, Hazlitt's is
located in the former
townhouse of the essayist
William Hazlitt (1778–
1830). The hotel's literary
feel is enhanced by its
library of books signed
by the many authors who
have stayed as guests
at the hotel.

Designer Hotels

ME London
MAP N3 ▪ 336–37 Strand
WC2 ▪ 020 7395 3400
▪ www.melia.com ▪ £££
With its black-and-white,
classy decor and stunning
pyramid-shaped reception,
a visit to ME London
is like stepping into a
sci-fi film. The futuristic
feel continues with the
ground-floor restaurants,
guest lounges and the
Radio Rooftop Bar, which
has panoramic views of
the city skyline.

art'otel Battersea
MAP D6 ▪ 1 Electric Boule-
vard SW11 ▪ 0333 400
6154 ▪ www.artotel-
londonbattersea.com ▪ ££
Playful artworks greet
guests in the lobby of this
cool new hotel, and the
rooms are full of designer
chic. The jewel in the
crown is the stunning
rooftop terrace, with an
infinity swimming pool
seemingly within touching
distance of Battersea
Power Station's chimneys.

Eccleston Square Hotel
MAP D5 ▪ 37 Eccleston
Sq SW1 ▪ 020 3503 0750
▪ www.ecclestonsquare
hotel.com ▪ ££
Overlooking the lush
gardens of Eccleston
Square, this luxury bou-
tique hotel is aimed at
the ultra-sophisticated
and offers high-tech
facilities, including uber-
comfy Hästens beds.

Hoxton Hotel
MAP H2 ▪ 81 Great Eastern St EC2 ▪ 020 7550 1000 ▪ www.thehoxton.com ▪ ££

Set in the trendy area of Shoreditch, and with branches in Holborn and Southwark, the Hoxton offers plenty of industrial chic, with small but cool individual rooms at reasonable prices. A US-style grill and roof-top Mexican restaurant complete the picture.

St Martins Lane
MAP L3 ▪ 45 St Martin's Lane WC2 ▪ 020 7300 5500 ▪ www.sbe.com/hotels/originals/st-martins-lane ▪ £££

In the heart of the West End, the Sanderson's sister hotel has a lobby of theatrical proportions. The rooms have floor-to-ceiling windows and even the bathrooms (all of which have big tubs) are 50 per cent glass.

The Zetter Hotel
MAP F2 ▪ 86–88 Clerkenwell Rd EC1 ▪ 020 7324 4567 ▪ www.thezetter.com ▪ ££

Modern with retro touches, this laid-back option offers luxuries such as the latest in-room entertainment and walk-in rain showers. The rooftop studios feature private terraces and out-door bathtubs. The Zetter has a sister hotel, the stunning Zetter Town-house, in Marylebone.

Charlotte Street Hotel
MAP K1 ▪ 15–17 Charlotte St W1 ▪ 020 7806 2000 ▪ www.firmdalehotels.com ▪ £££

This is a tasteful and comfortable hotel, with padded armchairs, antiques and log fires in the drawing room and library. A "Bloomsbury Group" theme runs through the entire hotel, complete with original artworks and a mural in the bustling Oscar bar and restaurant.

COMO Metropolitan
MAP D4 ▪ Old Park Lane W1 ▪ 020 7447 1000 ▪ www.comohotels.com/metropolitanlondon ▪ £££

Contemporary and stylish, this was one of the first of the classy modern hotels in London, with black-clad staff, cool interiors and bright, airy bedrooms and suites. Go celebrity-spotting in Nobu, the hotel's fashionable Japanese-Peruvian restaurant.

COMO The Halkin
MAP D4 ▪ Halkin St SW1 ▪ 020 7333 1059 ▪ www.comohotels.com/thehalkin ▪ £££

A startlingly beautiful hotel in a Georgian townhouse on a quiet street, which has been given a thoroughly modern overhaul with luxurious marble, glass and dark wood details. The relaxed Halkin Bar is chic and the rooms are equipped for modern communication.

No. 5 Maddox Street
MAP J3 ▪ 5 Maddox St W1 ▪ 020 7647 0200 ▪ www.living-rooms.co.uk/no-5-maddox-st ▪ £££

Glass, vintage prints and large plants feature in the decor of these sleek and well-appointed serviced apartments, tucked away in a quiet Mayfair location with a restaurant delivery service, goodies on arrival and free gym membership.

Sanderson
MAP K1 ▪ 50 Berners St W1 ▪ 020 7300 1400 ▪ www.sbe.com/hotels/originals/sanderson ▪ £££

Originally designed by Phillipe Starck, this is one of London's most stylish hotels. Behind a 1950s office-block exterior, its plain decor is enlivened by Dalí-lips and Louis XIV sofas and a funky 80-ft (24-m) cocktail bar, while the sparsely decorated bedrooms retain their sense of whimsy. Facilities include a state-of-the-art gym. Make sure to book a table for the themed Mad Hatter's afternoon tea.

W London
MAP L3 ▪ 10 Wardour St, Leicester Sq W1 ▪ 020 7758 1000 ▪ www.marriott.co.uk/hotels/travel/lonhw-w-london ▪ £££

This glamorous West End hotel will have you feeling like the star of the show. The rooms feature designer beds and spa products. They offer good in-room dining options, while cocktail-lovers will enjoy the extensive menu at the bar. There is also an on-site fitness centre and a spa with a variety of relaxing treatments.

The Bloomsbury Hotel
MAP L1 ▪ 16–22 Great Russell St WC1 ▪ 020 7347 1000 ▪ www.doylecollection.com ▪ £££

This stylish red-brick hotel, originally designed by Edwin Lutyens, started life in the 1920s as the Central Club of the YWCA. In summer, the gorgeous, flower-filled Dalloway Terrace *(p117)* is the highlight, while the dazzling Coral Room bar brings a dash of glamour and decadence.

Business Hotels

Holiday Inn Express London City
MAP H2 ■ 275 Old St EC1 ■ 020 7300 4300 ■ www. ihg.com/holidayinn express ■ £
One among a chain of value-for-money London hotels, the Holiday Inn Express London City is not actually in the City, but backs onto fashionable Hoxton Square *(see p159)*, an area known more for art than for business. The hotel offers complimentary breakfast. There are several branches across London.

Andaz Liverpool Street
MAP H3 ■ 40 Liverpool St EC2 ■ 020 7961 1234 ■ www.hyatt.com ■ £££
Built in 1884 as the railway hotel serving Liverpool Street station, Andaz fuses a 5-star hotel with boutique design flair. Set in a red-brick building with stylish, minimalist rooms, it has five restaurants and bars offering a great range of eating and drinking options.

London Bridge Hotel
MAP T4 ■ 8–18 London Bridge St SE1 ■ 020 7855 2200 ■ www.london bridgehotel.com ■ ££
Situated just over the river from the City, this

handsome, modern, independently owned hotel is well equipped for business guests, with modern conference facilities. Breakfast is served in the Londinium restaurant, and the Quarter Bar offers afternoon tea (book ahead).

The Tower Hotel
MAP H4 ■ St Katharine's Way E1 ■ 020 7523 5063 ■ www.guoman. com/the-tower ■ ££
Many of the 800-plus rooms in this vast block close to Tower Bridge and St Katharine Docks boast spectacular river views.

Canary Riverside Plaza
46 Westferry Circus E14 ■ DLR Westferry ■ 020 7510 1999 ■ www.canary river sideplaza.com ■ £££
As smart and stylish as you would expect from a Canary Wharf hotel, this is a straightforward, well-equipped, contemporary-looking affair. Some rooms have window seats with river views, there's a spa, a fitness centre and indoor pool. The restaurant opens onto a terrace during summer.

Marble Arch Marriott
MAP D3 ■ 134 George St W1 ■ 020 7723 1277 ■ www.marriott.co.uk ■ £££
A modern hotel near the western end of Oxford Street. Rooms, in white, grey and aquamarine, are bright and cheerful, and facilities include a bar, restaurant and fitness centre. There

are also complete business facilities in the executive lounge.

The Park Tower Knightsbridge
MAP C4 ■ 101 Knightsbridge SW1 ■ 020 7235 8050 ■ www. marriott.co.uk ■ £££
Housed in a circular 1970s tower, this plush hotel is a Knightsbridge landmark. The rooms and suites, with chaise longues and window-side desks, offer views over Hyde Park and the city's skyline. Business guests are well catered for.

St. Pancras Renaissance Hotel
MAP E1 ■ Euston Rd NW1 ■ 020 7841 3540 ■ www.marriott.co.uk ■ £££
Located in front of St Pancras International Station, home of the Eurostar, this is the perfect hotel for those who commute regularly from Europe. It also happens to be one of London's grandest and most palatial Victorian buildings, designed by Sir George Gilbert Scott.

Mid-Priced Hotels

Langham Court Hotel
MAP J1 ■ 31–5 Langham St W1 ■ 020 7436 6622 ■ www.gemhotels.com ■ ££
Located in a side street close to Oxford Circus, this hotel, with its attractive façade, is as friendly inside as its exterior promises. The terrific Langham Brasserie serves both French and Spanish cuisine, including tapas.

For a key to hotel price categories see p174

Apex City of London Hotel
MAP H3 ■ 1 Seething Lane EC3 ■ 020 7702 2020 ■ www.apexhotels. co.uk ■ ££
The four-star Apex has rooms with state-of-the-art facilities and a smart restaurant. Special offers are often available. There are two more Apex hotels in the City – on Fleet Street and off London Wall.

DoubleTree by Hilton London West End
MAP E2 ■ 92 Southampton Row WC1 ■ 020 7242 2828 ■ www.hilton.com ■ ££
Behind the Edwardian façade of this veteran Bloomsbury hotel are smart rooms and luxury suites with state-of-the-art facilities. There is also a fitness centre, bar and a good restaurant.

Hotel La Place
MAP D2 ■ 17 Nottingham Place W1 ■ 020 7486 2323 ■ www. hotellaplace.com ■ ££
This townhouse in Marylebone is quirky and unique. Decor in the 20 rooms and Le Jardin wine bar is chintzy and ornate. A full English breakfast is included in the room rate. The owners take great care of their guests.

Malmaison London
MAP G2 ■ 18–21 Charterhouse Sq EC1 ■ 020 3750 9402 ■ www.malmaison. com ■ ££
Located in Smithfield, this boutique chain hotel is charming and reasonably priced. As well as

the comfortable rooms, it offers a chic restaurant and a lounge bar.

Meliá White House
MAP D2 ■ Albany St NW1 ■ 020 7391 3000 ■ www.melia.com ■ ££
Close to Regent's Park, this classic four-star hotel was originally built as a block of model apartments in 1936. Now run by Spanish chain Meliá, the hotel boasts 581 spacious, comfortable and light-filled rooms, a swish Spanish restaurant and a cocktail bar.

Mercure London Bridge
MAP R4 ■ 71–9 Southwark St SE1 ■ 020 7902 0800 ■ www.all.accor. com ■ ££
Situated close to the Tate Modern, Borough Market and The Shard, this hotel boasts a smart contemporary design plus a high level of facilities, including Marco's New York Italian restaurant by celebrity chef Marco Pierre White.

Bedford Corner Hotel
MAP L1 ■ 11–13 Bayley St WC1 ■ 020 3004 6000 ■ www.bedfordcorner hotel.com ■ ££
The artworks adorning the walls of this modern Bloomsbury hotel, housed in a Georgian building just off Tottenham Court Road, nod to the area's literary connections. Rooms are simply decorated but comfortable. Also on site are a branch of CAIL's Bakery and a co-working space.

Bedford Hotel
MAP E2 ■ 83–95 Southampton Row WC1 ■ 020 7636 7822 ■ www. imperialhotels.co.uk ■ ££
One of six large, good-value Bloomsbury hotels run by Imperial London Hotels, the Bedford's advantages are a good restaurant and a sunny lounge and garden. It has simple yet comfortable rooms, some of which overlook the garden.

The Culpeper
MAP H3 ■ 40 Commercial St E1 ■ 020 247 5371 ■ www.theculpeper.com/ bedrooms ■ ££
With artfully distressed walls, open fireplaces and colourful woven fabrics, the rooms above this lively refurbished pub feel right at home in trendy Spitalfields. Don't miss dinner in the excellent first-floor restaurant, which has a small but impeccably sourced menu. In summer enjoy a set lunch on the lush rooftop terrace.

Thistle Trafalgar Square
MAP L4 ■ Whitcomb St WC2 ■ 020 7523 5064 ■ www.thistle.com ■ ££
The Thistle Group has eight hotels in London. This one is next door to the National Gallery, close to Leicester Square, so staying here will save on transport costs. Rooms are stylishly furnished with all mod cons.

The Fielding Hotel
MAP M2 ■ 4 Broad Court, Bow St WC2 ■ 020 7836 8305 ■ www.thefielding hotel.co.uk ■ ££
Named after the novelist Henry Fielding and ideally

situated right opposite the Royal Opera House, this charming hotel is a warren of oddly shaped rooms, with showers and basins tucked in corners. Outside there is all of Covent Garden to breakfast in. All rooms are equipped with amenities such as digital TV and air conditioning.

The Resident Kensington

MAP A5 ▪ 25 Courtfield Gardens SW5 ▪ 020 7244 2255 ▪ www.resident hotels.com ▪ ££

Occupying a set of grand Edwardian townhouses in salubrious Earls Court, this "luxury budget" hotel offers mini-kitchens with a Nespresso coffee machine in every room. Its 65 rooms, each of which is decorated in contemporary style, range from singles and luxury bunks to family rooms.

Inexpensive Hotels

Church Street Hotel

29–33 Camberwell Church St SE5 ▪ Tube Oval, then 12, 36 or 436 bus ▪ 020 7703 5984 ▪ www.church streethotel.com ▪ £

Enjoy a vibrant slice of Latin America in this cheerful Hispanic-themed establishment in South London. Rooms are bright and colourful, with bathrooms clad in Mexican tiles. Many art galleries, pubs, and live music venues dot the area.

easyHotel Victoria

MAP D5 ▪ 34–40 Belgrave Rd SW1 ▪ 020 7834 1379 ▪ www.easyhotel.com ▪ £

The company behind easyJet offers a fleet of budget hotels with small, functional rooms. Expect no frills as they are the cheapest en-suite double rooms in town. There are three more easyHotels in central London (in South Kensington, Paddington and Old Street) and also at Heathrow, Luton and Croydon. Wi-Fi costs extra.

The Corner London City

42 Adler St E1 ▪ Tube Aldgate East ▪ 020 3021 1440 ▪ www.thecorner londoncity.co.uk ▪ £

Sustainability is the watchword at this hipster hotel in the East End. Rooms are cube-shaped pods, and the cheapest lack windows, but bespoke furniture and fittings add a touch of luxury.

The Columbia

MAP B3 ▪ 95–9 Lancaster Gate W2 ▪ 020 7402 0021 ▪ www.thecolumbia.co.uk ▪ £

With a delightful leafy setting overlooking Hyde Park and Kensington Gardens, the Columbia is cosy family-run hotel. Originally townhouses, one of which was used as an American Red Cross Hospital during World War I, the hotel offers everything from dinky singles to four-bed rooms for friends and families.

Millennium Gloucester Hotel

MAP B5 ▪ 4–18 Harrington Gardens SW7 ▪ 020 7373 6030 ▪ www.millenniumhotels.com ▪ £

Located at a minute's walk from Gloucester Road tube station, this hotel is close to attractions such as Kensington Gardens and the museums of South Kensington The modern rooms are spacious and reasonably priced. Three restaurant options offer East Asian, Indian and classic British pub cuisine in Humphrey's Bar. Other facilities include a fitness centre.

Morgan Hotel

MAP L1 ▪ 24 Bloomsbury St WC1 ▪ 020 7636 3735 ▪ www.morganhotel.co. uk ▪ £

This family-run hotel has several rooms overlooking the British Museum, as well as serviced apartments, and all have air conditioning. The cosy breakfast area has framed London memorabilia on the walls.

Z Soho

MAP L2 ▪ 17 Moor St W1 ▪ 020 3551 3701 ▪ www.thezhotels.com/ soho ▪ ££

Set in the heart of Soho, this hotel – the original of a burgeoning chain – offers 85 tiny rooms (some with no windows) and a small café. It is close to Theatreland.

B&Bs and Hostels

Barclay House

21 Barclay Rd SW6 ▪ Tube Fulham Broadway ▪ 07767 420942 ▪ www. barclayhouselondon.com ▪ ££

A classy B&B in an exquisite Victorian property. It shows impressive attention to detail in the three luxurious guest rooms, from the underfloor heating to the rainforest showers. Minimum stay is three nights.

For a key to hotel price categories see p174

Clink261

MAP F2 ▪ 261–5 Grays Inn Rd WC1 ▪ 020 7833 9400 ▪ www.clinkhostels.com ▪ £

Clink hostels have private rooms with shared bathrooms and dorms, maintained by a friendly staff. A self-catering kitchen and laundry are available. There's no bar here but a lively one nearby at Clink78.

Astor Hyde Park Hostel

MAP B5 ▪ 191 Queen's Gate SW7 ▪ 020 7581 0103 ▪ www.astorhotels.com/hostels/hyde-park ▪ £

Located close to Hyde Park, this hostel offers spacious dorms and comfortable private rooms. There is also a homely Victorian lounge, featuring plush leather sofas and wood-panelling.

Dover Castle Hostel

MAP S6 ▪ 6a Great Dover St SE1 ▪ 020 7407 9777 ▪ www.dovercastlehostel.com ▪ £

This privately run hostel offers great value-for-money accommodation for backpackers. There are 60 beds in total, in mixed dorms sleeping from 4 up to 12. The late-licensed bar has reasonably priced drinks.

Generator Hostel London

MAP E2 ▪ 37 Tavistock Place WC1 ▪ 020 7388 7666 ▪ www.staygenerator.com/hostels/london ▪ £

With decor somewhere between sci-fi and industrial chic, this youth-orientated hostel provides budget solutions for impecunious travellers. Private rooms are available as well as dorms. There's a café and bar, and the hostel organizes theme nights and other regular events.

Wombat's City Hostel

7 Dock St E1 ▪ Tube Aldgate East ▪ 020 7680 7600 ▪ www.wombats-hostels.com/london ▪ £

Housed in a refurbished former sailor's hostel, this chilled option is handily located for City attractions such as the Tower of London and not far from Shoreditch's nightspots. Accommodation is in 4–8-bed dorms, both mixed and female-only, and spacious private rooms, including with a rooftop terrace. The cavernous, bare-brick womBar is a convivial place for a pint, and plenty of activities, from walking tours to karaoke, are organized.

St Christopher's at The Village

MAP S5 ▪ 161–5 Borough High St SE1 ▪ 020 7939 9710 ▪ www.st-christophers.co.uk ▪ £

This is the largest of three hostels around London Bridge run by St Christopher's Inns.It was also the UK's first hostel with capsule beds, which are fitted with curtains as well as USB chargers. There are other branches in Camden, Greenwich, Shepherd's Bush, Liverpool Street and Hammersmith. Private capsules, two-bunk rooms and female-only and mixed dorms are available along with complimentary buffet breakfast. Belushi's bar is great for partying and there's a resident DJ at weekends.

YHA Earl's Court

MAP A6 ▪ 38 Bolton Gardens SW5 ▪ 0345 371 9114 ▪ www.yha.org.uk ▪ £

Set in a Victorian building with a courtyard garden, the rooms in this back-packers' hostel are minimalist in decor. Guests have access to comfortable shared areas.

Arosfa Hotel

MAP E2 ▪ 83 Gower St WC1 ▪ 020 7636 2115 ▪ www.arosfalondon.com ▪ ££

In the heart of Bloomsbury, near the British Museum, this Georgian townhouse – once the home of artist John Everett Millais – has been renovated as a comfortable B&B, with modern bathrooms attached to its small but cosy rooms. There's a pleasant guest lounge as well as a little garden at the back.

Aster House

MAP B5 ▪ 3 Sumner Place, SW7 ▪ 020 7581 5888 ▪ www.asterhouse.com ▪ ££

This B&B in a Victorian townhouse has just 13 rooms. It is within walking distance of the Science, Natural History and Victoria and Albert Museums. The buffet breakfast is served in the orangery.

B+B Belgravia

MAP D5 ▪ 64–6 Ebury St SW1 ▪ 020 7529 8570 ▪ www.bb-belgravia.com ▪ ££

Set within two Grade II listed Georgian

townhouses, this B&B offers 17 en-suite rooms, as well as a range of studios and apartments in a separate building. Guests have 24-hour access to a lounge with an open fire, a laptop, a TV, a printer, daily newspapers and a coffee machine. There's also a garden. Guests can borrow bikes for free.

Smart Hyde Park View
MAP B3 ▪ 16 Leinster Terrace W2 ▪ 020 7262 8684 ▪ www.smart hostels.com ▪ ££
Situated just off Kensington Gardens, this is a comfortable variation on a hostel, offering double rooms with private bathrooms as well as traditional dormitories. There are branches in Camden and Russell Square too.

Out of the Centre

Hotel 55
55 Hanger Lane W5 ▪ Tube North Ealing ▪ 020 8991 4450 ▪ www. hotel55-london.com ▪ £
The decor of this hotel is bright and modern, with character. Dine in the in-house Indian restaurant, Royal Shezan and unwind in the landscaped garden.

The Lodge Hotel
52–4 Upper Richmond Rd SW15 ▪ Tube East Putney ▪ 020 8874 1598 ▪ www. thelodgehotellondon. com ▪ ££
Leafy Putney isn't that far from the centre of London, but this hotel has a calm out-of-town feel to it. Two Victorian mansions and a former coaching stable have

been joined together to provide 73 bedrooms along with a lounge, gym and restaurant-bar.

Martel Guest House
27 The Ridgeway NW11 ▪ Tube Golders Green ▪ 020 8455 1802 ▪ www. martelguesthouse.co.uk ▪ £
Hidden away along a quiet tree-lined road just a 5-minute walk from the tube station (15-minute journey to central London), this neat and clean guesthouse offers well-appointed rooms. The owner, Phil, is warm and friendly and helps with taxi rides and useful tips. .

The Mitre
291 Greenwich High Rd SE10 ▪ DLR Cutty Sark or train to Greenwich ▪ 020 8293 0037 ▪ www. themitregreenwich.co.uk ▪ £
Originally an 18th-century coaching inn, this bustling pub with 24 smart and comfortable rooms, including three family suites, is close to Greenwich's sights and transport links. Popular with locals, the pub serves good food, including hearty Sunday roasts. There is a conservatory and a garden but no parking on site.

Novotel London Stansted Airport
Round Coppice Rd, Stansted ▪ 01279 680 800 ▪ www.all.accor.com ▪ £
A modern hotel with standard facilities, this is just a 6-minute journey to the terminal at Stansted Airport via shuttle bus, making it an ideal choice for early flights.

The Pilot
68 River Way, SE10 ▪ Tube North Greenwich ▪ 020 8858 5910 ▪ www. pilotgreenwich.co.uk ▪ ££
Tucked away in Greenwich, this hotel and pub offers a refreshing change from central London. The decor flaunts a nautical theme, and each of the ten rooms has an individual style. The pub kitchen offers hearty favourites. It is a ten-minute walk away from the O2 (see p73).

Renaissance London Heathrow
Bath Rd, Hounslow ▪ Tube Heathrow Terminals 2 & 3, then Hoppa bus ▪ 020 8897 6363 ▪ www. marriott.com ▪ ££
This hotel with views of Heathrow's runways is handy for getting to the airport, and has a 24-hour fitness centre and soundproofed rooms.

Sofitel London Gatwick
North Terminal, Gatwick Airport ▪ 012 9356 7070 ▪ www.all.accor.com ▪ ££
Walk directly from Gatwick's North Terminal to this classy hotel, which has a full range of facilities. It is linked to London by the Gatwick Express train.

St Paul's Hotel
153 Hammersmith Rd W14 ▪ Tube Hammersmith ▪ 020 8846 9119 ▪ www. stpaulhotel.co.uk ▪ ££
Housed in a handsome 1884 Victorian building that was originally a school, this boutique hotel is just a short walk away from the Eventim (Hammersmith) Apollo and Olympia London.

For a key to hotel price categories see p174

General Index

Acknowledgments

This edition updated by

Updater and Project Editor Edward Aves

Senior Editor Alison McGill

Senior Designer Vinita Venugopal

Indexer Helen Peters

Picture Research Manager
Taiyaba Khatoon

Picture Research Administrator
Vagisha Pushp

Publishing Assistant Halima Mohammed

Jacket Designer Jordan Lambley

Senior Cartographer Subhashree Bharati

Cartography Manager Suresh Kumar

Senior DTP Designer Tanveer Zaidi

Senior Production Editor Jason Little

Production Controller Kariss Ainsworth

Managing Editors Shikha Kulkarni,
Hollie Teague

Deputy Editorial Manager
Beverly Smart

Managing Art Editor Priyanka Thakur

Art Director Maxine Pedliham

Publishing Director Georgina Dee

DK would like to thank the following for
their contribution to the previous editions:
Kate Berens, Vinny Crump, Joe Staines,
Anna Streiffert, Roger Williams

The publisher would like to thank the
following for their kind permission to
reproduce their photographs:

Key: a-above; b-below/bottom; c-centre; f-far;
l-left; r-right; t-top

Alamy Images: Archive Images 49; Mike
Booth 36bl; John Bracegirdle 52b;
BritishCeremonies 25br; David Coleman 4crb;
Ian Dagnall 160b; horst friedrichs 145br;
Kevin J. Frost 106cra; David Gee 4 90cra;
Granger - Historical Picture Archive 19tr;
Heritage Image Partnership Ltd 48br, 63clb;
IanDagnall Computing 17tl; Jack Hobhouse
51bl; IanDagnall Computing 114cra; IML
Image Group Ltd 69cra; PA Images / Katie
Collins 34clb; Jansos 156cl; Benjamin

John 99tr; Justin Kase zsixz 11cra; Lebrecht
Music and Arts Photo Library 30br;
Londonstills.com 100cl; migstock 121tl;
Beata Moore 67b; Eric Nathan 89cla; 8–9;
PA Images / David Parry 38cl; Stephen Porritt
62cra; Prisma Archivo / Portrait by Albert
Charles Challen (1847-1881) 19cla; Adrian
Seal 24–5c; Neil Setchfield 89br; Shawshots
49cla; Kumar Sriskandan 80bl; Anna Stowe
3tl, 84–85; Matthew Taylor 20br; Travel
Pix 27tl; Steve Vidler 90cra; Michael K
Berman-Wald 59br; World History Archive
48t; Gregory Wrona 97tl.

AWL Images: Ivan Vdovin 2tr, 46–7.

Bibendum: 131crb.

BOW WOW London Ltd: 109tr

The Trustees of the British Museum:
Christy Graham 12bl, 13tl, 13cla; Nick
Nicholls 12cra, 14bl; Doug Traverso 10tr.

Camera Press: Cecil Beaton 41b.

Cora Pearl: 111tr.

El Camion: Jake Baggaley 99br.

Cinnamon Club/Roche Communications:
93tl.

Corbin and King/David Loftus: 75b.

Corbis: 17cra; Arcaid/Jonathan Bailey 37tl;
Diane Auckland 106b; Chris Ball 60br;
Jean-Baptiste Rabouan 55cl; Quentin
Bargate 42cl; Massimo Borchi 92b; James
Davies 141br; Demotix/Malcolm Park 40c;
dpa/Peter Kneffel 32–3; Eurasia Press/Steven
Vidler 4cl, 88b; Dennis Gilbert 15cl; Grady:
Damian 55cr; John Harper 54br; Heritage
Images 62bl; Roberto Herrett 147cra; JAI/Alan
Copson 7tr; Pawel Libera 154t, Yang Liu
102–3, Loop Images / Dave Povey 104tr, Loop
Images / Eric Nathan 77tl; Leo Mason 70tl,
71cr; Robert Harding World Imagery 96b;
Napoleon Sarony 60tl; Hendrik Schmidt 61tl;
Splash News 68crb Homer Sykes 112tr,
Mark Sykes 144cr; The Gallery Collection
16–17c, 16bl, 58tl; Steven Vidler 57cr,142cr.

Dalloway Terrace: 117cra

Daunt Books: 138b.

Dean and Chapter of Westminster: Jim
Dyson 34bl.

Dorling Kindersley: Max Alexander 116b; Courtesy of the Natural History Museum, London/John Downes 10clb, /Colin Keates 20cl; courtesy of the Royal Festival Hall, and Park Lane Group Young Artists' Concert 81tr; Courtesy of The Science Museum/Geoff Dann 10crb; Courtesy of Benjamin Pollock's Toyshop/ Max Alexander 109br; Courtesy of the Wallace Collection, London/Geoff Dann 134tr.

Dreamstime.com: Acmanley 91tr; Andersastphoto 98b; Tudor Antonel Adrian 150b; Ajv123ajv 3tr, 164–5; Altezza 4clb, 87cra; Anizza 119tl; Ardazi 107tl; Arsty 86cla; Anthony Raggett 61br; Baloncici 59cl, 125tr; Bargotiphotography 135tr; Beataaldridge 54t; Michal Bednarek 108tr; Felix Bensman 27br; Christian Bertrand 73tr; Mikhail Blajenov 6cl, Bombaert 114b, Dan Breckwoldt 126b, 129tr, 136b, Anthony Brown 56t, Andrew Chambers 119b; Claudiodivizia 143bl; Mike Clegg 130 cla, 161br, 162tr; Cowardlion 28–9c, Cowardlion 50clb; Johanna Cuomo 68bl, 79tl; Chris Dorney 7cr, 51 tl, 54t, 120b, 127cla, 142bl; Mark Eaton 155clb; Jorge Duarte Estevao 161tl; Eric Flamant 83cl; Haircutting 152cl; Jodi Hanagan 158cla; Sven Hansche 132–3; Anna Hristova 163bl; Imaengine 15b; Irishka777 113t; Dragan Jovanovic 128cra; Kmiragaya 4cla, 105br, 146tr, 153tr; Georgios Kollidas 126cra, Jan Kranendonk 122b, Ingus Kruklitis 73clb; Frik Lattwein 129clb; Charlotte Leaper 118tl; Lowerkase 10–11b, 26bl; Maisna 137cl; Ac Manley 115bc; Mark6138 87br; Michaelimages 70br; Krzysztof Nahlik 94tl; Nadirco 4b; Dmitry Naumov 42br; Nhtg 55tr; Dilyana Nikolova 2tl, 8–9; Radub85 63tr; Sampete 64tl; Pere Sanz 26cla; Sinoleo 141tr; Spiroview Inc. 149bl; Stuart456 4cr; Thevirex 79bc; Alexandra Thompson 140cra; Travelwitness 64b; Tupungato 91clb, 100br; Florenta Vatavu 159tr; Paul Wishart 70cr; Yongong 135b.

Electric Cinema: 128bl.

Getty Images: AFP/Dan Kitwood 81cl; Bloomberg Anna Branthwaite 75tr; Corbis Historical / Fine Art 58br; DeAgostini 30–1; DESPITE STRAIGHT LINES (Paul Williams) 36–7c; Tabatha Fireman 72t; Furture Light 65clb; Heritage Images 40tr, 45b; Leemage 120cra; Moment / Peter Zelei Images 1; NurPhoto 83tr; Pawel Libera 4t, 27cl; Robert Harding World Imagery/Amanda Hall 38–9; Lizzie Shepherd 6tr.

Gordon's Wine Bar: 110b.

By permission of IWM (Imperial War Museums): Richard Ash 57tl.

Inn the Park/Peyton and Byrne: 123tr.

iStockphoto.com: MichaelUtech 95tr; violettenlandungoy 53cl

J Sheekey: 101cr.

KU Bar: 96cra

La Fromagerie: 139cr.

National Portrait Gallery, London: 18cr, 18bl; Marcus Gheeraerts the Younger, circa 1592 10cla.

The National Trust Photo Library ©NTPL: Andrew Butler 76bl.

The Trustees of the Natural History Museum, London: Kevin Webb 21tr, 20cr.

OXO Tower Restaurant/Harvey Nichols: Jonathan Reid 93cr.

Philip Way Photography: 44tr, 45cl.

The Royal Collection Trust © Her Majesty Queen Elizabeth II 2015: Crown © HMSO 41cl; Derry Moore 25tl.

Rules Restaurant: 74t.

© Science Museum Group: 23crb, 23tr.

Courtesy of the Trustees of Sir John Soane's Museum/Caro Communications: Gareth Gardner 113br.

St Paul's Cathedral: 42–3.

© Science Museum Group: 68t.

Shutterstock.com: Jananz 36cla.

Superstock: Stefano Baldini/age fotostock 19crb.

© Tate, London 2013: Norham Castle, Sunrise by Joseph Mallord William Turner 30cla; Carnation, Lily, Lily, Rose John Singer Sargent 31tr; Three Studies for Figures at the Base of a Crucifixion Francis Bacon 31crb; DACS, London 2016 /Whaam! (1963) Roy Lichetenstein 28br; /Three Dancers (1925) Pablo Picasso 28cla.

Tate Modern: Cildo Meireles Babel 2001 © Cildo Meireles 29tr

The City Barge Pub: 157tr.

Victoria and Albert Museum: 56bl.

192 » Acknowledgments

Cover

Front and spine: **Getty Images:** Moment / Peter Zelei Images.

Back: **Alamy Stock Photo:** robertharding tl; **AWL Images:** Hemis crb; **Alamy Stock Photo:** Helen Dixon cla; **Getty Images:** Moment / Peter Zelei Images b; **iStockphoto.com:** E+ / fotoVoyager tr.

Pull out map cover

Getty Images: Moment / Peter Zelei Images.

All other images are: © Dorling Kindersley. For further information see www.dkimages.com.

Illustrator Chris Orr & Associates

Commissioned Photography Susie Adams, Max Alexander, Demetrio Carrasco, Geoff Dann, Mike Dunning, Steve Gorton, Frank Greenaway, John Heseltine, Ed Ironside, Colin Keates, Laurie Noble, Stephen Oliver, Rough Guides/Victor Borg, Rough Guides/Suzanne Porter, Rough Guides/Natascha Sturny, Rough Guides/Mark Thomas

Penguin
Random
House

First edition 2002

Published in Great Britain by Dorling Kindersley Limited, One Embassy Gardens, 8 Viaduct Gardens, London SW11 7BW, UK

The authorised representative in the EEA is Dorling Kindersley Verlag GmbH. Arnulfstr. 124, 80636 Munich, Germany

Published in the United States by DK Publishing, 1745 Broadway, 20th Floor, New York, NY 10019, USA

Copyright © 2002, 2023 Dorling Kindersley Limited

A Penguin Random House Company

23 24 25 26 10 9 8 7 6 5 4 3 2 1

A CIP catalogue record is available from the British Library.

A catalogue record for this book is available from the Library of Congress.

ISSN 1479-344X
ISBN 978-0-2416-2105-9

Printed and bound in Malaysia

www.dk.com

As a guide to abbreviations in visitor information blocks: **Adm** *= admission charge.*

MIX
Paper | Supporting responsible forestry
FSC™ C018179

This book was made with Forest Stewardship Council™ certified paper – one small step in DK's commitment to a sustainable future.
For more information go to www.dk.com/our-green-pledge